Frank
& Al

Frank & Al

FDR, AL SMITH, and the
UNLIKELY ALLIANCE
THAT CREATED the MODERN
DEMOCRATIC PARTY

TERRY GOLWAY

ST. MARTIN'S PRESS ❧ NEW YORK

FRANK AND AL. Copyright © 2018 by Terry Golway. All rights reserved. Printed in the United States of America. For information, address St. Martin's Press, 175 Fifth Avenue, New York, NY 10010.

www.stmartins.com

Designed by Steven Seighman

Library of Congress Cataloging-in-Publication Data is available upon request.

ISBN 978-1-250-08964-9 (hardcover)
ISBN 978-1-250-08965-6 (ebook)

Our books may be purchased in bulk for promotional, educational, or business use. Please contact your local bookseller or the Macmillan Corporate and Premium Sales Department at 1-800-221-7945, extension 5442, or by email at MacmillanSpecialMarkets@macmillan.com.

First Edition: September 2018

10 9 8 7 6 5 4 3 2 1

For journalists, everywhere. Now more than ever.

CONTENTS

Frank

& Al

PROLOGUE

THE DULL LIGHT of a winter's afternoon in Albany was beginning to fade, and the men in stiff collars and dark suits who wrote New York's laws shuffled papers and tapped their desks while tiresome colleagues expounded on this or that, seemingly unaware that their impatient audience was making plans for the rest of the evening. Some, the more dutiful, would return to the cheap rooming houses they rented for the legislative session. Others would head for the city's legendary saloons or perhaps to the Ten Eyck Hotel, where it was good to be seen, and afterward stroll toward the Hudson River, to places where women made a living providing the comforts of home, an hour at a time.

In January 1911 the air was unusually warm, as it had been for more than a month. Doctors said the absence of snow and bone-chilling temperatures were to blame for a terrible outbreak of pneumonia that had claimed the lives of more than three dozen Albanians since the beginning of December.

The new majority leader of the New York State Assembly found himself alone and surprisingly unscheduled as his colleagues made their way into the delightfully temperate, if somewhat dangerous, Albany air. Had it been a Thursday, he would have gathered up three or four of his colleagues—men from the mountains of the North Country, the mill towns of western New York, the potato fields of Long Island—and walked down the hill from the capitol past St. Peter's Church to Keeler's Restaurant on State Street. As the streetcars clambered by, they'd talk politics, gossip about absent colleagues, or critique the day's debates. Once at Keeler's, they would feast on corned beef and cabbage in one of the fabulous restaurant's fourteen dining rooms, where dozens of waiters scurried about with heaping plates of crab, lobster, and shrimp for those with a bit more cash to spend. Later, when the cigars came out, they'd turn their attention to their host as he told stories in his carnival barker's voice about an exotic place called the Lower East Side of Manhattan, where, it seemed, people from half the nations on earth lived side by side in relative peace and even had a laugh together on occasion. The host had a gift for imitating accents the likes of which his listeners had never heard but found hilarious.

This was the world of Alfred Emanuel Smith, the very picture of a rough-and-tumble pol from the immigrant wards of urban America. He sang Irish songs and told Irish stories, but in truth, he was only half Irish. His father thought of himself as Italian-American, but, in fact, he was half German. Al Smith was a gregarious symbol of the new twentieth-century American who lived in tenement houses, not log cabins or mansions, and who worked in factories, not barns or office buildings. And like those other new Americans, he worshipped God in ways that many found offensive, dangerous, and utterly un-American. He was a Catholic, like many of his neighbors—except for those who were Jewish. He lived in a portion of America that other Americans would not recognize, where business was transacted in languages other than English, where the locals had long and strange-sounding names, where children played in streets rather than fields. He lived in a portion of America that frightened other Americans.

Al Smith had a honker of a nose, and his big smile revealed a mouthful of gold fillings. His wide-striped suits were brassy and loud. In his younger days, his five-foot, seven-inch frame was slender and lithe. Now, at age thirty-seven, there was a hint of a paunch underneath his vest. He was rarely without a cigar and smoked as many as eighteen a day. His voice, a laborer's bellow, was urban and ethnic, and in his everyday speech he displayed only the slightest familiarity with English as it was spoken in the Fort Orange Club, just around the corner from the capitol, or in the uptown neighborhoods of Manhattan. But a more refined colleague who was fond of Smith said he and other legislators overlooked Smith's "violations of the rules of grammar" because he was such an easygoing fellow, quick with a song and story and a slap on the back.

Except for Thursday night, nobody in Albany worked harder than Al Smith did. He was invariably described as a self-taught political genius, for he left school in eighth grade when he went to work to help his widowed mother and his younger sister. But he had some help in mastering the art of legislation: for a few years early in his political career, Al Smith roomed with a quiet young German immigrant with a law degree, Robert Wagner, who taught him the tricks lawyers played with the people's business. The two men, both products of the streets of New York City, became good friends, and now, in the winter of 1911, they were the talk of Albany. Smith was not only the assembly's majority leader but chairman of the all-powerful Ways and Means Committee. Wagner, at age thirty-three, was the youngest president of the state senate in New York history.

The press called Smith and Wagner the "Tammany Twins," for they were members of Tammany Hall, the infamous Democratic Party machine run by Charles Francis Murphy, a saloonkeeper who was said to treat politicians under his control as though they were waiters at his favorite dining establishment, Delmonico's.[1]

Because it was not a Thursday and there would be no corned beef and cabbage at Keeler's, Al Smith had nothing but his tedious homework to keep him busy until bedtime on this warm January night. But then he ran into his friend Wagner, whose business on this night was very much unfinished. Wagner was on his way to see a junior member of the state senate who was holding up business in Albany on an issue that had little to do with the making of laws and budgets, about which the young man knew very little. He had won election to the state senate in 1910 after promising the laborers, farmers, and mechanics in his rural district that he would protect them from the evils of city politicians, and everybody in the district knew who and what he meant. Now he was making good on his promise and, not coincidentally, adjusting the beam of publicity from Wagner and Smith to himself.

Wagner sought to put an end to the nonsense, so he donned a sack-cloth of humility, placed his hat in his hand, and prepared to walk across State Street to meet with the new state senator from Dutchess County, Franklin Delano Roosevelt.

Roosevelt! Smith had never met the man, but he had heard all about him. Who in Albany had not? Two weeks into his career as a public servant, the twenty-eight-year-old with the brilliant smile and impeccable pedigree had proclaimed himself the new archenemy of Tammany Hall and Murphy the saloonkeeper. He was serving as the spokesman for about two dozen dissident Democrats who refused to attend the party's voting sessions to choose a new U.S. senator from New York. These were the dying years of the old way of electing senators, when state legislatures, not the people, made the choice. Democrats controlled both houses of the legislature, so they were ready to send a fellow Democrat to Washington as the term of the Republican incumbent, Chauncey Depew, expired.

Murphy the saloonkeeper supported the candidacy of a onetime state legislator and lieutenant governor named William Sheehan, known to friend and foe alike as "Blue-Eyed Billy," a charming if not necessarily remarkable politician who had grown rich as a lawyer in New York City. But Roosevelt, with his hours of experience in government to draw upon, decided that Sheehan was not fit for the U.S. Senate, a place where men with faces meant for marble pillars debated great issues of the day in language that would make Shakespeare weep with envy. Roosevelt preferred Edward Shepherd, an earnest reformer from Brooklyn with a summer house on Lake George's Millionaire's Row. The *New York Times* described him as a man who was "born into politics of the higher sort."[2]

Newspapers reported on the emergence of a new Roosevelt, a distant cousin of the former president and the husband of his niece, who was fearlessly taking on Murphy the saloonkeeper and his minions like Smith and Wagner. "There is nothing I love as much as a good fight," he told reporters. "I never had as much fun in my life as I am having right now."[3]

Word spread from Albany about this new prince of reform with his Teddy-like pince-nez and a similar sense of his own righteousness. Letters filled the new senator's mailbox from admirers near and far. "Although I live in New Jersey," wrote one correspondent, "I wish to encourage you in the magnificent fight you and your associates are making to save the Democratic party . . . from destruction by its alleged 'leaders' in corrupt alliance with 'the interests.' . . . You and your associates in this fight represent democratic Democracy, while Sheehan and his backers represent plutocratic Democracy."[4]

Plutocratic Democracy? Represented by Al Smith, with his eighth-grade education and workingman's bellow? Democratic Democracy? Represented by Franklin Roosevelt, a wealthy Harvard graduate elected to office with no qualification other than his kinship with a popular former president? It was a strange business, politics.

Robert Wagner told Al Smith of the humiliating task he was about to perform—here he was, the president of the state senate, a man who could kill a bill or approve a contract without a word of explanation, going off to negotiate with a troublemaking freshman in *his* parlor, on *his* turf, on *his* terms!

Smith's reaction was instant and unexpected. I'll come along with you, he said.

It was just a short walk, a few minutes, from the capitol to Roosevelt's residence at the corner of State Street and South Swan Street, but it would have been more than enough time for Smith to vent about Roosevelt and his friends. The press may have seen them as steadfast defenders of good government, but Smith saw something quite different: bigotry disguised as principle. "There's nothing the matter with Sheehan," Smith had said. "He's all right, except he's an Irishman. That's all they've got against him." The father of young Senator Roosevelt once decreed that he would not hire any Irishmen to work the grounds of his estate. Smith would not have been surprised to hear it.[5]

Franklin Roosevelt lived in what he called a "palatial" townhouse, which he rented for $400 a month at a time when he and Smith and Wagner and their colleagues earned $1,500 a year as legislators. But the young senator from Dutchess County did not lay awake at night in the upstairs bedroom wondering how to pay the rent. He was, after all, a Roosevelt.[6]

Smith and Wagner climbed the seven stairs from street level to the building's impressive doorway and announced their presence with a knock. The door opened, revealing neither Senator Roosevelt nor his wife Elea-nor, but a butler. A butler, in Albany, working for a state senator! The two visitors surely were either shocked or amused, or perhaps a little of both.

Wagner, with his law school polish, announced in an appropriately for-mal tone that he and Assemblyman Smith had an appointment to see Senator Roosevelt.

The butler found this puzzling. "I know the senator is expecting Sen-ator Wagner," he said, his voice trailing off as he examined this uninvited guest with his cigar and gold fillings.

Smith gave the butler a smile as he brushed passed him. "That's all right," he said. "I'll come along, too."[7]

Smith would tell the story of his first meeting with Roosevelt many times in the prosperous years of his later life, perhaps over drinks in his Fifth Avenue apartment as the sun descended below the tree line of Central Park, perhaps at one of the many dinners and receptions held in his honor as a martyr in the fight for a more pluralistic, tolerant Ameri-can democracy. But he never said what he discussed with Roosevelt that night in Albany because, after all, it was a private conversation, and Al Smith learned from his mentors that when you made a promise—to deliver a contract, to hire a friend, or to keep a conversation private—you kept your word. And he always did.

The result of the meeting, however, was clear: it was a waste of time. Roosevelt continued to speak for the dissidents who held up the senate vote until Murphy the saloonkeeper abruptly changed tactics, dropping Sheehan in favor of a prominent judge who just happened to be a friend of his, and the rebellion disintegrated. Roosevelt, who had said he would never compromise with the Tammany boss, cast his vote for Murphy's choice. The caucus room erupted in hoots and laughter.

Franklin Roosevelt's time in Albany was short. He was soon off to Washington to serve the new president, Woodrow Wilson, as assistant secretary of the navy—the post his famous fifth cousin, Theodore, held just over a dozen years earlier.

Al Smith, like many of his colleagues, was not unhappy to see Roosevelt leave. He told friends that the young man from Dutchess County didn't understand politics, and what's more, he simply wasn't likable. "Franklin," he told a friend, "just isn't the sort of man you can take into the pissroom and talk intimately with."[8]

With Roosevelt gone, Smith continued his extraordinary rise to power, winning election as governor four times and, in 1928, becoming the first Catholic to be nominated for president of the United States.

To deliver his nominating speech that year, Al Smith chose a man the press had been describing as his protégé and friend—Franklin Delano Roosevelt, or "Frank," as Smith now called him. Weeks after Smith won the nomination, he called Roosevelt in Warm Springs, Georgia, and persuaded him to run for governor of New York, never mind that Roosevelt had not been able to move his legs for seven years. Roosevelt agreed, reluctantly. Smith lost the 1928 presidential election, but Roosevelt won the governor's race and became a national figure.

Four years later, both men sought their party's presidential nomination, setting off one of the most epic feuds in American political history. Roosevelt captured the nomination when he cut a shrewd backroom deal with Smith's bitter enemy, William Randolph Hearst, a deal that two men who once worked for Smith, James A. Farley and Edward Flynn, helped to broker. Roosevelt went on to win the presidency and make history with his New Deal reforms, thanks in no small way to the persistence of one of the era's greatest U.S. senators, Robert Wagner. The Social Security Act, the National Labor Relations Act, laws that virtually outlawed child labor, established a federal minimum wage, imposed new regulations on business, and established a federal role in public housing all echoed in some way measures Smith had advocated during his years as a state legislator and as governor. Roosevelt would point out that most of what he did to lift the nation out of the Great Depression had already been done by Al Smith in New York.

And yet, by the mid-1930s Al Smith had become one of Franklin Roosevelt's most embittered critics. They would eventually reconcile, but the feud that began when they were in each other's way in 1932 became one of the New Deal's most fascinating, and tragic, storylines.

In 1944, when both men had only months to live, an acquaintance asked Smith at a summer barbecue what he thought of Roosevelt, who was running for a fourth term as president of the United States. It was an innocent question, but Smith's friends cringed when they heard it. Certain topics were best left alone.

Smith's unmistakable voice, so harsh and so New York that men and women in the heartland covered their ears when they first heard it through the miracle of radio in the 1920s, quickly filled an awkward silence. "He was the kindest man who ever lived," he said. There was a pause, and then he said what he really meant. "But don't ever get in his way."[9]

one

RIVER FAMILIES

IN THE DRY SEASONS of the late nineteenth century, salt water from New York Harbor churned upstream from lower Manhattan to a bend in the Hudson River north of Poughkeepsie called Crum Elbow. There, brine from the harbor mixed with clear water flowing south from pristine streams in the Adirondack Mountains to form something not quite sea water, but not quite fresh water either.

From a bluff on the river's eastern bank overlooking Crum Elbow, the mixing and matching of north and south, upstate and downstate, country and city passed without notice. The river's surface was tranquil and timeless, a good deal like life itself at Springwood, the estate of James Roosevelt and his bride, Sara Delano. The back of their manor house faced the majestic waterway that was the source of so much of New York's power and wealth. The daily drama of Gilded Age commerce unfolded before their eyes: steamboats transporting goods from the farms, orchards, and quarries of the Hudson Valley to the markets of New York City ninety miles to the south; belching locomotives crawling along the river's banks, connecting the economic and cultural power of Manhattan to the state's center of politics and government, Albany. In the late afternoon, as the sun set behind the dark outline of Shawangunk Ridge to the west, the pace of commerce slowed and the river disappeared from view, with only the occasional blast of a night ship's horn reminding neighbors that it was never truly at rest.

As James and Sara Roosevelt awaited the birth of their first child together in January 1882, the river was untamed and unconquered, a divide that seemed impossible to bridge. Then again, the Hudson's resistance to modernity added to its charms, and those charms would not be lost on the baby boy born to the Roosevelts on January 30, 1882. "All that is in me," Franklin Roosevelt would later say, "goes back to the Hudson."[1]

South of Crum Elbow, the river returned to its relatively straight path toward New York City and the Atlantic Ocean beyond. On either bank were the farms, orchards, and vineyards that fed the ravenous appetites of the great cities to the south—not just New York, but Brooklyn as well. Their combined population in 1880 was closing in on two million and growing with each immigrant ship that passed into the harbor on its way to the piers of lower Manhattan.

The river narrowed as it passed the gentle slope of Storm King Mountain on its western bank, famed for inspiring the artists of the Hudson River School. It was squeezed even tighter as it paraded past West Point, headed for the twin sentinels of Bear Mountain on the west and a sweeping peak known as Anthony's Nose to the east. Workers picked at granite deposits in Anthony's Nose and sent them off to the city, where builders needed all the raw material the valley could provide.

The river turned gently to the east as it approached Iona Island and back again to the west as it turned past the town of Peekskill toward the ancestral manor house of the Van Cortlandts, one of the many Dutch families that settled in the valley and gave the region place names that looked in English like typographical errors—Spuyten Duyvil, Gansevoort. Two miles south of the old mansion, on the opposite bank, was an enormous ice house, painted white to reflect the sun's rays. Ice was a commodity as critical to the valley's economy as grain and fruit, and the market for it just as insatiable. Ice on the river could measure as much as ten or twelve inches thick, and it provided work for twenty-five thousand people, most of them farmers who relied on the river just as surely as they depended on the land. Without ice, they could go hungry.

James Roosevelt's brother, John, had no such concerns. The uncle of young Franklin was the commodore of the Poughkeepsie Ice Yacht Club and owner of what was said to be the largest ice yacht in the world, named *Icicle*. For Roosevelt and his fellow club members, the frozen river meant not bread, but recreation and competition. If the wind was right, *Icicle* could easily achieve speeds of more than sixty miles an hour. Crowds gathered along the river banks to watch *Icicle* and its competitors from other clubs glide along the ice on weekend afternoons.

The river expands again south of Haverstraw until it reaches its greatest width of three and a half miles near Nyack, where the Erie Railroad ended and passengers boarded ferries to take them south to the great city. Within minutes ferry riders were treated to one of the Hudson's most glorious works of nature, a long stretch of monumental cliffs on the western bank known as the Palisades. They rose five hundred feet high along the New Jersey bank of the river, preening in their stark, jagged beauty.

As the river approached the slender finger of upper Manhattan, a portion of it peeled off to the east, creating the Harlem River, which joined with the Long Island Sound to form the East River. The Hudson, however, continued south, becoming in equal parts a great urban highway and an open sewer.

Humble ferryboats plying the New York–New Jersey route and great passenger ships powered by steam and sail from ports around the world shared this portion of the river, not just with each other but with the factories and slaughterhouses that relied on the river's current to dispose of chemicals, blood, bone, and human waste. Here there were no ice yacht races in wintertime, no green open spaces for weekend picnics or baseball games. Sanitary inspectors from the city Board of Health dutifully filed reports about odors wafting from the riverfront to the tenement districts of Manhattan's West Side, but action rarely followed, even as parents told of children vomiting because of the air they breathed, of scorching summer afternoons spent with windows closed to keep out the odor of decaying animal parts and foul liquids in the river. A West Side resident told the Board of Health that the riverfront air was so thick with offensive smells that he and his family could barely breathe, but when he complained to the local police captain, he was told that it was no use. There was too much money at stake, the captain said.[2]

Straight ahead, as the river emptied into the harbor, was a small bit of land called Bedloe's Island. There were plans to erect an enormous statue, a gift from the people of France, on the island. Supporters said the statue of a woman with a torch would one day redefine the sky in the great harbor, but nobody seemed interested in funding the project. When the city sought the state's permission to spend $50,000 on the project, Governor Grover Cleveland vetoed the appropriation as wasteful. James Roosevelt, Franklin's father, was a good friend and admirer of the stout governor—Grover Cleveland understood the proper role of government, which was to stand aside and let the markets perform their magic.

Near the southern tip of Manhattan, a large, oval-shaped government building topped with a small dome and a tall flagpole served as an entrance point for the immigrants who once again were streaming into the city after a pause during and just after the Civil War. The facility, called Castle Garden, opened in 1855, when many of the newcomers were from northern Europe, especially Germany and Ireland. But after the war came a new wave from southern Italy and Eastern Europe, places of hopeless poverty and primitive conditions that rarely if ever saw a visitor from the great cities of Europe and North America. Among the new immigrants were Achille La Guardia and his wife Irene Coen, who arrived at Castle Garden in 1880 after a long journey from Italy. The couple barely had time to adjust to their new life when Irene gave birth to their first child, Fiorello, in December 1882.

The Hudson's long journey from the Adirondack Mountains comes to an end as it empties into the upper reaches of New York's harbor. But on the other side of the island, separated by less than a mile of lower Manhattan, was the East River, just as busy, just as much a part of the great city as the Hudson. A steamboat following the curved tip of lower Manhattan from west to east would present passengers with one of the great vistas in all the world as it turned up the East River: the Gothic towers and magnificent tangle of cables of a bridge that would unite the cities of New York and Brooklyn.

The Brooklyn Bridge was nearly done in early 1882. It would cost an astonishing $15 million and the lives of more than twenty men, among them its chief engineer, John Roebling, who died of tetanus back in 1869 when his foot was crushed in an accident during the very early stages of planning. His son, Washington Roebling, took over, but the bridge cost him life as he knew it—at age thirty-five, he was overcome by the bends while working in one of the bridge's caissons. He became an invalid, watching from his apartment window in Brooklyn as the bridge neared completion.

Almost directly across the river, another set of eyes watched as small figures high atop the towers put the finishing touches on their work before turning it over to the public. Years later, Al Smith would write of the "sense of admiration and envy I felt toward the men who swarmed like flies stringing the cables and putting in the roadways as the bridge slowly took shape." Al Smith was eight years old in early 1882, and he and his sister and their parents lived in a five-room apartment on the third floor of a small building on South Street under the bridge's roadbed. The apartment's two front windows looked out on the river and its ceaseless activity and energy—schooners from another era sharing space with modern steamships; truckers hauling great boxes of tea, coffee, fruit, and spices from far-flung islands and nations; children who saw the great seaport as a playground as they raced from pier to pier, leaping to touch the long bowsprits reaching out from the water's edge.[3]

In the summertime, with the windows open, young Al could hear the sounds of a city putting aside its childhood and embracing maturation and growth: rough sounds—shouts and curses, orders barked from ship to shore, the crash of cargo moved too quickly, the click of wheels negotiating with cobblestones, the barking of dogs who had free run of the waterfront, the raucous laughter of sailors leaving their ships for a few hours of entertainment on the Bowery. At night, when commerce was done, creaky wooden ships groaned with exhaustion, rocking gently with the current until they were awakened at ungodly hours by the arrival of the fishing boats. All of this took place in the shadow of the bridge that would change the destiny of the humid islands gathered in the great bay. The bridge would knit together the cities of New York and Brooklyn, so much so that less than two decades after its opening, the two would become one, with the stepchildren of Queens, Staten Island, and the Bronx invited to join the blended family.

Strung across the great granite towers of the bridge was a catwalk designed for workers as they made their way from one end of the span to the other. Al Smith made that walk from New York to Brooklyn and back again one day with his father, Alfred Emanuel Smith Sr., who was determined to say that he and his son crossed the bridge before it was even completed. Father and son had little problem evading authorities to gain access to the bridge, as the elder Smith was employed part time as a security guard whose job it was to keep people off the narrow, wind-blown catwalk.

If he raised his eyes from the wooden planks below him and looked up as he made the return walk from the Brooklyn side, young Al Smith could see the city as few others ever had. To his left, looking south, was the steeple of Trinity Church, the most prominent landmark of lower Manhattan. Scanning from south to north, he would have seen rows of low-rise buildings seemingly gathered for protection around some larger structure: the post office near City Hall; the new Tribune building on Park Row, its magnificent clock tower rising two hundred and sixty feet into the air; the whitewashed headquarters of Harper & Brothers on Pearl Street. If he looked to the right, he would see the city advancing up the island, following the elevated train lines under construction above the north-south avenues (save for Broadway and Fifth Avenue, which were kept light and airy thanks to the influence of the wealthy who lived on those streets).

High above the river, young Al Smith was given a glimpse of the possibilities of the coming years, of the new century less than twenty-five years away.

"The bridge and I grew up together," Smith would later write. Joining them on the journey to maturity was the city itself.[4]

He was born on December 30, 1873, the first child of Catherine Mulvehill but the second for her husband, the thirty-eight-year-old widower Alfred Emanuel Smith, whose daughter had been sent to live with her grandmother when Smith's first wife died. A strapping man of 225 pounds and more than six feet tall, Alfred Smith worked hard as a trucker with his own carts and horses, and he was rewarded, modestly, for his sweat and effort. He was not rich by any means, but compared to the wretched immigrants packed into the airless buildings of Manhattan's Fourth Ward, he almost qualified as gentry, even if he was the poorly educated son of immigrants from Italy and Germany. He was able to afford a fifteen-dollar-per-month apartment with more rooms than family members, no small accomplishment, and he made sure his son and namesake and, later, his daughter had toys and clothing and food, and that was about all one could ask of life.

Catherine Mulvehill was the daughter of Irish immigrants who left County Westmeath together in 1841, just a few years before the potato crop in Ireland turned black and inedible, season after season, until there were parts of Ireland that were home only to the dead and the departing. Thomas and Maria Mulvehill landed in lower Manhattan and rented an apartment just a few blocks from the waterfront. The young couple found other men and women who sounded and looked like them in St. James Roman Catholic Church, a few blocks from their apartment on Dover and Water Streets. In the manner of the country they left behind, the Irish flocked to the church for the pleasure of each other's company, whether gathered in pews with heads bowed or dancing a jig at a parish social.

Thomas and Maria Mulvehill had six children, four boys and two girls.

Thomas was a skilled tailor who found work at Brooks Brothers, so he and Maria were blessed with the stability of a regular paycheck, and that blessing made others possible. The children were educated and sent off to useful careers in the police and fire departments. Catherine Mulvehill was born in 1850, the fifth of the six Mulvehill children, and she was sent to the girls' school at St. James parish.

Alfred Smith's stables were in a building on Dover and Water Streets, adjacent to the apartment building where Thomas and Maria Mulvehill and their children lived. At some point after his wife died, he took notice of Catherine, now finished with school and learning the umbrella trade. He summoned the courage to speak with her, and from there a romance blossomed.

He was fifteen years older than Catherine. He had a daughter somewhere in Brooklyn, a daughter he never saw and perhaps never spoke of. He was not Irish, but he was Catholic—a fellow parishioner at St. James Church—and at least he had an Irishman's love of storytelling. He had his own business, and he worked hard at it. He would take care of Catherine. Her parents could sense that.

Alfred and Catherine were married in St. James in the fall of 1872 and moved to the South Street apartment where Alfred E. Smith Jr. was born just over a year later and another child, Mary, arrived two years later on the very same day, December 30.

Young Al Smith never learned much about his father's family, mostly because Alfred was never around much. He rose early and came home late, and that was a good thing, because it meant he had work even during the lean times following the financial panic of 1873. They were lucky, because all around the great city men without work were begging in the streets, sleeping under lampposts and in parks, and wandering from place to place in search of a job. The *New York Times* noted that "the main thoroughfares seem absolutely blockaded with beggars." A quarter of the city's workers were unemployed, thanks to the cascade of closings and bankruptcies that followed the collapse of a Philadelphia-based investment house, Jay Cooke & Co. An official with the city's charity commission wrote that "men come to us hungry with hollow cheeks. . . . It is terrible, terrible." The city's mayor, William Havemeyer, a banker who owned a sizable chunk of the Long Island Rail Road, told a gathering of poor men that they ought to be saving their money rather than going "to the beer shops and theaters every night." The mayor would not order construction of public works or raise taxes to support relief. The jobless had only themselves to blame, he said. They had gone on strike and agitated for better working conditions. Did they expect the rich, who "by thrift and industry had built up their houses," to bail them out?[5]

The tensions between labor and capital during the early Gilded Age were an abstraction, if that, for Alfred Smith. He simply went about his business, lifting and trucking heavy loads from place to place, keeping his stables in good order and his precious horses in good health. On Sundays, the Smiths and many of their neighbors filed into a music hall called the Atlantic Garden, where adults drank beer and children ate cake and other treats while singers, musicians, and comedians entertained them. The Atlantic Garden was young Al Smith's introduction to the bustling, sinful, raucous, and sometimes violent neighborhood known as the Bowery, the poor man's theater district, a place of music and laughter and, for those so inclined, vice and sin. It was where the families of the Lower East Side and, more particularly, those in the Fourth Ward spent their precious spare time, so often squeezed into a few hours on Sunday.

The Bowery was where wisecracking adults stood in front of crowds and told jokes that depended on pitch-perfect timing, voice inflection, and, when all else failed, a pratfall or a funny face. Young Al Smith was enthralled and would remember into his last years the spectacle of singers and actors and dancers performing for his amusement while he and his little sister devoured chocolate and watched as the well-worn faces of their parents and neighbors brightened, if only for a few hours. And then night fell and the kerosene lamps were extinguished and all too soon it was Monday morning again.

It was a hard life, and, in the view of some, it was no way to raise a family. One of the men who employed Alfred's trucking services took him aside one day and presented an alternative: The employer owned a farm in the wilds of south Brooklyn, far from the chaos of the waterfront and the temptations of the Bowery. If Alfred wanted to move, he could rent the farm for a modest fee. Surely the children would be safer there, away from the streets that led so many astray. Wasn't the country preferable to the city?

Alfred Smith said no, for he loved the excitement of the city, the bustle, the chaos, the melding together of different people and beliefs and languages and customs. And he passed on that love to his son. Many years later, Al Smith would write, "I thank God I am part of this glorious metropolitan life, a part of its art and industry, its culture and recreations— and I would not trade my lot with a citizen anywhere."[6]

On a brilliant early afternoon in May 1883, forty mounted police officers and members of the 7th Regiment, New York Militia, escorted the president of the United States, Chester Arthur, from his hotel near Madison Square to the Brooklyn Bridge's New York entrance. Arthur would have been able to make the two-and-a-half-mile journey on his own if he had to, for the president was a New Yorker who owned a townhouse in Manhattan's Murray Hill neighborhood, not far from Theodore Roosevelt's home. Joining Arthur for the procession to the bridge was the governor of New York, Grover Cleveland, a stout man with a walrus moustache and a reputation as a reform-minded politician who sneered at the patronage requests of his fellow Democrats in New York City. Solid business Democrats like James Roosevelt loved Cleveland, and so did the earnest men in the city's reform clubs, where members gathered in well-appointed meeting rooms to mutter about the awful people who occupied public office at taxpayer's expense. Cleveland's reputation as an efficient, free-market reformer made him a national figure, and in 1885 he would be sworn in as the nation's twenty-second president, succeeding his fellow New Yorker, Arthur.

As crowds cheered, Arthur, Cleveland, and New York mayor Franklin Edson began their journey across the bridge's roadbed, suspended in midair by the network of steel cables. They were met at mid-span by Brooklyn's boy mayor, thirty-three-year-old Seth Low, and together they walked to the Brooklyn side, where there were prayers and music and speeches. And then the great bridge opened, and thousands of people came to see this modern marvel.

Decoration Day, a holiday set aside for the decoration of Civil War veterans' graves but, in fact, an excuse for picnics and games, fell six days after the opening ceremony, on May 31. The Smith family took advantage of Alfred's day off by boarding a ferry from lower Manhattan to Brooklyn, crossing the river the old-fashioned way. They returned over the bridge, taking in the sights and spectacle of the two cities at play. The wealthy mixed with the poor, united in their curiosity and their pride as they stopped mid-span with nothing beneath them but the East River. The ferries looked quaint and small and very outdated from the roadbed, nearly 150 feet above the river.

After the Smiths returned to Manhattan, at about 3:30 in the afternoon, a woman lost her footing on the steps leading to a walkway near the New York side of the bridge. The crowd on the bridge was immense, and when the woman who fell began to scream, others did, too. Somebody screamed that the bridge was falling. And then more people screamed, and more people panicked.

Al Smith and some of his friends were playing under the bridge. He saw bits of clothing, shoes, parasols, and hats falling from the roadbed above. Men, women, and children were being pushed, or doing the pushing, as they tried to flee the span before it crashed into the river. Smith and his friends raced over to Park Row, near the approaches to the bridge, and saw the injured being taken away and police officers gathering clothes and hats ripped from the bodies of the dead, the injured, and even the survivors.

Twelve people were trampled to death. About three dozen were injured. "That was my first view of a great calamity," Smith would later write.[7]

The bridge was new and modern. Why did people think it would fall?

two

FATHERS, MOTHERS, AND SONS

A HONEY-HAIRED CHILD wearing a flowing dress took one waddling step after another until the short journey was complete and the child was smothered in the arms of smiling adults.

It was May 1883, and while the cities downriver prepared to commemorate the completion of the great bridge, James and Sara Roosevelt celebrated the first unaided steps taken by little Franklin Delano Roosevelt, all of fourteen months old. His mother noted in her diary that the child seemed "quite proud of his new accomplishment."[1]

He was by all accounts a happy toddler, who won the approval of the adults in his life with a heartwarming smile and pleasant demeanor. An older, distant cousin, Mittie Roosevelt, described baby Franklin at five months as "sweet" and "cunning," a formidable combination at any age. Mittie Roosevelt was the mother of one of Franklin's two godfathers, Elliot Roosevelt, who would soon marry Anna Rebecca Hall. They would have a baby girl in 1884 and name her Anna Eleanor Roosevelt.[2]

He was born on January 30 and christened on March 20, 1883, in St. James Chapel in Hyde Park, just east of the Albany Post Road. The chapel was an adjunct of Saint James Church, a Gothic Revival structure a mile north of the chapel where the Episcopalians of Hyde Park gathered to worship on Sunday mornings. James and Sara Roosevelt sat in the third pew, and James, who helped run the parish through his elected position as a vestryman, rose from his place during the offertory to assist in collections. The parish's most prominent families lived in homes with names rather than addresses, and, in the manner of the English gentry, would expect the town's laborers to doff their caps as they passed by in their carriages on their way to Sunday services, and women would expect gentlemen in a coach to do the same. People knew their place in Hyde Park, and daily life was carried out as it was in the past and as it seemingly always would be.

Young Franklin's early childhood was just as orderly as the rituals of his church, his community, and his class. He was given instruction at home, following an exact routine his mother put together and supervised. He rose at seven. He was in bed by eight. Lessons started at nine and ended at four, with a break for play and lunch. His mother bathed him until he was nearly nine years old.

Summers were spent on Campobello Island, a bit of Canada lurking off the coast of Maine. There were trips across the Atlantic to England and the Continent, and domestic journeys to places like Chicago's World Columbian Exposition and Washington, DC. When they journeyed to other American cities, they traveled in James Roosevelt's elegant private railcar, which had multiple bedrooms and a sitting room.

At fifty-four years of age, James Roosevelt was nearing the end of his middle years and preparing to cross the line into old age when Franklin was born. He put aside the aches and pains familiar to anyone in middle age to introduce Franklin to his passion for the outdoors, and the two rode, fished, and sailed together in the warm weather; when winter came and snow covered the grounds, James and Franklin went sledding, skating, iceboating, and tobogganing.

The river and the timeless beauty of the Hudson Valley provided young Franklin with a sense of place far from crowded cities filling up with strangers. But there were signs of change as the final decade of the nineteenth century approached. From the veranda of Springwood's manor house, young Franklin marveled at the progress of a magnificent new bridge making its way across the Hudson between Poughkeepsie and Highland, just to the south of Hyde Park. It was made of steel and iron, and, at more than sixty-seven hundred feet, it was the longest double-track railway bridge in the world, standing more than two hundred feet above the river. Three thousand workers and four hundred and fifty horses worked on the bridge itself or on connections between the bridge's approaches and the various rail lines on both sides of the Hudson that sought access to the span.

The bridge certainly changed the view from the Roosevelts' veranda— where once they looked out on a lovely portrait of the river as it flowed south toward Newburgh, now there was a slash of steel across the landscape. But for James Roosevelt, a vice president of the Delaware and Hudson Railway, the bridge represented the inevitability of progress and expansion.

The Fourth Ward of Manhattan was home to nearly twenty thousand people, including Catherine and Alfred Smith and their two children, in the mid-1880s. Almost half the Smiths' neighbors were born outside the United States, and while many were from Ireland, others were not. It was possible to stroll through the ward and not hear a word of English.

But, diverse and chaotic and crowded though it was, the Fourth Ward really was a small town, one of the scores of small towns that made up the great metropolis of New York City. It seemed as though everybody knew somebody who was somehow different in any number of ways— skin color, language, religion. A newspaper reporter took note of the vast experiment in toleration and collaboration that was underway in Al Smith's small part of the world, writing that he found "Chinamen eating chili con carne, Italians eating chop suey, Irishmen talking Yiddish." The mixing and matching of cultures, cuisines, languages, and religions was not without tension, and the relative absence of African Americans in the ward was conspicuous, but for the most part, Al Smith's diverse neighbors found a way to get along.[3]

"When I was growing up," Smith wrote decades later, "everybody downtown knew his neighbors—not only people who were immediate neighbors but everybody in the neighborhood." What's more, Smith noted, in the small town of his big-city youth, "every man, woman and child knew the alderman."[4]

The alderman was indeed a familiar face in the neighborhood, as were the local leaders of the city's Democratic machine, Tammany Hall. They sponsored picnics in the woods of the Upper East Side, where an ox was roasted, carved up, and distributed in thick slices. A great bear of a man with a big black moustache, Tom Foley, was one of the neighborhood's most prominent characters, in part because he owned a popular saloon but more because he was a local Tammany leader in Smith's neighborhood. Another Tammany politician said of Foley that if you asked him for a hundred dollars to pay the rent and care for a sick family, "he'd dig down in his jeans and look over his pile. If there was a hundred in it, you'd get the hundred. If there was fifty, you'd get the fifty."[5]

The Smiths never had reason to call on Foley for help. They were lucky. Others, stricken by the loss of a job, poor health, or an accident, sometimes found themselves with little choice, for there was nothing else to protect them from falling into the abyss. There were plenty of private charities, but many were run by well-meaning but highly judgmental religious organizations, some of them seemingly more concerned with preaching than providing. Others were run by moral reformers who believed that charity only encouraged laziness and sloth, so only the deserving should be shown pity and a pittance.

Politics provided families with help and entertainment. The church offered comfort and education, and here the Smiths gladly availed themselves of both. They were regular churchgoers at St. James, a parish community of sixteen thousand souls. Young Al attended the parish school along with about fourteen hundred other children, including his sister. Nothing marked Al as out of the ordinary. Quite the opposite: one of Al's teachers took aside his sister, whom everybody called Mamie, and told her that it was pointless for Al to remain in school because he was a "great mischief."[6]

Smith's mother chose to ignore the teacher's advice, and the teacher no doubt was surprised when mischievous Al Smith developed into something of an orator, winning a prize at an elocution contest and earning an invitation to perform at the St. James School's graduation ceremony for the Class of 1886, when he was in sixth grade.

As young Al entertained the graduates and their families on that June afternoon, his father was barely able to get out of bed. He was ill and weak, unable to continue the heavy lifting required of his trucking business. The Smiths had just moved to a cheaper apartment at 12 Dover Street, again quite literally in the shadow of the Brooklyn Bridge.

Alfred Smith had worked hard for a long time and had been able to keep his family fed, educated, decently housed, and even entertained. But not long after the family moved from South Street, this proud man with a trucker's broad shoulders and strong back began to feel weak and tired. He sold his horses, and then his wagon. The Smiths' move to Dover Street, hard by the Brooklyn Bridge's Manhattan anchorage, was another attempt to save a few dollars on rent as the family's income dwindled.

He continued to decline through the summer and fall of 1886, so weak he spent his days propped up in bed. But on Election Day, he found the strength to climb down two flights of stairs, leaning on the arm of a friend, and shuffled through the streets to cast his ballot for Tammany Hall's candidate for mayor, Abram Hewitt. He returned exhausted, collapsing on the sidewalk outside his apartment. Catherine, whose anxiety and fear can only be imagined, brought out cushions so her husband could rest comfortably while he sought to regain his strength for the trip back upstairs.

He couldn't do it. His body, withered and brittle, was spent. Catherine and his friend helped Alfred into a chair and, slowly and lovingly and fearfully, they carried the sick man up the darkened stairs to his bedroom.

"I guess this is the last ballot I'll ever cast," Alfred Smith said.[7]

He died just over a week later, on November 11.

Al Smith was just a few weeks shy of his thirteenth birthday when his father died. Mamie was exactly two years younger. They had seen their father, big, burly, and hard-working, transformed into a frail weakling barely able to lift his head from a pillow, and now he was gone. What were they going to do?

Alfred's friends paid for his funeral. Afterward, Catherine and her two children returned to their joyless, chilly flat, just the three of them now. Near despair, Catherine blurted out a thought she might have kept to herself rather than have her children hear it. "I don't know where to turn," she said.

Al Smith, all of twelve years old, replied, "I'm here. I can take care of you."[8]

Catherine very quickly made it clear that she was capable of taking care of herself and her family. The following morning, she rose early, made her children their lunches, and went to work at an umbrella factory.

As the summer of 1896 began to fade, Franklin Roosevelt made his way down the riverbank from Springwood and plunged into the Hudson for a late-summer swim just a few days before he was to head off to Groton, the renowned boarding school for boys in Massachusetts. Sara Roosevelt watched her only child from a discreet distance. "I looked on and with a heavy heart," Sara wrote in her diary. James and Sara brought him to Groton on September 15. They returned home, just the two of them now, in James's private railroad car. "James and I feel this parting very much. It is hard to leave my darling boy," Sara wrote. James, ill since suffering a heart attack several years earlier, retired to his bedroom after returning from Groton. He remained there for several days as his ailing heart sought to regain its strength.

In his final year at Groton, Franklin was awarded a prize for a Latin essay, but his parents missed the ceremony. James was ill and weak; Sara thought it best to stay with him rather than travel to Groton for the ceremony. They summered in Campobello that year before sending Franklin off to Harvard as a member of the class of 1904. In late October, James fell seriously ill again, and yet again in early December. His mother summoned Franklin to their apartment in New York City as his father continued to weaken. "It was sweet just to be together," Sara wrote.[9]

James Roosevelt died in his bed at 2:20 on the morning of December 8, 1900. He was buried in the graveyard behind St. James Church in Hyde Park. It was just the two of them now.

three

YOUNG MEN IN A HURRY

THE STREETS OF THE LOWER East Side were never quiet, not even in the predawn darkness of a Friday morning. As Al Smith wiped the sleep from his eyes at the ungodly hour of 3:00 a.m. and started on his short walk to work, the hooves of horses clipped and clopped along South Street, pulling carts to the waterfront to await the morning's haul of tea and vegetables and spices. The walk took only a few minutes, but on some days—when he turned down his face from blasts of cold air off the river, or when late-summer storms turned the streets into streams—it was a few minutes too long. He began his journey every morning just before four o'clock, except on Fridays, when he was due in at three. Friday was a big day for fish in New York, or, more precisely, for the sellers and consumers of fish. The city's large and growing Catholic population was prohibited from eating meat on Friday, so the market was always packed that morning and demand was strong. Al had to get to work an hour early to put things in order for his employer, Joseph Feeney & Co.

He held the title of "assistant bookkeeper." Mostly, though, he transported fish, he packed fish, he wrapped fish, he gutted fish. He dreamed about fish—a live one, chasing after him and looking to take revenge for what he had done to all those other fish in all those barrels. And he ate fish, lots of fish, because he got it for free as a perk, and the Smiths were not about to turn down free food.

A few hours into his day's work, when the sky over Brooklyn brightened, Smith climbed to the market's roof and looked out to the east through a pair of strong binoculars, trying to spot his employer's fishing boats making their way into Buttermilk Channel, a narrow strait separating Brooklyn from Governor's Island. As the boats turned gently to the port side and sailed toward South Street's piers, Smith zoomed in to see how high, or low, they were in the water. If they were low, it meant they were weighed down with an impressive catch. If they were riding high, it meant the night's fishing had been frustrating and the results meager. Smith, known for his leather lungs, shouted his observations to his bosses, who quickly calibrated the prices they would charge for the day's catch. Lots of fish meant low prices. A scarcity allowed dealers to charge more, especially on Fridays, when demand was high and dogma emphatic. Having that extra bit of intelligence helped Feeney & Co. get a slight edge on the competition.[1]

Hard though it was, Al Smith enjoyed his job at the Fulton Fish Market, although some of that enjoyment may have been in retrospect. Later in life, when he had earned many titles and honors, Al Smith still told stories of the lessons he learned while slinging the morning's catch into barrels on the market's floor. "I speak the fish language," he once said. As a member of the New York Assembly, he once found himself in conversation with colleagues who brandished their college credentials in a series of initials, leading Smith to describe himself as an FFM man. They were puzzled, until Smith explained that the initials stood for Fulton Fish Market.

Al Smith started at the fish market in 1892, when he was nineteen years old. He had been working full time at various jobs since the spring of 1888, when the family's finances took a turn for the worse and he quit St. James School just two months before his eighth-grade graduation. Since the death of her husband in 1886, Catherine Smith did everything she could to keep her family fed, housed, and together, one of the many women on the Lower East Side who carried on and raised their children after their husbands died or disappeared. Al delivered newspapers after he got home from school, and his sister helped out whenever she could.

Still, it was not enough, and when Al had an opportunity to make three dollars a week in the trucking business—his late father's trade—he took it.

He moved from job to job quickly, more than doubling his salary when he took a job as a clerk for an oil company for eight dollars a week. Feeney & Co. hired him to work in the fish market for twelve dollars a week—another impressive raise. The job was physical and draining, but because he started so early, he was released from his obligations relatively early as well, generally at about four in the afternoon. He returned home, changed out of his sweaty, smelly work clothes and then transformed himself into an aspiring actor.

He was a member of the St. James Players, an amateur theatrical company associated with his parish and well-known beyond the parish's borders. Some members of the troupe graduated from the eight-hundred-seat space in the basement to the theaters of the Bowery and even to the more respectable venues uptown.

There were moments when young Al Smith saw himself making that same journey. He was, as he later wrote, "dead stuck on acting." The more he performed, the more confident he became in all parts of his life. When he overheard several young women talking about a picnic they were planning, he made it clear that he'd like to join them. One of the women, apparently not particularly enamored with the boisterous young man and his loud clothes, replied, tersely, "You haven't been asked to go."

"Oh, you'll ask me," Smith told her. "You won't be able to get along without the talent."[2]

He wasn't wrong. The young man had that certain something that the local power brokers could spot a mile away. People liked him, and he seemed to like them. He worked hard. And he knew how to give a speech—he had the timing, the theatrics. He knew when to flail his hands, when to bring his voice to a whisper (perhaps his hardest assignment), and how to rouse the crowd. For the Irish who ran Tammany Hall, speechmaking was not just an art but a part of the culture they inherited from the old country. The men who succeeded in public office were as eloquent as the men who operated behind the scenes were taciturn. They were the New World successors to the storytellers of rural Ireland, the *shanachie*, men and women who entertained the villagers with stories of heroes and villains, great deeds and misdeeds, courage and infamy. There was more than a little of the shanachie in this young man from St. James parish.

Al Smith began drinking beer with the older men in Tom Foley's saloon, where the local political power brokers gathered to talk over the latest gossip from City Hall—just a few blocks to the west—or from the outer reaches of civilization up in Albany. Politics was not a spectator sport in the Fourth Ward. The game was about participation.

Smith's choice of drinking establishments was no accident, for he had known Tom Foley for years and fondly remembered the annual Foley-sponsored outings and picnics. Foley knew something about Smith, too. He knew that Al had lost his father at a young age, just as he had. He knew that Al was trying to find his place in the world, despite his lackluster scholastic career. Tom himself went to work as a blacksmith at the age of thirteen to help support his widowed mother.

They got along, and Foley helped arrange a job for Smith on the public payroll. For $800 a year, the twenty-one-year-old was given the task of delivering summonses for jury duty and investigating the excuses the good citizens of New York had for avoiding the assignment. His work sometimes took him across the Harlem River into the Bronx, a sparsely populated region under the jurisdiction of Manhattan-based courts. The journey to deliver a jury summons to these northern woodlands would consume the better part of a day, requiring multiple transfers from elevated trains to horse-drawn streetcars.

It was adventure rather than business that brought him to the Bronx one day in 1894, when he tagged along with an acquaintance who needed the signature of a relative, Emily Dunn, on some family papers. She lived in a small house on 170th Street and Third Avenue in the Claremont section of the Bronx, surrounded by vast open spaces and people who seemed more like pioneers on the edges of the western prairie than fellow New Yorkers. The little house also was home to Catherine, daughter of Emily and her husband and fellow Irish immigrant, Simon. Katie, as everybody called her, was refined and educated, and she lived in a house with a parlor and went to an academy for young ladies. She had been taught to sing, a skill the young entertainer Al Smith never quite mastered. Her family was so much better off than his, and she was so very different, even though she and her family had lived in Al's neighborhood until 1889 or so, when she was about ten years old.

She was just sixteen now, but Al, six years her senior, was smitten. He insisted on accompanying his friend when family business took him to the Bronx again. Soon it became acceptable for Al to visit on his own, and he did so, often, even though it took about ninety minutes to travel about a dozen of the longest miles he'd ever know: The Third Avenue El. The horse-drawn streetcar on the Bronx side. The walk to the Dunn house. And back again. He often fell asleep on the ride home, but he saw no reason to complain.

It was a protracted courtship for lots of reasons: She was very young, Al was a busy fellow, they were separated by geography, and there was the whole business of Al and his love of the stage. That was something of a problem for the Dunns. They had sent Katie to a finishing school run by nuns; they had this nice house with a parlor in the Bronx, far from the teeming masses of the old neighborhood; and they very likely had dreams of Katie marrying a college boy, maybe a young man from St. John's College—the future Fordham University—just a few miles to the north.

It soon became clear that if Al was intent on winning his Katie, something would have to change. *The Paper Chase*, produced in 1898, became one of Al's final curtain calls. He gave up the stage for love.[3]

Katie Dunn and Al Smith were married on May 6, 1900, in the Church of St. Augustine, just a few blocks from the Dunn household. The newlyweds spent the summer at Bath Beach in Brooklyn, and then Al Smith brought his bride back to her old neighborhood on the Lower East Side.

In the winter of his freshman year at Harvard, weeks removed from burying his father, Franklin Roosevelt set his sights on winning election to the staff of the *Crimson*, the school's renowned student-run newspaper. Only a select few volunteer journalists were invited to join the paper's staff of editors, and Franklin was determined to be one of them. He often spent up to seven hours a day in the *Crimson*'s office on Massachusetts Avenue trying to make himself useful and, in turn, ingratiating himself with his elders. "I have worked again for the *Crimson* from 4 p.m. to 11 p.m. [and] I am now off for bed," he wrote his mother on the night of April 7, a Sunday. He hoped the editors took note of his enthusiasm.[4]

Then again, there were lots of enthusiastic young Harvard students scurrying around campus on behalf of the *Crimson*. What Franklin Roosevelt needed was not enthusiasm but a good story. And on the evening of April 29 he got one: he learned that the vice president of the United States, a member of the Harvard Class of 1880, would deliver an unannounced lecture in Professor A. Lawrence Lowell's government class the following morning. Even the best-informed political reporters at the *Globe*, the *Herald*, the *Evening Transcript*, and all the other Boston papers were not aware of this. The vice president, Roosevelt learned, would discuss his recent tenure as governor of New York, where he proved to be so disruptive that the party bosses decided to promote him to a meaningless job in Washington so they could return to business as usual in the country's most powerful state.

Franklin Roosevelt obtained his exclusive about the vice president simply by calling him on the telephone to say hello. He had this kind of access because he was, after all, Vice President Theodore Roosevelt's fifth cousin. Theodore told Franklin all about his upcoming visit to his alma mater and his plan to deliver a lecture in Professor Lowell's class. That was news to Franklin, who was enrolled in the very class the vice president would address. In fact, it was news to everybody. Professor Lowell had kept the vice president's lecture quiet because he didn't want other students to overrun his class. So Theodore Roosevelt's visit was something akin to an academic state secret.

The boy reporter saw his opportunity. He quickly made his way to the

Crimson's offices and typed out his exclusive. The next morning, his story led the *Crimson*'s front page, splashed across four columns. He was overjoyed. "Last night I got a 'scoop' about Cousin Theodore's talk," he dutifully informed his mother.[5]

Two thousand people showed up in a venue that held five hundred. Professor Lowell was livid. The vice president no doubt was delighted—he always was. Franklin Roosevelt was elected to the *Crimson*'s staff later that year.

He returned home when the academic year ended, home to a lonelier Springwood with his father gone. Sara and Franklin chose not to make their usual excursion to Campobello, where memories would be too fresh and sad. Instead, they sailed to Europe in early July, visiting Norway, Germany, and Switzerland before finishing up their journey in Paris. It was there, on September 7, that they learned that President William McKinley had been shot two days earlier while visiting Buffalo in western New York. The president was still alive, and as they set sail for home on September 11, reports indicated that he would likely survive.

He died on September 14. The Roosevelts learned the tragic news while still at sea. It was, Franklin noted, a "terrible shock."[6]

Cousin Theodore was now president of the United States.

Upon his return to Harvard in the fall, Franklin found there was even more magic in his last name. He was elected secretary of the *Crimson* and was duly described in the Boston press as, alternatively, President Roosevelt's cousin or his nephew. A newspaper reporter wrote that the new *Crimson* secretary "has many of the qualities that have put his uncle at the front. He is a hard worker [and] thoroughly democratic." The comparisons with his fifth cousin made Franklin "excessively tired," or so he told his mother. In fact, he seemed to enjoy every minute of it.[7]

The familial connection to the president became stronger still in late 1902 when Franklin began courting cousin Ted's niece, Eleanor, a shy nineteen-year-old who was orphaned at the age of nine. They attended a White House New Year's party to ring in 1903, and she was on hand to celebrate his twenty-first birthday several weeks later. He asked her to marry him on a mid-November afternoon in 1903 as they strolled together along the banks of the Nashua River.

As Al Smith celebrated Thanksgiving in 1903, he and his family were utterly astonished as well as thankful. Just a few weeks earlier, Alfred E. Smith, grade-school dropout, had been chosen by the neighborhood's voters to be a member of the state assembly. In a little over a month, he would take his place in the lavish assembly chamber in Albany, where men of far greater learning and experience made the laws that governed the richest and most powerful state in the union.

His political career had unfolded almost as fast as his family life did. He and Katie quickly became the parents of two children, born twelve months apart. Alfred E. Smith Jr. was born in January 1901, and Emily Smith in late December of the same year. In the fall of 1903, the family of four was living on Peck Slip, within walking distance of St. James Church, the South Street waterfront, and Tom Foley's saloon.

It was Foley who sent Al Smith to Albany to represent the voters of the 2nd Assembly District. To be sure, there was the whole business of elections, and the voters of the neighborhood had the right to turn down Foley's choice. But they trusted big Tom Foley with his blacksmith's arms and barrel chest, a man who was not afraid of getting dirty if that's what it took to earn and keep the loyalty of his neighbors and friends. The *New York Times* said of him, "He founded clubs where he and his district captains acted as a sort of permanent committee to give everybody in the district who needed it, whether a voter or not, advice, assistance, work. For a good many years his part of the east side and its inhabitants were as familiar to him as if it were a village."[8]

Voters ratified Foley's choice of Smith on Election Day, casting 4,942 ballots for the young man from Saint James parish. His Republican opponent received about 1,500, the Socialist 106, and the Prohibitionist 5. The prospect of representing his neighbors in the state legislature didn't exactly fill young Al Smith with humility and awe. "Acting is a lot harder work than helping make the laws," Smith told a newspaper reporter on the night of his election. But, he added with a wink, "politics pays better." That certainly was true: Smith's salary, beginning January 1, would be $1,500 a year, which was about $1,500 a year more than he ever made on stage. But it was the stage that gave him the confidence to play the new role he had been assigned: "If I'm not exactly a star in the House yet," he said, "I guess I'll get to the center of the stage."[9]

Eleanor and Franklin Roosevelt were married on March 17, 1905, Saint Patrick's Day, when the bride's uncle, the president of the United States, was scheduled to be in New York. At the reception afterward, guests gathered not around the happy couple but the boisterous president.

Franklin was enrolled in Columbia Law School at the time of his marriage, but his studies were short lived. He left school in 1907 after passing the bar exam in New York but before receiving his degree. Membership in the bar was the only credential he needed to begin practicing law; the degree from Columbia was not worth his time and effort. So while his erstwhile classmates continued to plow through case law and precedents, Franklin Roosevelt, Esq., now the father of two toddlers, Anna Eleanor and James, spent several months at Hyde Park and in Campobello before accepting a job as a junior lawyer at the Wall Street firm of Carter, Ledyard and Millburn in September 1907. The firm made a specialty of defending corporations from the trust-busting proclivities of Franklin's cousin in the White House.

Franklin quickly found the whole business tiresome, not remotely the sort of work that suited his personality and his ambitions. He had other things in mind, and he was not afraid to say so. In one of his many idle moments in the firm's office, as he and other junior staffers chatted about the future, he said he would like to run for a seat in the state assembly. After that, well, he loved the sea, and so he could see himself one day as the assistant secretary of the navy. Franklin's sharper listeners would have realized that he was, in fact, describing his famous cousin's career. Following his stint at the Department of the Navy, Franklin said, he would run for governor. And then?

"Anyone who is governor of New York has a good chance to be president," he said.[10]

As one of Franklin's friends put it, it all sounded entirely reasonable.

four

ALBANY

AL SMITH SPENT his first night in Albany—his first night away from home in five years—awake, alert, and deathly afraid.

It wasn't the weather that frightened him, although it surely was fearsome in early January 1904. It was fifteen below zero when Al Smith arrived at Union Station in Albany. He and a fellow freshman legislator, Tom Caughlan, raised their collars and made their way to Keeler's Hotel on Broadway and Maiden Lane. They arrived half frozen and were delighted to see a roaring fireplace in the lobby.

Smith and Caughlan planned to board together during the four-month legislative session to save on expenses. They were assigned a room on one of the creaky hotel's upper floors, which ordinarily would not have caused Smith much anxiety. But only a week earlier, on December 30, 1903, more than six hundred people were killed in a fire in Chicago's Iroquois Theatre. The aftermath of the ghastly tragedy still dominated the front pages of newspapers across the country.

Al Smith kept thinking about that roaring fireplace in the hotel's lobby and the thought kept him awake and afraid. In his mind, he could hear the logs hissing and the crackle of bark catching fire. Smoke filled his nostrils, or so it seemed. He checked for any sort of fire escape but found that his room's window led to an interior corridor. There was, as far as he could tell, no way out.

There would be no sleep for Al Smith, or for his roommate, on that night, the night before they were to be sworn in as members of the New York Assembly. Smith persuaded Caughlan to stay up and play pinochle, which they did until five in the morning, when they then took turns sleeping for an hour. Then it was time for breakfast and a short journey to the state capitol just a few blocks away. Bleary-eyed and exhausted, they passed the Ten Eyck Hotel on State Street, where a large sign on the building's exterior taunted them. The hotel, the sign said, was "fireproof." It was also too expensive for their budget. They booked rooms in a low-rise boarding-house for the rest of the session.[1]

The capitol building at the top of State Street was so much more than just another statehouse in just another political backwater. Dedicated five years earlier, in 1899, after three decades of construction, it was designed to show off the imperial ambitions of the men who walked its high-ceilinged hallways, cut deals behind huge wooden doors seemingly designed for defense rather than privacy, and made laws in the ornate splendor of the senate and assembly chambers. It was built for men like Theodore Roosevelt, the first governor to take his place in the second-story offices built for the state's chief executive. He wasn't there very long. He lived in the White House now.

The building cost $25 million, the most expensive state capitol of its time. The capitol's red-gabled turrets, its baroque stonework, its gorgeous interior staircase, its cathedral-like ceilings inspired those who wrote and executed New York's laws to dream big dreams. Albany gave New York's politicians the energy and ambition they needed to begin their climb to the top, to embrace the state's motto: Excelsior. Ever upward.

Bundled against the arctic air, Al Smith climbed the capitol's enormous staircase facing State Street, an onerous task in the best of weather. If only he had known that there was an elevator on the first floor, hidden behind the staircase. If only he had known that the staircase itself was put in place not so much to convey people from the street but to prop up the building after architects determined that one day it might begin to slide down the steep hill it was built to dominate. There was no investigation of this rather striking design flaw.

Al Smith took the oath of office as a member of the New York State Assembly at eleven o'clock on the morning of January 6, 1904. He took his place at the very back of the assembly chamber, in the last row, where freshman members of the minority party were closer to visitors and pass-ersby than they were to the chamber's Republican leaders. From Smith's vantage point, procedural motions and the introduction of bills and the rulings of the Speaker of the Assembly passed by in a blur. Nobody had prepared him for this, not even Tom Foley. He had given Smith a single piece of guidance: "Don't speak until you have something to say."[2]

And so, for the first time in his life, Al Smith was speechless. He duti-fully scooped up the papers that piled up on his desk and brought them home to study, but the words meant nothing. "I never knew there was so much law," he said. He found himself reading amendments to laws he had never heard of, written in opaque phrases and clauses that only the chamber's growing population of lawyers could understand. He turned in frustration to his roommate, Caughlan: "I can tell a haddock from a hake by the look in its eye," he said, "but in two hundred years I could not tell these things from a bale of hay."[3]

He was assigned spots on two committees: Banks, and Public Lands and Forestry. "I knew nothing about banking laws and had never been in a bank except to serve a jury notice," Smith said, "and I had never seen a forest."[4]

But personal experience, or experience of any kind, was not a prereq-uisite for a committee assignment. His roommate Caughlan, who lived in and represented lower Manhattan, was assigned to the Committee on Indian Affairs. If he had ever laid eyes on an American Indian, it was of the cigar-store variety.[5]

Smith slogged through the session, trying his best to make sense of the parliamentary maneuvering, the back-and-forth between colleagues whose names he did not know and the dreary prose of the bills brought to his desk every day. Through it all, Al Smith kept his mouth shut. He had nothing to say, and so he said nothing.

Without the starry eyes of his first campaign, he went through the motions of reelection in the fall of 1904, hiding his frustration behind a mask of good cheer, playing the part of a backslapping politician. He easily won, more than doubling the total of his Republican opponent. On the day he cast his ballot for himself, Smith and his family moved to a new apartment, a five-room walkup at 28 Oliver Street, still in St. James parish, still in the neighborhood that defined him, and just steps away from Tom Foley's headquarters, the Downtown Tammany Club. He would live on Oliver Street for twenty years, moving to a larger apartment at number 25 in 1909. His neighbors celebrated his election that night and Al smiled through it all, not showing even a hint of second thoughts.

Albany's rituals were more familiar to Smith when he returned to the capital for the new legislative session in 1905, but familiarity did nothing to ease his frustration. The bills were still incomprehensible. The debates were still impossible to follow. After a particularly frustrating day in the capitol, he went for a walk with Tom Caughlan, who found the bills and the speeches and the debates equally mystifying. They walked down State Street and wound up by the Hudson River.

"Tommy," Smith finally said, "we're in the wrong place. Whoever thought we were assemblymen?"[6]

It was Tom Foley who thought Al Smith was an assemblyman. When the session finally ended in the spring of 1905, Al Smith made an appointment to see Foley, to tell him that he had made a poor choice. Al Smith was not cut out for politics.

They met for breakfast and talked over Al's frustrations at a downtown restaurant not far from a civic center that would one day bear Foley's name: Foley Square. Smith told him that Albany was no place for a boy from the Fulton Fish Market, no place for a man who didn't finish grade school. Foley considered the young man who was so eager just two years earlier, who predicted that he would be a star of the show in Albany. Now he wanted out, beaten by the system.

He told Smith that his timing was good, because the city was looking to hire a superintendent of buildings. The job was Al's if he wanted it. Tom Foley could find somebody else to represent the voters of the 2nd Assembly District. Al just had to say the word and it would be done.

Days passed. Tom Foley waited and Al Smith thought it over. And perhaps Foley knew how this would end up. Smith decided that he would stand for reelection after all, and he vowed that after he won reelection— victory was a given—things would be different. He wouldn't let the debates and the paperwork get him down. He would teach himself, just as he had been teaching himself for years. "I just hated the idea that I should have to admit there was anything I could not understand," Smith said.[7]

Tom Foley might well have folded his blacksmith's arms and smiled at his own wisdom.

Al Smith headed back to Albany in January 1906.

Albany!

Franklin Roosevelt might well have wondered what he had done to deserve this stroke of good fortune. The district attorney of Poughkeepsie, a man named John Mack, had stopped by to see him in his Wall Street office to talk over some legal business. Then, seemingly out of nowhere, Mack asked him if he might be interested in running for a state assembly seat in Dutchess County in the fall.

Interested? Roosevelt could hardly contain himself.

Roosevelt had been slogging away at the law firm for a little more than two years but it felt more like twenty. Roosevelt could barely disguise his disinterest. Colleagues noticed that he was hardly a go-getter. He was, they concluded, a "harmless bust."[8]

It simply was not the life he imagined. He wanted something else, and John Mack was offering it to him. All he had to do was say yes, and so he did. Mack was delighted: he had recruited a candidate with one of the most famous last names in the nation, and he was a Democrat!

The man who currently held the assembly seat was a Hudson Valley stalwart named Lewis Stuyvesant Chanler, a blue-blooded lawyer who was a shoo-in for reelection in 1910 but had seemingly lost interest in running for another term. Mack's fellow Democrats in Dutchess County needed a strong candidate to hold onto the seat; and who better than a man named Roosevelt?

Franklin Roosevelt began to act like a candidate even though nothing was quite official just yet. He spent more time in the Hudson Valley, making sure to be seen and acting like a neighbor even though he and Eleanor and their two children were living in a townhouse on East 65th Street in Manhattan that Sara Roosevelt had bought for them as a wedding present. (She moved into the adjacent apartment.) He plunged into retail politics that summer under the watchful eyes of the valley's political professionals, drinking beer and smiling broadly at events like the Poughkeepsie Police Department's annual clambake.

Just as Roosevelt was getting a taste of the excitement of a political campaign, the incumbent, Chanler, had an apparent change of heart. He told Roosevelt over lunch that he would run for reelection to the assembly after all. The conversation did not go well, at least not from Roosevelt's perspective.

He was furious, believing he was played for a fool, and he told the Dutchess County party bosses that he might well run an independent campaign, just to spite them and Chanler. That would very likely lead to a split in the Democratic vote and a Republican victory. Was he bluffing? The party bosses could hardly take that chance.

They quickly presented the impatient young man with a Plan B. It wasn't particularly attractive, but it was all they had. Would Roosevelt be interested in running for state senate? They didn't have a candidate yet, and with good reason. The senate district was larger than the assembly district and took in a lot more farmers and rural communities, including parts of neighboring Putnam and Columbia Counties. It was a safe

Republican seat, held by a nondescript but capable incumbent named John Schlosser, who had offended nobody. But then again, a Democrat named Roosevelt just might stand a chance. About one in five, they said.

Roosevelt took the offer. He had five weeks to impress his would-be constituents in a district that spanned three mostly rural counties connected by pitted, dusty roads built for the nineteenth century. He set out on them almost immediately, although before doing so he checked in with the other Roosevelts to make sure that cousin Theodore had no objections. Theodore was now a former president—a very young former president, at age fifty-two—and in 1910 he was campaigning across New York on behalf of progressive Republicans. Word was passed to Franklin that Theodore would not campaign for his Republican opponent.

Franklin rented an automobile, a bright red Maxwell, and paid a driver to take him the length and breadth of the district he wished to represent, giving speeches, shaking hands, complimenting villagers for the beauty of their trees, their civic buildings, their belief in progress, a belief, as it happened, he shared with them. "This country has progressed since its beginnings more than any other probably in the history of the world," he told one group of potential voters.[9]

The vagueness of his speeches mattered less than the effort he put into them. Wherever two or three were gathered, alongside a road, in front of a general store, at a crossroads, there was Franklin Roosevelt and the red Maxwell. He called these people "my friends," and he was happy to tell them that he would represent them and only them—not those other, corrupt interests that were based elsewhere, and they knew exactly what he meant. Even several Italian laborers lingering alongside a road were not immune from a Rooseveltian peroration. The candidate spotted them, ordered the Maxwell halted, hopped out of the flashy car, and spoke to them in a Hudson Valley version of their native language. Their astonishment was no doubt profound.

Franklin Roosevelt was in Springwood on election night to monitor the results. Republicans, badly divided in 1910 thanks in part to Theodore Roosevelt's war on the party's conservatives, got their electoral heads handed to them. The Republican nominee for governor, Henry Stimson, lost badly to the Democratic nominee, a pleasant nonentity named John Dix. And in the 26th Senatorial District, so reliably Republican for so many years, Franklin D. Roosevelt piled up majorities in towns in all three counties, winning by more than a thousand votes out of about thirty thousand cast. Democrats won both houses of the legislature and the governor's office, meaning they would have complete control over state government for the first time in years.

Ninety miles to the south, Roosevelt's fellow Democrats in Manhattan were celebrating the party's big sweep. But one Tammany Hall veteran saw trouble as he scanned the returns from upstate. State senator Timothy Sullivan, who had risen from terrible poverty to become the boss of the Bowery, took note of the sensational victory in the Hudson Valley. It was impressive, but, he noted, the winner was a Roosevelt, and he had seen what another Roosevelt, the former president, who was still called by his old military title of colonel, had done to his own party that very year.

"If we've caught a Roosevelt," Sullivan told his smoke-wreathed friends at Tammany, "we'd better take him down and drop him off the dock. The Roosevelts run true to form, and this kid is likely to do for us what the Colonel is going to do for the Republican party—split it wide open."[10]

Senator-elect Franklin Delano Roosevelt started looking for suitable accommodations in Albany. A friend advised him to make sure he joined the Fort Orange Club, where Albany's elite gathered, the local country club, and St. Peter's Episcopal Church just down the hill from the capitol. The music at St. Peter's was lovely, the friend assured him, perhaps unaware that Roosevelt would more likely be found at the country club than in church on Sunday, to the consternation of the more dutiful Eleanor.[11]

Franklin Roosevelt soaked it all in. He had accomplished the improbable and had a ball doing it. He and Eleanor and their three children packed up and set out for Albany, where he was sure he'd have the time of his life.

five

LEADERSHIP

A LITTLE MORE than five years had passed between Al Smith's heart-to-heart talk with Tom Foley and the great Democratic sweep of 1910. In that time, Smith transformed himself from a widely ignored functionary in the state assembly to one of the chamber's most popular members. Republicans and Democrats alike found themselves under the spell of this rough-hewn character who told colorful stories from the sidewalks of New York.

Al Smith was as sociable as any of them, and he was not one to turn down the chance to have a few beers and tell a few stories. But after closing time at the saloon, when his colleagues spilled into the street in search of other entertainment, Smith returned to his boardinghouse, parked himself behind a cheap desk, lit a cigar, and began decoding into plain English the bills his learned colleagues wished to become law.

There were proposals to build bridges and highways, there were requests to hire state workers in counties he would have a hard time finding on a map—where in the world were Cattaraugus and Herkimer Counties anyway?—and, most intimidating of all, there was the appropriations bill, a massive document outlining the ways in which the state planned to spend more than $36 million. It was a given that nobody read the bill in its entirety as it was too tiresome and boring, and besides, individual lawmakers generally cared only about the appropriations in their own district.

Al Smith began reading the whole bill, every page, and as he did so he transformed himself from an insecure near quitter to an expert in the ways and means of New York State government. "There is no better way of becoming acquainted with the business of the state than to study the appropriation bill," Smith said. He was being modest: he was not merely acquainted with the bill, he knew it intimately. A newsman noted that when the assembly took up the appropriations bill, most members found convenient excuses to leave the floor. But when Al Smith rose to criticize or praise portions of the massive bill, members stayed in their seats. "He could keep the members in their seats hours on end with his masterly dissection of that measure," the reporter noted.[1]

Like the legislators, newspapermen began to take notice of this Tammany man from the Lower East Side who insisted on being called Al. He was a diligent member of the insurance committee, immersing himself in the nitty-gritty of arcane regulation. He became a regular visitor to the state library in the capitol, where he'd inquire about copies of old laws and books about laws, tempering the gravel in his voice so that he might not disturb the scholars and staff in the room. He soon knew more about New York government than any of his better-educated colleagues. And he understood how all those bills and all those spending measures affected the people he was sworn to represent.

He returned home after the 1906 session exhausted but satisfied. The following year, after his usual smashing reelection, he wrote and introduced his own bills, handfuls of them, and they reflected the views of a man who had spent hundreds of hours thinking about laws and government's place in this new world of the twentieth century. He proposed new regulations for the fire insurance industry aimed at cracking down on what he called the "arbitrary fixing of rates." He joined with his New York City colleagues in fighting for the repeal of laws that prohibited the playing of baseball—a workingman's game—on Sunday. He argued for tougher regulations of narcotic drugs and cigarettes (he was silent on the subject of cigars, his particular vice) and for a nascent movement to create a workers' compensation fund. And he teamed with his friend and roommate, Robert Wagner, in pushing a bill mandating that the fare on the Coney Island rail line should be cut to five cents from a dime to allow city dwellers cheaper access to the waves and breezes of Brooklyn's seaside resort.[2]

Many of the bills he wrote and supported did not pass. Still, Al Smith was making his voice heard in all its Lower East Side glory.

A young, idealistic woman named Frances Perkins arrived in Albany in 1910 to lobby for the New York Consumers League. She was thirty years old, a child of New England privilege, and her idea of a progressive reformer was Theodore Roosevelt, with his high-pitched, high-minded appeals to reason in public life and noblesse oblige in private. Roosevelt's words helped inspire Perkins to work with the poor in settlement houses in Chicago and New York City after graduating from Mount Holyoke College. She went to Albany hoping to work with legislators interested in passing new bills to ease the burdens of factory workers, seamstresses, and their families, especially when illness, an accident, or a financial panic took control of their lives.

Her immediate cause was a bill that would limit the workweek to fifty-four hours for women, and in the winter of 1910 she became a familiar figure in the high-ceilinged hallways of the capitol as she sought to win support for her bill. Some version of it had been kicking around Albany for several years, but the factory owners and their friends in high places and in both parties made certain that it was never considered. What right did the government have to tell the owners of private property how long their employees should work?

Perkins, her hair short, her dresses sober, her demeanor earnest, was making the rounds in the assembly chamber with a colleague one day when she spotted Al Smith at his desk—now moved considerably closer to the action. While other politicians gathered in small circles and gossiped with each other during a break in the debates, Smith remained seated, looking serious and scholarly as he stared at the papers in front of him. Perkins noticed and asked her colleague about the solitary hard worker in the chamber. That's Al Smith, Perkins's colleague said. "He's reading the bills introduced last night." Perkins decided to approach him. Al Smith rose, as any gentleman would, and greeted the young woman, who told him about the fifty-four-hour bill and how important it was. Smith said the bill had his support, but it was stalled in committee. She should ask for a hearing so she could make her case in public and perhaps generate publicity and fight the battle again some other time.[3]

Smith's blunt assessment impressed Perkins—he seemed very different from the popular image of a ruthless machine politician. Her colleague agreed that Smith was a decent sort but was less optimistic about how effective he might be. "Pity he's a Tammany man," Perkins's colleague said.[4]

While it was notable that Al Smith was winning over reformers like Frances Perkins with his warmth, intelligence, and honesty, there was only one person whose good opinion Smith needed, and that person was Charles Francis Murphy, the head of Tammany Hall.

Murphy, a reserved man with round spectacles, his once athletic frame now flabby around the middle, was looking to create a new kind of Tammany Hall, with a new breed of lawmakers: respectable, responsible, and, most important, electable. Al Smith was all of those things, and Charlie Murphy was quick to realize it. Smith, he decided, was going places.

But some of Murphy's allies believed that there were limits to just how far Smith could climb. It was unfortunate, nobody's fault really, but facts were facts. Smith was a kid from the streets, popular on the Lower East Side but hardly the type who could bridge the gulf between New York City and the rest of the state. "He's a nice fellow," a friend of Murphy's said of Smith. "He has a lot of ability. It's too bad he isn't a college man."

Murphy, a high school dropout who had the sort of power that Harvard men found irritating if not corrupt, had a ready response.

"If he was a college man," Murphy said, "he wouldn't be Al Smith."[5]

As Democrats prepared to take over state government after their electoral sweep in 1910, there were rumors that Lewis Stuyvesant Chanler, the Hudson Valley patrician whose decision to run for reelection in 1910 led to Franklin Roosevelt's senate bid, was in line to be the new majority leader of the state assembly, second in command to the incoming Speaker, another upstater named Daniel D. Frisbie.

But Charles Francis Murphy had another idea, and it was communicated to Chanler in no uncertain terms. The press soon reported that Chanler was quietly withdrawing his name as a candidate for the leadership post. Murphy, who was now the most powerful man in the state, decided that Al Smith should be the new majority leader *and* the chairman of the all-powerful Ways and Means Committee. No member of the assembly had ever been given such power before (and none would again, for the following year it was agreed that the majority leader should not also be a committee chairman).[6]

Smith celebrated his thirty-eighth birthday on December 30, 1910, just a few days before he headed north to assume responsibilities he could not have imagined on that day five years earlier when he met with Tom Foley to talk about how miserable he was in Albany.

At noon on January 2, 1911, members of the state assembly and senate filed into the spacious assembly chamber on the third floor of the state capitol to take their oaths of office. Through all the pomp and speechmaking, the faint sound of music wafted into the chamber. Freshman state senator Franklin Roosevelt, seated in the chamber while his wife and mother watched from the gallery, recognized the sounds of the Hyde Park Fife and Drum Corps, whose stalwart members had made the trip to Albany to salute their new state senator. Roosevelt's new colleagues, who didn't think to bring their own marching bands to Albany for the occasion, exchanged annoyed looks.[7]

Al Smith, seated with assembly members apart from Roosevelt and the other senators, took his oath for the eighth time and none, save for perhaps the first, was more significant. His party had full control of state government, and he was about to take on the dual duties of majority leader and chairman of Ways and Means. He left the capitol after the ceremony for his new room in the Ten Eyck Hotel.

Meanwhile, the crowd from Dutchess County piled into the townhouse Roosevelt rented on State Street near the capitol to feast on chicken salad, sandwiches, beer, and cigars. The telephone rang at about five o'clock—it was the new governor, Dix, and he wished to invite Franklin and Eleanor to a small reception at the executive mansion, just about a half-mile from the Roosevelts' townhouse. No other legislator received such a summons. He and Eleanor spent the night chatting with the governor, his family, and a few aides.

Dix was so taken with the charming young man from the Hudson Valley that he spoke of putting Roosevelt, with his several hours of seniority, in charge of the state senate. This was a curious notion, suggesting that the governor had only the slightest understanding of how politics worked in Albany, or anywhere for that matter. The choice of senate president was not the governor's to make. It was Murphy's call, and Murphy had decided on thirty-three-year-old Robert Wagner, Al Smith's good friend and former roommate. Democrats gathered for a caucus the following morning and gave their assent to Murphy's choices. Roosevelt told himself that Wagner's election was a blessing. "I am most thankful that nothing further came of the Governor's suggestion of my name as President pro tem," he wrote with a modesty few associated with his demeanor and his pedigree.[8]

Smith and Wagner were now among the most powerful men in the state of New York. They knew from personal experience the struggles and hardships of the immigrants and children of immigrants who lived in cities and at the mercy of decisions and forces that were quite beyond their power and comprehension. Smith's rise from grade-school dropout to political fame already was becoming a New York legend. Wagner himself was slightly more fortunate, but only slightly. His immigrant family remained intact, his father working as a janitor for five dollars a week in the German enclave of Yorkville on Manhattan's Upper East Side. All six of the Wagner children were sent to work as adolescents even while they attended school. Wagner, with his law school degree, seemed like the proverbial urban Horatio Alger, a child who crossed the Atlantic at the age of nine, the son of a janitor, and now a lawyer and president pro tem of the New York State Senate. He could sense the pointing of fingers from the comfortable and content—see that young man, they were saying. He picked himself up by his own bootstraps. And if he could do it, why couldn't those others? Robert Wagner knew that's what people were saying about him. And he knew how wrong it was, how unfair it was.

"My boyhood was a pretty rough passage," Wagner once said. And as for those who believed that character and hard work were all anyone needed to escape poverty and alienation, Wagner had two words in reply: "That's bunk."

"For every one who rises to the top," Wagner said, "a thousand are destroyed."[9]

From his desk on the senate floor, the Bowery's "Big Tim" Sullivan—the man who had advised his colleagues to dump the new Roosevelt off a pier before he split the party—took the measure of the tall young man in seat twenty-six. Franklin Roosevelt, the congenial Sullivan soon decided, was an "awful arrogant fellow."[10]

The young reformer who portrayed himself as the scourge of patronage was on the job no more than two days when the realities of local politics began to pile up on his desk. A man named Samuel Beskin of Fishkill wrote on behalf of a friend, a good Democrat, who was looking for an appointment as a commissioner of road work. Should Roosevelt wish to reach him to discuss the matter, Beskin's letterhead listed his two phone numbers—310 and 235. Another man, W. J. Kiernan, wrote that he was "badley in need of a job and I am shure it is hard to get a job at Albany." Hard though it was, Kiernan hoped Roosevelt would help him get an appointment as a mail carrier.[11]

Other constituents had broader concerns. One asked him to support a measure permitting the hunting of rabbits with ferrets but prohibiting the killing of more than five gray squirrels per day. Two clergymen wanted his assurance that he would oppose a measure to allow gambling at the racetrack. Roosevelt noted that while he was personally devoted to horses and racing, he believed that "a sport cannot be a healthy one when its existence depends on gambling." A Hyde Park neighbor, C. F. Shaffer, asked Roosevelt to prevent Big Tim Sullivan from passing a bill to allow the playing of baseball on Sunday, a pet cause of Roosevelt's father. Roosevelt said he had not made up his mind, although he told another letter-writer that because his constituents opposed Sunday baseball, he would as well.[12]

Interesting though these issues were, Franklin Roosevelt had not traveled the length and breadth of the lower Hudson Valley and shaken calloused hands by the thousands in 1910 in order to arrange for jobs for postal workers or to debate the finer points of rabbit hunting. He had campaigned as a political independent, pledged to no boss, no special interest. He wanted to live up to his words, to show that he was his own man. And he soon had the chance to prove it.

On the morning of January 22, 1911, a Sunday, the *New York Times* introduced readers to the man who had become the talk of state politics in New York. A banner headline read simply, "Senator F.D. Roosevelt, Chief Insurgent at Albany." A sub-headline noted that "he's a Fifth Cousin of the Colonel." A pen-and-ink portrait of the chief insurgent stared back at readers from behind the inevitable pince-nez: he was handsome and impeccably groomed, his lips bearing just a faint trace of a smile, but with no Teddy-like exposure of his teeth. The reporter, W. A. Warn, declared that Roosevelt was so attractive "he could make a fortune on the stage and set the matinee girl's heart throbbing with subtle and happy emotion."

The article focused on the new senator's pedigree and his emergence as the chief spokesman for a new group of Democrats seeking to foil the corrupt plot to appoint Blue-Eyed Billy Sheehan as the next U.S. sena-tor from New York. The coming weeks, the *Times* announced, "will tell whether Franklin D. Roosevelt is the man of this Democratic hour." It was very likely around this time that Al Smith and Robert Wagner made their short and humiliating walk over to Roosevelt's townhouse, where nothing of note happened, save that two future governors and presiden-tial candidates shook hands for the first time.[13]

Political reformers and newspaper reporters concluded that they had found a new champion for clean government in this young Roosevelt, so confident and self-assured, so undisguised in his contempt for the uncouth men who held power in the legislative chambers. They loved hearing about his lonely battles against the political barbarians in his chamber, the hacks who had taken control of the ship of state and sought to plunder its stocks of gold. During a debate on state appropriations, Roosevelt stood up and demanded to know why the state of New York proposed to spend nearly $900 for a small bridge in his district. The chairman of the assembly's Ways and Means Committee, Al Smith, had found unspent funds in the state budget and directed that the money go to various public works projects, including a bridge in Wappingers Falls just south of Hyde Park.

Roosevelt found this outrageous. "But the appropriation is not needed, and I don't see why it was made without consultation with the represen-tatives of the district," Roosevelt told his fellow senators, some of whom might well have wondered if their hearing was failing them.

Two senators, however, heard every word Roosevelt said. One of them, Harvey Kinman, an upstate Republican and protégé of Theodore Roose-velt, declared that it was "the first time in my experience that I have heard such talk in the Legislature." He proposed, perhaps with tongue in cheek (but perhaps not), that the state erect a monument in Franklin Roose-velt's honor.

Senator Tim Sullivan, a man who handed out free shoes to his im-poverished constituents because he remembered what it was like to walk the streets of New York in bare feet, had a rather different view of his colleague's outburst.

"Frank," he muttered, "you ought to get your head examined."[14]

The bridge was not built.

As Al Smith went about the daily business of trying to pass laws and write a new budget, he could only shake his head in disgust as Senator Roosevelt conducted his daily press conferences in his salon, insulting the motives of men with far more experience in public life. The young man was the star of the moment, but he knew nothing about state government. He had never read a bill. He had never traded a vote. Who was he, after all, to lecture seasoned politicians on how to do their business?

Smith vented about Roosevelt to the young reformer he met a year earlier, Frances Perkins. They were an unlikely pair: Smith with his loud suits and foghorn voice and his ward heeler's demeanor; Perkins, earnest and well-educated, the sort of do-gooder that Tammany politicians like Smith tended to regard as naïve at best, natural-born enemies at worst. And yet, as Perkins continued to lobby for her fifty-four-hour bill, the Lower East Side pol and the good-government reformer were forming a bond that would last a lifetime. "I became considerably attached to Al Smith as a human being and as a politician," Perkins would say many years later. "He didn't make false promises. He told me the truth."[15]

Even as early as 1911, when they had known each other only about a year, Smith felt he could confide in Perkins, not just about legislation but about the troublemaker in the state senate, Franklin Roosevelt. "He can't get ahead in politics," Smith told Perkins. "He doesn't have any idea of how you get on in politics." Perkins had no reason to disagree. She had seen him operate in the capitol, seen the looks of disgust on the faces of other senators as Roosevelt walked by without saying a friendly word, and would always remember the image of the tall, slender young man atop the capitol's exterior steps, looking down at colleagues from behind his pince-nez. What a shame, she thought, that this young man chose to keep his distance from the city politicians she was growing to appreciate.[16]

The deadlock in Albany came to an abrupt and unhappy end in late

March when Tammany boss Charlie Murphy dumped Blue-Eyed Billy Sheehan and put forward a friend of his, state Supreme Court justice James O'Gorman, a man of impeccable integrity and a spotless reputation despite his association with a saloonkeeper. Franklin Roosevelt, who vowed he would never submit to the saloonkeeper's dictation, voted for O'Gorman when the final vote came in the legislature. In the following day's *New York Times*, a headline proclaimed Murphy as the "victor" in the long standoff.[17]

Roosevelt tried to persuade himself that he had played the winning hand, that he had gotten what he wanted. He wrote to a friend, "I think we finally secured a man not only of great ability but of independence. It certainly cannot be said that he is representative in any way of the protection [of] privilege and as far as one can judge by his record he will uphold the true democratic doctrine of equal opportunity for all."[18]

It was a delightful piece of fiction.

six

FIRE

THE TELEPHONE WAS RINGING. It was four o'clock in the morning, and it was dark and cold in Albany. Who in the world would be calling in the middle of the night? One thing was certain: it was nobody from the old neighborhood. Nobody on Oliver Street had a telephone.

Al Smith fumbled in his bed in the Ten Eyck Hotel and picked up the receiver. The voice on the other end was familiar, a colleague in government. Al, the voice said, the capitol is on fire.

Smith didn't believe it. It was a practical joke, and not a particularly funny one at this hour. But it wasn't. Smith made his way to a window that looked out on State Street and the great building itself. He saw red and orange against the black sky. The capitol was engulfed in an inferno fed by thousands upon thousands of books and documents in the state library.

He dressed quickly and raced up the hill to the stricken building. Firefighters had been on the scene for more than an hour, summoned there after a restless newspaper correspondent named Louis Howe spotted the fire during a solitary, post-midnight ramble. Smith stepped gingerly around the fire hoses stretched from nearby hydrants and was allowed to pass through the fire lines into a relatively safe portion of the building. He made his way to the assembly chamber and watched with fascination and horror as water and smoke filled the room he had come to love. His eyes moved up to the ceiling, and he remembered hearing years ago that the capitol's designers called for a ceiling of oak, but a contractor looking to cut corners ignored the design and used plaster instead. Thank God for shifty contractors, Smith thought as he kept his eyes above him. The ceiling never buckled, even though the inferno was just above the assembly chamber. But the damage to the chamber, mostly from water and smoke, was severe.[1]

The great capitol fire of March 29, 1911, turned old state documents and books to cinders, ruined priceless antiquities held in the state museum, and would require $5 million of repairs. Old Albany hands would tell stories decades later of the night the capitol burned, adding with a whisper a conspiracy theory or two about its actual cause.

But it was another fire, four days earlier, that history would remember and that would change the course of Al Smith's career. On March 25, 146 workers in the Triangle Shirtwaist Factory in Manhattan, most of them women and many of them immigrants or the children of immigrants, were killed when a fire broke out on the eighth and ninth floors of the building that housed the sweatshop. There were no sprinklers in the building. There had been no fire drills. There were no emergency exits. A rickety fire escape collapsed, dooming dozens. One of the factory doors was locked. Bodies piled up behind it. Young women stepped to a window and jumped, and jumped, and jumped. Perhaps they were lucky. Their deaths were quick. Those they left behind were burned alive.

The city was not shocked. It was enraged. The tears that were shed were those of anger and bitterness and solidarity. The young workers who lost their lives were transformed from victims of an accident to martyrs for a cause, all within days of the catastrophe. For the working poor in the tenements of the Lower East Side and Hell's Kitchen and the Brooklyn waterfront, and in far-off neighborhoods in Boston and Philadelphia and Chicago and Baltimore and wherever else men and women and children worked in dimly lit, unsafe factories, this moment had been a long time in coming. Everybody knew what went on inside the workplaces of industrial America, and whether the process involved the slaughtering of cattle or the stitching together of fabric, it was no secret that the work was dangerous and unhealthy, and worse yet, nobody seemed to care.

Children were awakened in the morning and sent off to canning factories in upstate New York, where they worked twelve, thirteen, fourteen hours a day, stuffing fruit and vegetables into cans for shipment to the city. Men worked from dawn to dusk in the slaughterhouses of Back of the Yards in Chicago, and they came home exhausted and smelling of dead animals. Women hunched over tables for hours at a time, piecing together garments in rooms that were hot and poorly ventilated and barely lighted, in the textile mills of New England. They grew old before their time, and if they were injured on the job or could no longer perform the tasks required of them, they were shunted aside.

The fire in the Triangle Shirtwaist Factory did not surprise the working poor. It infuriated them. And they knew who was to blame for these needless deaths: everybody. The landlords, the factory owners, the aldermen in City Hall, the mayor, the lawmakers in Albany, the governor, the police, the laws. The system.

The smashed bodies of those who threw themselves from the eighth floor and the charred remains of those who died inside the building were brought to a pier on the west side to await the horrendous process of identification. Fathers and mothers, sisters and brothers, waited in line to examine bodies placed awkwardly in one-size-fits-all coffins, some unrecognizable save for a piece of jewelry, a ring, a gold filling. And as loved ones endured this unimaginable ordeal, the women who belonged to the International Ladies' Garment Workers' Union, who knew what conditions were like in Triangle and scores of other factories around the city, raised their voices so that little else could be heard. They walked in the rain four days later, tens of thousands of them, in a silent protest march. Civic meetings were held in Cooper Union and the Society for Ethical Culture and the Metropolitan Opera House as speaker after speaker demanded not condolences but change.

Some of the dead lived in Al Smith's district. He visited the grieving families and heard the sounds of unknowable anguish. He went to the morgue with some as they sought to find and identify their loved ones, if they could. He would never write about this, not in his autobiography or in the newspaper essays to which he signed his name in later life. And perhaps that silence suggests just how profoundly moved he was.[2]

The Sheehan business in Albany was wrapped up days after both fires, and perhaps that was no coincidence. The next fire could very well consume dawdling lawmakers who could not even pick a senator, never mind deal with the problems of the men and women and children who worked day and night to keep a roof over their heads and who prayed that they might be spared a crippling injury or worse, for it would mean catastrophe in a society that believed character, not luck, determined who rose and who fell.

A coalition of government reformers and labor activists formed what it called a Committee on Safety to demand that state lawmakers put aside their petty squabbling and address the conditions that led to the Triangle Shirtwaist catastrophe. The committee named Frances Perkins as secretary and lobbyist for its Albany delegation, knowing that she was familiar with the landscape in the capitol but perhaps not realizing that she felt more at home with the tough urban politicians than the virtuous reformers who delivered earnest speeches to the like-minded.

The reformers had a plan: Governor Dix should appoint a blue-ribbon commission of people like themselves, the finest people in the state of New York. These fine people would investigate conditions in the state's factories, meet regularly, perhaps form committees and subcommittees, gather around them policy experts and professors, and then present their findings to the public, which, having been educated in the finer points of public policy, surely would rise up and demand that the recommended reforms be passed.

This was the plan they proposed when they met with Governor Dix, who suggested that they meet with the assembly's majority leader, Al Smith. They did, and he listened respectfully as they made their case.

When they finished, Smith had a question for them: Had they ever noticed that the finest people in the state of New York often were so busy that they never seemed to have time to actually do the things that were asked of them?

The delegates might well have shifted uncomfortably in their seats. The man wasn't wrong.

"Besides," he said, "it isn't the 'finest people in the state' that have the most influence in the legislature. . . . If you want to get anything done, you got to have this be a legislative commission. If the legislature does it, the legislature will be proud of it, the legislature will listen to their report and the legislature will do something about it."

This was not what the reformers had in mind. They did not trust the legislature, for it was filled with men who operated on behalf of the inter-ests, not the people. Reform had to come from the disinterested, from the civic elites who knew what was best for society, who were independent of tawdry politics. Smith could sense what they were thinking.

"These fellows in the Assembly are good men at heart," he said, know-ing full well that this observation would come as a revelation to the group. "They don't want to burn up people in factories. They just don't know anything about how to prevent it, and they don't really believe that there is any hazard until you show them. And they'll be more impressed if it is shown them by their own commission and own members."

Frances Perkins, who was part of the delegation, thought Smith's ad-vice was ridiculous. But he persisted. "That is the way to do it," he said. Get Democrats and Republicans on board, along with the experts. Let the politicians feel as though they're part of the process rather than keeping them on the outside and then expecting them to sign off on whatever is presented to them.[3]

The Committee on Safety gave in. There would be no blue-ribbon commission of civic leaders appointed by the governor and independent of the political process. Instead, there would be a commission of the leg-islature, funded and directed by the very politicians the reform-minded committee loathed. It was to be one of the best compromises any reform-minded group ever made.

Al Smith was named as the commission's vice chairman. The chairman would be his friend Robert Wagner. Joining the politicians were experts and advocates who ordinarily would have never associated themselves with a couple of politicians from Tammany Hall, who would have looked upon Al Smith as everything they loathed about tawdry, corrupt politics. He was uneducated, he was coarse, he told stories in saloons, he reeked of cigar smoke. But they gave it a chance, putting their faith in politics and politicians rather than simply issuing meaningless white papers that nobody would read. Frances Perkins would serve as its chief investigator. Doctors, labor union activists, and social workers eagerly joined the effort. Before the year was out, the commission held fourteen public hearings and heard from 222 witnesses who spoke about conditions in the state's factories and who helped to reshape the commission's agenda. The stories they were hearing—of rank exploitation, of dangerous conditions that had nothing to do with the threat of fire, of families living at the mercy of bosses, profit margins, and simple bad luck—led Smith and his colleagues to expand their inquiries. What was the proper role of government in regulating work carried out in the tenements? What could be done about the long hours women and children were forced to endure or risk dismissal and perhaps financial disaster for their families? At what age should children be barred from working? Could government regulate wages and other conditions of employment? Shouldn't government protect women from being forced to return to work after giving birth?

Al Smith stood outside a factory in Auburn and watched as holloweyed women emerged from the plant after working the night shift, passing their husbands as they stood in line to take their place on the day shift. Smith turned to Frances Perkins, who was standing nearby. "It's uncivilized," he said. A few hours later, Smith and Perkins met with one of the women who had worked the night shift. Tired and in the midst of getting her three children off to school, she nevertheless invited the two strangers into her home and offered them a cup of coffee. "See here," Smith said, "we ought to get you a cup of coffee." Gesturing to a chair, he said, "You sit right down there and put your feet up on the other chair."

When the children were gone, she told her guests of her life of unceasing labor—she worked nights, her husband worked days, she cared for the children and cooked their meals and then tried to sleep for a few hours before reporting back to the factory. It was a hard life, and she had little time to spend with her family. But she was not alone. Her neighbors in Auburn could tell similar stories, or worse. Some could get through the day only by starting it with a drink, she said.[4]

Smith heard more stories, saw more suffering as the commission conducted its hearings and carried out its inspections. He saw parts of his home state that he would never have stepped foot in were it not for this work. He saw what life was like in the canning factories upstate, where children as young as three years prepared fruit and vegetables to be placed in cans for sale in the cities. The canning industry dealt with extremely perishable merchandise that had to move quickly from farm to factory to the grocery store. The bulk of the work was done in the late summer and early fall—harvest time—and it was grueling even by the standards of the time. Adults commonly worked a hundred hours a week; children worked until they dropped, literally. An inspector reported that children were working in one canning operation from 4:00 in the morning until 9:30 at night.[5]

Conditions in the factories were equally abysmal. The commission found worksites with a single toilet for hundreds of workers, or, even worse, nothing more than a barrel in a basement. Smith climbed to the third floor of a factory, worked his way around obstacles to get to a window, and discovered that the fire escape that ought to have been there had been removed. The building's owner was having trouble with vandals, Smith was told.[6]

Al Smith was known for his good cheer and humor and companionship, but the sights and sounds and smells were getting to him. A member of the city's powerful real estate industry showed up at Smith's Oliver Street apartment on a Sunday morning in a fancy yellow touring car the likes of which nobody in the neighborhood had ever seen before. The real estate man was looking to speak with Smith, but the assemblyman was in church. He waited. And when Smith finally appeared, full of grace and peace, the real estate man cornered him and began to complain about the factory investigation. Smith cut him off: "If you've got anything to say to me, you come down before the whole commission and say it. Don't you try to approach me in any private or secret way. This is where I live. Goodbye!" He turned on his heel, leaving the real estate man to dwell on his breach of decorum.[7]

When the legislature reconvened in January 1912, Smith was no longer majority leader, as the Republicans had won back control of the assembly in the fall of 1911. But his friend Wagner still ran the senate, and together the Tammany Twins began formulating new laws to correct the abuses and exploitation they were witnessing firsthand. Factories would have to register with the state so that inspectors would know of their existence; children would have to undergo a medical examination before being allowed to work; factory owners would be required to install sprinklers and conduct regular fire drills; the state's labor commissioner would get new powers to clean up unsanitary factories, and women were barred from working for four weeks after giving birth—a measure intended not to discriminate against women but to protect them from unscrupulous bosses.

They all passed, and if the lawmakers paused for a moment to consider what they were doing, they may have realized that Smith and Wagner and their new allies among the reformers were doing something nobody envisioned when the legislature authorized the Factory Investigating Commission. Back then, people were talking about fire prevention. Now, Al Smith and his friends were talking about regulating the relationship between employer and employee, about imposing conditions on the ownership of private property, about expanding government's role in the workplace and in society itself. This was no small change. This was almost a revolution.

And it continued. The Factory Investigating Commission, now Al Smith's life's work, continued to hold hearings, conduct inspections, and gather together a remarkable group of supporters from good-government organizations that had been established to oppose the likes of Tammany hacks like Al Smith. Representatives of groups with names like the National Consumers League, the Child Welfare League, the American Association for Labor Legislation, and the United Charities Association found themselves testifying before the commission or working with Smith, Wagner, and their fellow commissioners on reports and investigations. Young women from Vassar College in Poughkeepsie and Radcliffe College in Cambridge volunteered to inspect factories on the commission's behalf.[8]

A bridge was under construction, spanning the gulf between idealistic reformers and pragmatic politicians, between civic elites and men and women from the sidewalks of the city, between blue bloods and immigrants, between progressives with their agendas and liberals with their lunch buckets. Crossing it would require faith in the good intentions of those who poured the anchorage and strung the roadbed. Crossing it would require a suspension of long-held fears and anxieties, of the natural tendency to glimpse down at the abyss below. But cross it they did.

Like many state senators in the spring of 1912, Franklin Roosevelt was a busy man. The Triangle fire and the work of the Factory Investigating Commission had transformed the debates in Albany and inspired legislation and regulations that historians would later celebrate as milestones of progressive thought. In the byzantine corridors of the capitol, beefy men from the city like Big Tim Sullivan and Thomas McManus, Roosevelt's colleagues in the state senate, proceeded to their offices with a new urgency, for there were bills to pass and causes to adopt and constituents to satisfy—constituents who were making it clear that times had changed and they wanted more than a friendly ear in the clubhouse and a chance to line up for free shoes for their children.

But Franklin Roosevelt's crowded schedule in the spring of 1912 had little to do with Albany's new agenda. In fact, the earnest lobbying for new social welfare and labor laws was becoming downright tiresome. As lawmakers were beginning to pass the bills Smith and Wagner wrote, Frances Perkins seized on the momentum to get her fifty-four-hour bill passed. It was a critical piece of the reformers' agenda, and, she reckoned, the practical politicians could no longer run away and hide from the issue just because a few factory owners objected. She was right: lawmakers like Sullivan and McManus and other roughnecks, as she called them with increasing affection, were lining up in support of the bill.

The bill was a natural, she figured, for Franklin Roosevelt. She saw him one day as he was preparing to leave the senate chamber, tall and handsome and utterly unapproachable. She approached him anyway. As other senators brushed by, Perkins raised her eyes to Roosevelt's and told him about the fifty-four-hour bill, explaining how it would improve the lives of working women and would help, in some small way, to ease the exploitation of industrial workers.

The young senator did not attempt to disguise his utter lack of interest. "No, no," he said as he waved her way. "More important things. Can't do it now. Can't do it now. Much more important things." He rushed away, head in the air, leaving Frances Perkins to wonder how this man Roosevelt could be so "absurd"—a favorite word of hers.[9]

Roosevelt did indeed have many other things to keep him busy as Smith and his allies devoted themselves to the concerns of working men, women, and children. He had formed a new law partnership with a fellow Groton and Harvard graduate, Langdon Marvin, and another lawyer, Harry Hooker, within weeks of being sworn in as a state senator, and Marvin was making it clear that he expected business to boom thanks to Roosevelt's connections in Albany. "We want more business and big business," Marvin wrote, underlining the words "business" and "big business," just in case FDR didn't get the point. "Keep this in mind and watch for legislative committee work, etc. We can investigate anything the State thinks needs looking into."[10]

The state, in the form of the Factory Investigating Commission, was looking into a good many things in the spring of 1912, but it did not require the assistance of Marvin, Hooker & Roosevelt, Counsellors at Law.

Edward Litchfield, on the other hand, did.

Edward Litchfield was a fabulously wealthy New Yorker reared in a mansion off Prospect Park in Brooklyn. He fell in love with the castles he saw during a childhood trip to Germany and was now in the process of building himself a palace of his own in the tiny village of Tupper Lake in the Adirondack Mountains near Lake Placid. It would have a hundred rooms, each with a custom ceiling. There would be dozens of fireplaces and a veranda measuring seven hundred feet. A special trophy room, with a thirty-five-foot ceiling designed by Louis Tiffany, would show off his collection of art and furniture. The driveway from the gate of the estate to the chateau itself would be five miles.

It all sounded quite lovely. There was, however, a problem, which is why Litchfield presented himself to the offices of Marvin, Hooker & Roosevelt at 52 Wall Street one day in early 1912. He wanted a road built between Tupper Lake, home to his dream castle, and Long Lake, a nearby town. He expected the state to build it, and to achieve that goal he expected Marvin, Hooker & Roosevelt to make the necessary arrangements. He gave Marvin a blueprint of the planned road and, in essence, told him to make it happen. There would be more business for the firm, he promised.

Marvin immediately sensed the possibilities. This wasn't just business, this was *big* business. He began a yearlong correspondence with Roosevelt about getting Litchfield's road built. Legislation to fund the road already was in the works in both the assembly and senate, but Litchfield needed somebody to make sure it passed. Marvin wrote to Roosevelt, "He is very anxious indeed to have this bill go through. Will you, therefore, see what can be done to advance this bill?"[11]

Through the remainder of the 1912 legislative session and beyond, Roosevelt made the case for Litchfield's road to colleagues with more power and influence. Roosevelt reported that "through a good deal of diplomacy" he had succeeded in getting the necessary legislation reported out of the senate's Finance Committee, a crucial step forward for Litchfield's road. "I do not believe that there will be more trouble passing it," FDR said with the confidence of a freshman legislator new to the intrigues of Albany. Marvin remained nervous about satisfying the firm's wealthy client. He told FDR, "I want . . . every effort made to get this bill pushed now before the opposition becomes . . . acute."[12]

The fight for the Litchfield road bill was a classic case of a private interest seeking to benefit from the expenditure of public money, and as Roosevelt himself pointed out, it was hardly the only one of its kind. But Franklin Roosevelt had run for election and, in 1912, was running for reelection as a progressive politician in debt to no boss, no special interest.

In the end, Litchfield did not get his bill. Roosevelt was informed in February 1913—as the state legislature was passing bill after bill upon the recommendation of the Factory Investigating Commission—that any new funding for roads had to be used for roads designated in a state bond issue, and the Litchfield road was not among them.

As Roosevelt reported this bad news to Marvin, he was just about done with Albany, and Albany was just about done with him. He was hoping to land a job with the new administration of Woodrow Wilson, who won the presidency in 1912 over two Republicans, incumbent William Howard Taft and Roosevelt's cousin Theodore, who finished in second place running on the Progressive Party line.

Franklin had his eye on cousin Teddy's old job as assistant secretary of the navy. The offer came on the very day that Wilson was inaugurated as president, March 4, 1913, and when Roosevelt returned to Albany after attending the inauguration, he felt obliged to ask for the advice of his legislative leader, Robert Wagner. Should he take the job?

Wagner never hesitated.

"Go, Franklin, go," Wagner replied. "I'm sure you'll be a big success down there." The taciturn German immigrant no doubt tried his best to contain his relief.[13]

He was in Washington days later, sworn into office on March 17, the eighth anniversary of his marriage to Eleanor. Cousin Ted dropped him a note of congratulations. "It is interesting to see that you are in another place which I myself once held," he wrote.[14]

He was glad to be away from Albany, away from men like Tammany's Murphy, whom he compared to a "noxious weed." But, oddly, he also wanted to make sure that he was remembered there for the right reasons. He had kept his distance from the social legislation that was making New

York a leader in a new kind of progressivism, but he did agree to sponsor a bill requiring employers to give their workers a day off every seven days. Practically speaking, it guaranteed a day of rest on Sunday.[15]

The bill had the support of Christian clergymen in his district who otherwise had little to say about the new social legislation, so their approval may have had something to do with Roosevelt's interest. Whatever the case, just a few weeks before he headed to Washington, he made a point of writing to the Factory Investigating Commission's lead attorney, Abram Elkus. "I hope you are not going to forget my small contribution to this legislature, the so-called One Day Rest in Seven bill," he wrote. Perhaps sensing, at last, the historic work of the Factory Investigating Commission, Roosevelt wished to note that he was on the right side of history, that he was at the ramparts when the status quo was overthrown. In later years, he would concoct a story that placed him at the center of change in Albany, an audacious claim that few would bother to check.[16]

But people like Abram Elkus and his colleagues knew who was carrying on with the hard work of reform, and it wasn't Franklin Roosevelt. It was Al Smith.

seven

CHANGING TIMES

AL SMITH WAS SPEAKER of the state assembly in 1913 and he was unlike any other man who had ever held the position. Nobody could recall the sight of a Speaker eating his lunch at this desk, banging his gavel with one hand while stuffing a sandwich in his mouth with the other. He was crude and uncouth and loud, and all of this made him larger than life, quite literally. Men commented that Smith seemed taller than his relatively modest five feet, seven inches.[1]

He had a way of getting to the point of an issue despite his presumed limitations, and this rarely failed to startle or delight his colleagues, depending on their own views of the issue at hand. He was the assembly's most powerful advocate for the bill Franklin Roosevelt sponsored in the senate requiring employers to give their workers a day off once a week. The state's canning industry, which had a powerful friend in Tammany boss Charles Murphy, argued that ruin and disaster would follow such meddling in their private business. The industry argued that it simply could not give workers a day off during the peak harvest season.

Al Smith heard these arguments again and again, until one day, while presiding over a hearing during which the canners made their case for a seven-day workweek for all their workers, including women and children, he exploded. "If these distinguished champions of women and children were to rewrite the Divine Law, I have no doubt that they would change it to read, 'Remember the Sabbath day, to keep it holy—except in the can-neries," he bellowed. The bill passed the assembly and became law.[2]

By the time the session ended in 1913, the assembly under Speaker Smith and the senate under President Wagner passed a new workers' com-pensation bill, required that workers on state canals received a minimum wage of two dollars a day, imposed a ten-hour limit on the workday for railroad workers, created a state-funded college scholarship program for poor children, banned child labor in trades deemed to be dangerous, strengthened workplace safety laws, gave new powers to the state Labor Department—all in addition to passing the Roosevelt bill requiring a day off once a week. It was an extraordinary session.

Smith also introduced a bill to grant state pensions to widows with children. It would mean that the children of the twentieth century would not have to look for jobs when their fathers died, would not have to leave school to help their mothers and siblings, would not be sent to institutions if government-supported private charities added to a widow's sorrows by taking her children away if she was judged to be incapable of supporting them. Had his mother not been healthy, not been able to work, Smith said, he and his sister surely would have wound up in an orphanage. It was luck, not character, that kept some families together and broke up others. A state pension would remove luck from the question and help character to tri-umph over adversity. The bill failed in 1913, but it passed two years later, and Smith would regard it as one of his greatest legislative achievements.[3]

His tenure as speaker lasted just a single, albeit memorable, year, for Republicans captured control of Albany in 1914 after Tammany boss Murphy ordered the impeachment of the sitting governor, William Sulzer, a Tammany man himself who decided he no longer had to bow to Mur-phy's request. As fortune would have it, Sulzer had played fast and loose with campaign money—Tammany was shocked to hear of it—and the impeachment was quick and clean. But voters saw it as a power play, one that Smith had opposed, and they punished Murphy's Democrats. Smith was reduced to the role of minority leader.

He would now be forced to defend the laws he helped write and pass, and did so with the enthusiasm and energy he had summoned when he was on offense, when the bridge he helped build between advocates and politicians, townhouse and tenement, seemed to offer a way forward. Now the alliance was in danger of falling apart as Franklin Roosevelt and his new friends in Washington, including Treasury Secretary William Gibbs McAdoo, were attempting to form a rival Democratic faction to overthrow Tammany and Murphy and his minions like Smith in the name of progressivism.

Smith refused to accept his diminished role in the legislature. Rather than simply serve as the voice of "no" in a Republican-controlled chamber, he was able to cajole and charm and engage his colleagues so that in 1915 the legislature passed his bill granting widows with children a pension. Lawmakers voted after hearing Smith describe what happened to so many poor families after a husband and father died, leaving behind a widow with no visible means of support. "The mother stands in police court," he said. "She witnesses the separation of herself and her children. They are torn away from her and given over to the custody of an institution, and nothing is left for her but to go out into the world and make her own living. What must be her feelings? What must be her idea of the state's policy when she sees these children separated from her by due process of law?" The state's policy changed. The mother would receive money not as a charity but as a sign of society's commitment to her and her children.[4]

Several years of breathtaking change led New York's elected and self-appointed leaders to call for a convention in 1915 to add to and rewrite the state's constitution. Smith was among the delegates who spent five months debating the basic premises of government's role in a modern, industrial society. The Republicans sent the great and the mighty to the convention—Elihu Root, a Nobel Peace Prize winner who served Theodore Roosevelt as secretary of war and secretary of state; Seth Low, who had been mayor of Brooklyn when it was its own city and then was elected mayor of New York City itself, the only person who would ever achieve that distinction; Charles Evans Hughes, former governor, current U.S. Supreme Court justice, and future presidential candidate; and Henry Stimson, who had been President William Howard Taft's secretary of war.

The Democrats sent Al Smith. To be sure, they sent others, but he was all they needed. He became the voice of New York City when upstaters sought to take away some of its lawmaking powers. He took up the cause of workers and families when others sought to roll back the reforms he wrote and pushed through the legislature. He stood up for immigrants in opposing a measure that would have required voters to pass English literacy tests. "The ability of a man to write," Smith said, was "no indication of his character." There were men in Sing Sing who knew how to sign their names, he said. Seth Low told Smith that Albany ought to have more power over how New York City was governed, pointing to California as an example of a state where cities had limited control over their own affairs. Smith could only shake his head. California? Since when did New Yorkers compare themselves to a backwater with just a million and a half people? That was no argument at all, Smith said. "I would sooner be a lamppost on Park Row than the governor of California." Delegates tried to hide their smiles, but Smith wasn't kidding.[5]

Through it all, he showed off a working knowledge of state government that left his social superiors in the Republican delegation astonished, and mightily impressed. "Al Smith," said the convention's chairman, Root, "knows more about the real needs of the state than do most of us."[6]

And he was at his best when the leader of the state Republican Party, William Barnes, offered a blandly worded amendment that would have barred the state from granting "any privilege or immunity not granted equally to all members of the State." Smith immediately understood what Barnes was up to: the abolition of all the new laws that singled out certain groups—injured workers, children, widows—for special assistance. Barnes dressed up his argument in the language of equality, but Smith was no fool. He also knew that the moderate and progressive Republicans in the convention had no desire to side with Barnes in turning back the clock, but they were relying on Al Smith, the champion of social reform, to make the case against the Barnes proposal.[7]

And so he did, in a memorable speech of thirty minutes. "The gentlemen around this chamber would lead us to believe that law in a democracy is the expression of some divine or eternal right," he said. "I am unable to see it that way. My idea of law and democracy is the expression of what is best, what fits the present needs of society, what goes the farthest to do the greatest good for the greatest number of people. . . . Is it prudent for this convention to do what it can to reduce the basic law to the level of the caveman's law, the law of the sharpest tooth, the angriest brow, and the greediest maw?"[8]

Smith's assault on the Barnes bill was a farewell speech of sorts, for it was announced during the constitutional convention that he was to be the Democratic Party's nominee for the position of sheriff of New York County, which made him responsible for collecting an assortment of fees for the city. The job paid $12,000 a year, and by law he was allowed to keep half of whatever he and his deputies managed to collect from recalcitrant businesses and individuals. Smith and his wife, Katie, were the parents of five children in 1915, and they had been living for years on his legislative salary of $1,500 a year plus whatever small patronage favors Tammany could throw his way. Many of his colleagues had other sources of income. Lawyers like Robert Wagner and Franklin Roosevelt maintained their practices, others relied on rackets and payoffs, and still others did both. As Smith was neither a lawyer nor a crook, he and Katie struggled to maintain a modest (though hardly impoverished) existence in the old neighborhood. Charlie Murphy thought it was time that Smith made a little money before moving on to bigger and better things. And so his nomination was arranged, and there wasn't a chance in the world that he would not be elected.

On election night, 1915, men, women, and children from Oliver Street and beyond gathered outside the Smiths' apartment to cheer for their hometown hero. Organizations representing the neighborhood's Jews, Italians, and Chinese hailed the half-Irish, half-Italian, all–Lower East

Side Al Smith as their champion, the man who understood them even if he could not speak their language. Smith stood on the stoop of 25 Oliver Street wearing a bow tie and a black derby, waving his arms, shaking hands, posing for pictures with his family. It felt like a homecoming for a man who had spent a dozen years making laws 150 miles away, and now those laws were making the lives of his neighbors not just more tolerable but infinitely better.

His earliest mentor, Tom Foley, was astonished. Nobody gathered outside his door when he had been elected to the very same position years ago. There were no cheering crowds, no words of praise from the newspapers and the reformers. Why, he wondered to a friend, did he miss out on all the excitement?

"You're not Al Smith," his friend replied.[9]

In years to come, it would be said of Franklin Roosevelt that he learned important lessons about progressivism, about politics, about the real-world problems of government during the years he spent with the formidable men who ran Woodrow Wilson's Washington. As a Democrat with a golden last name, as a Roosevelt who held a position made famous by another Roosevelt, as the assistant secretary of the navy at a time when the United States was emerging as a world power, FDR had access to key decision makers and was given the opportunity of a lifetime to see how the federal government operated at the highest levels. He developed important relationships with the next generation of Democrats, especially William Gibbs McAdoo, the dour, long-faced Treasury secretary who fell in love with and married the boss's daughter, Eleanor Wilson, in 1914.[10]

But if Roosevelt's new friends did indeed inspire him to think long and hard about the proper role of government in a modern industrial society, he kept those thoughts to himself. He seemed more interested in the crude machinations of New York politics than in the applications of high-minded progressive theory. He and his devoted personal assistant, the former newspaperman Louis Howe, spent many fruitful hours looking for opportunities to build their own army of political loyalists in New York through the judicious use of the federal payroll, especially the Post Office Department. Self-styled independents and reformers from New York saw Roosevelt as their point of contact as they applied for minor federal jobs in preparation for a coming war against Tammany Hall's horrifying abuse of the public treasury. Roosevelt made his intentions clear: "I am going to clean out that old gang if it takes twenty years," he told a friend, referring to Murphy the saloonkeeper and his allies. He and Treasury Secretary McAdoo exchanged notes about finding jobs for like-minded reformers, and there was no shortage of positions: collector of the Port of Rochester, recorder of deeds, assistant appraiser, impressive-sounding titles that may have entailed little work on behalf of the taxpayers but many duties related to politics.[11]

Barely a year into his job at the navy, Roosevelt was already thinking of his next move—there would be elections for governor and U.S. senator in New York in 1914—and he and Howe knew that having an army of well-placed loyalists throughout the state would help counter Tammany's famously organized troops when the time came. They placed postmasters in strategic locations, encouraged reformers in their battles with Democratic machines in places like Buffalo, and closely followed a piece of legislation in Albany near and dear to Roosevelt's heart—a new bill to allow primary elections, not political bosses, to decide party nominations. It was a compromise bill, one that Tammany's Murphy approved of, and it was on its way to passage. That meant some insurgent stood a decent chance at winning the nomination from Tammany's handpicked candidate for governor or U.S. senator.[12]

Perhaps Franklin Roosevelt could be that insurgent. Perhaps he could be the candidate who finally slew the Tammany beast. In August 1914, as Europe's armies mobilized for war and the United States remained resolute in its neutrality, Franklin Roosevelt announced that he would be a candidate for the Democratic Party's nomination for U.S. Senate from New York. His friend McAdoo was delighted and sent him a long list of "friendly Democrats and a few progressives" from each of the state's 150 assembly districts who might be of help.[13]

As for the pressing issues in the upcoming campaign, Roosevelt made it clear that everything else—the war in Europe, the economy at home— was of secondary importance to defeating Tammany's Murphy and whoever his choice might be. In a letter addressed to enrolled Democrats, his campaign stated that the party must be "freed from the . . . destructive bossism of Charles F. Murphy."[14]

A day before nominations were due, Murphy announced that Tammany Hall would support as its Senate candidate the Honorable James Gerard, a prominent New York Democrat who happened to be U.S. ambassador to Germany, an appointee of Woodrow Wilson. Gerard accepted the nomination but said he would not be able to campaign for the office because he was busy in Berlin.

It was a political master stroke, one that Roosevelt never saw coming. He sputtered and thrashed about, demanding that Gerard denounce the very man who had selected him, Murphy. He sounded shrill and unprepared. The support he was counting on from the Wilson White House evaporated, for Gerard was a Wilson man, just as Roosevelt was. He traveled the state to rail not so much against Gerard but against his sponsor, Murphy. He was anything but impressive. Roosevelt, a newspaper said, "cuts a sorry figure."[15]

Franklin Roosevelt did not simply lose the primary election. He was crushed. His opponent never issued a statement of any sort on any position, never made a campaign promise. But with the support of Tammany's get-out-the-vote operation, Ambassador Gerard won more than 210,000 votes to Roosevelt's 77,000. Roosevelt lost New York City by a four-to-one margin and lost upstate, his base, by two to one.

The insurgent organization that Roosevelt was counting on to boost his own career and take down Tammany wound up dying a slow and painful death after his loss in the primary. His fellow progressives in the Wilson administration saw no reason to further antagonize Tammany

Hall, not with the president up for reelection in 1916. The tide of battle in New York had turned, and the assistant secretary of the navy sensed it.

July 4, 1917, was a pleasant summer day in New York City. Skies were clear and the air warm as crowds began to gather outside Tammany Hall on 14th Street. It was an annual ritual, going back as far as anybody could remember—every Independence Day, the children and grandchildren of immigrants met at Tammany Hall to hear long patriotic orations and otherwise celebrate the nation's birth. On this occasion in 1917, the words and the rituals figured to be somber, for the United States was now at war and its young men were preparing to cross the Atlantic and take up positions on the battlefields of France.

Tammany, eager to show off its loyalty at a time when hyphenated Americans, especially the Irish, were thought to be less than committed to the war effort, chose to invite a representative from the Wilson administration to deliver a suitably patriotic oration on this wartime Independence Day. The spokesman was none other than the assistant secretary of the navy, Franklin Roosevelt. He arrived at the organization's headquarters as the crowd began to gather, and the men and women from the tenements of Manhattan would have been forgiven if they stared and pointed at the tall man in the straw hat wearing a bow tie and a double-breasted summer suit. That was Franklin Roosevelt! What in the world was he doing in Tammany Hall?

When the time came to address an organization for which he had expressed such scorn and contempt during his earliest years in public service, Franklin Roosevelt could only smile and acknowledge the obvious. "I am not entirely a stranger to Tammany Hall," he said, and everybody who heard him must have chuckled. The man who invited him to address the organization, Roosevelt said, had put it to him this way: if Tammany Hall could stand to have him as its guest, he should be able to stand its company.

The audience laughed. The rest of Roosevelt's talk was quite serious. His topic was the war in Europe and the nation's unprecedented decision to mobilize for war in the Old World. Very soon, he said, the newspapers would begin printing the names of American boys cut down in the trenches. "Lest we forget," he said, solemnly.[16]

Somewhere in the crowd was the sheriff of New York County, Al Smith, and perhaps Roosevelt's charm, seriousness of purpose, and courage in facing old and bitter foes made an impression on him. This surely was not the Frank Roosevelt he had come to know back in their Albany days, the young, humorless prig who wanted nothing to do with city people and politicians who stuck cigars between their teeth.

Reformers, however, were aghast. Franklin Roosevelt in Tammany Hall?

Not the end of times. Changing times.

Al Smith had been sheriff of New York County for two years. He attended political dinners and shook hands and met people of influence. He delivered speeches and developed such a reputation for wit and good humor that he worried that the city's powerful opinion makers wouldn't take him seriously. "I am in danger of being classed as a humorist," he told a friend. He was bored with the job, and when the time came for a return to political leadership, he did not want to be dismissed as a mere "humorist."[17]

The time came in 1917, not long after Roosevelt's appearance at Tammany Hall. With the United States at war, the embattled incumbent mayor of New York, a reformer named John Purroy Mitchel, alienated his friends and allies when he questioned the patriotism of his enemies, including those in Tammany Hall, as he sought reelection. "It would appear that certain members of the Legislature are working in the interest of the German government," Mitchel declared. "Of course you know . . . I mean Bob Wagner." It was a horrifying libel. Mitchel's progressive allies knew Wagner was not only a loyal American who happened to be born in Germany but also was a voice for social progress. Mitchel's lies were the mark of a desperate and unpleasant man.[18]

There had been talk of running Smith for mayor against Mitchel, but

Tammany chose a mediocre nonentity from Brooklyn named John Hylan while offering Smith a consolation prize: president of the Board of Aldermen. They were elected easily. The defeated mayor, Mitchel, left office a bitter man, joined the Army Air Corps, and was killed in a training accident. He was thirty-eight.

The presidency of the Board of Alderman had the merit of allowing Smith to play the part of acting mayor whenever Hylan was out of town or otherwise unavailable. But the new job was hardly a good fit. Smith was in the prime of life at age forty-four, and he burned with the ambition of a kid from the streets who knew he had what it takes. He was not a man cut out to play a supporting role. He saw himself as a star.

The Democrats needed somebody to run for governor in 1918 against a two-term Republican incumbent, Charles Whitman. The press reported in July that Democrats were privately talking up the prospects of Franklin Roosevelt, and President Wilson himself encouraged him to run. An emissary from Tammany Hall leader Charles Murphy visited Roosevelt in Washington and let it be known that the boss was interested in him if he was interested in the job. Wilson and Roosevelt discussed the matter on the White House lawn in the spring of 1918. Somebody mentioned Al Smith's name as a possible candidate and Roosevelt quickly reminded the group that Smith was a Catholic. No Catholic had ever been elected governor of New York, and Catholics were not particularly popular upstate.

Wilson was horrified. Religious differences shouldn't matter when Americans of all creeds were dying on foreign fields, the president said. Of course, Roosevelt replied. Of course.[19]

But some of the pragmatists in Tammany Hall shared Roosevelt's skeptical view of Smith's prospects. They were desperate to win back the governor's office and the patronage that came with it. They loved Al Smith, but they needed a win, and as they considered their prospects in 1918, they thought about the man who once upon a time treated them as though they were thieves and grafters: Franklin Roosevelt. State senator Jimmy

Walker told Roosevelt that it was "always a pleasure" to hear talk about his eventual return to New York politics.[20]

Roosevelt was delighted to have his name bandied about but he had his sights set on Europe, not Albany. He was desperate to get to the war zone, desperate to be able to tell people—voters, for sure, and perhaps cousin Theodore, whose three sons were already over there—that when duty called he got himself out from behind his desk and took part in the war. He announced in midsummer that he would not be a candidate for governor and suggested instead an old friend and longtime reformer, William Church Osborn, who saw politics as a contest between purity and evil. Murphy had a good long laugh over that one.

It was, Murphy decided, Al Smith's time.

The party's state convention in the resort town of Saratoga Springs became a full-throated celebration of Alfred Emanuel Smith and his unlikely and unprecedented rise from the Lower East Side to the corridors of power and influence in the most important state in the union. He was nominated for governor on July 24. It would have been a unanimous vote of the convention but for a delegate from Suffolk County named Samuel Seabury, a righteous soul whose ancestors were Episcopalian clergymen. He demanded a place at the political pulpit so that he might explain why he and he alone cast his vote against Al Smith. As Smith supporters hissed and Charlie Murphy sat serenely in a prominent place on the convention floor, Seabury delivered a fiery homily about the depravities Tammany had visited upon the state. Tall, austere of bearing but filled with indignation, Seabury was so irate that his memory failed him and he neglected to mention several of the reforms Tammany had forced on an unsuspecting electorate, including workers' compensation, tighter restrictions on workplace safety, the beginnings of a minimum wage measure, and other post-Triangle laws.

"Mr. Smith," he declared, "is the best representative of the worst element in the Democratic Party in the United States." Seabury cast his vote for Franklin Roosevelt's ally, William Church Osborn, as Smith's supporters hooted him off the convention stage.[21]

Al Smith accepted the party's nomination with humility and gratitude, displaying not the slightest notice of Judge Seabury's well-publicized dissent. "No man owes more to this country than I do," he said. "No man has been more benefitted by the free institutions of the State of New York than I have. I know what the people want." Many politicians had made such claims. But the words meant something more when they came from a man who had gone to work at the age of fourteen and who knew that it was luck more than grit that had given him a chance in life. He easily defeated Church in a Democratic primary.[22]

Good-government types, labor union activists, and social reformers saw in Smith something that critics like Seabury either missed or chose to ignore. His record spoke for itself—he had achieved reforms they had only dreamed of in the past, and he did so from the inside. No doubt to their own surprise, they came together to form an independent citizens campaign committee on Smith's behalf. There was a conspicuous number of Jews among the independent committee's leaders, including Joseph Proskauer, a well-known lawyer. Women, too, were prominent among the committee's leaders, and that was no small factor given that women would be voting in New York for the first time in 1918. Among them was Belle Moskowitz, a social reformer first attracted to politics by the late mayor of New York, John Purroy Mitchel.

It was an extraordinary collection of men and women who had come of age believing that it was their duty to oppose the dictates of machine politicians but who were open-minded enough to see in Al Smith something quite unexpected and surprising. He shared their goals—he favored municipal ownership of utilities and complained about Whitman's lax enforcement of the regulations he wrote and passed while in the legislature. He supported a minimum wage for women and children. He paid special attention to New York City's transit facilities, which were privately owned and operated. The state's regulation of the subway companies, he said, was a failure.[23]

Even with the help of the reformers and independents, and even with the enthusiasm of Tammany Hall's rank and file, Al Smith's chances of becoming governor in 1918 were not good. The incumbent, Whitman, had won reelection in 1916 by more than 150,000 votes. What's more, Smith opposed the growing movement against alcohol consumption. He was from the city. He was Catholic. The one clear advantage Smith had over his opponent—his winning personality—was neutralized as campaign rallies and personal appearances were canceled time and again because the flu was killing people in the fall of 1918—millions worldwide, thousands in New York—and voters were afraid to gather in crowds, afraid even to step out of their homes. Smith was forced to cancel plans for personal appearances in Syracuse, Buffalo, and Rochester. Hands would not be shaken. Backs would not be slapped. Stories would not be told. Al Smith, political showman, would be denied center stage.

It did not look promising.

The well-ordered life of Franklin Delano Roosevelt was anything but in the fall of 1918. He was back from Europe, where he had dined with politicians and generals in London and Paris and toured the killing fields of France: Chateau-Thierry, Belleau Wood, Verdun. He came home to New York on a stretcher, having contracted double pneumonia in France. While he recuperated, Eleanor came upon love letters to her husband written by Lucy Mercer, her onetime personal secretary. She offered him a divorce; his mother said she would cut off his income and his inheritance if he left Eleanor. Louis Howe provided even more pragmatic advice: divorce would ruin his political ambitions. The unhappy couple remained married, performing their respective roles in public, sleeping separately in private.

He was exhausted in body and in spirit, but he managed to find the energy and psychic space to keep up with local politics. He was following the race for governor of New York, and on October 14, 1918, as the trees outside Springwood's parlor windows relieved themselves of their leaves, he sent a letter to a man he had met in Albany a lifetime ago.

"My dear Al," he wrote. He was sorry for not having written earlier, but he had been away for a while, and then he was sick and only now was he feeling well enough to write. But he wanted to make sure that Al knew that he could count on Franklin Roosevelt's support in the closing weeks of the campaign. He included a second letter that Smith could use as he saw fit to publicize Roosevelt's support, and he offered to speak at any meetings in New York City in the days before the election.

"I see that you have been called the 'best equipped man' for this office," Roosevelt wrote. "May I tell you that this is not only true but that I trust that the people of this State will realise this. . . . Many men have served as you did for a long period of time in the Assembly or in the State Senate, but very few men, indeed, have served with a record of painstaking work and intelligent interest in the public good as yours." He went on to talk briefly about the old days, about "our personal friendship, dating from the time when we both served in the Legislature." He closed by calling himself, "Always your sincere friend."

Al Smith showed Franklin Roosevelt's letter to some of his advisers. It made "quite a hit with all the men around me," Smith told Roosevelt in his reply. It certainly must have.[24]

But at some point, one of those men around Smith must have asked: Al, were you and Frank Roosevelt friends in Albany?

Al Smith surely would have laughed at the thought.

eight

BRIDGE BUILDING

EDWARD LUCIANO WAS NOT SLEEPING well. He had been sick with the flu, and then he and his wife watched as their baby died of the same dreaded illness. He was weary, far wearier than any twenty-five-year-old ought to be. But he had buried a child, a baby, and it aged him as nothing else could.

On November 1, 1918, Edward Luciano was asked, or was told, to operate a train on the Brooklyn Rapid Transit's Brighton Beach line. He did not operate trains for a living. His job was to dispatch them. But the BRT's motormen were on strike and employees like Luciano who were not on strike were expected to pitch in and keep the trains moving and the customers happy.

He had already worked a long day, nineteen hours, but at six o'clock on Friday evening—prime rush hour—he took command of a five-car train crammed with about nine hundred passengers at the BRT's station at Park Row near City Hall in Manhattan. The cars were made of wood and completely out of date. Luciano was unfamiliar with the Brighton Beach line and had received just two hours of training as a replacement motorman. The striking motormen were given sixty hours of training before they were allowed to operate trains on their own.

The Brighton Beach line was elevated in some portions, at street level in others, and underground elsewhere. The grades and curves presented challenges absent from more run-of-the-mill trips to and from Manhattan.

After crossing the Brooklyn Bridge, Luciano struggled to bring the train to a halt at several stops, leading some to exit the train earlier than they planned. He lost time backing up to correct his mistakes, so as the train approached an S-turn heading toward the Malbone Street station, it was traveling much faster than the posted speed of six miles an hour. The train careened off the rails and crashed into a concrete wall as it entered a tunnel at Malbone Street. The first car exploded in splinters. Everyone who was in it died. Bodies and body parts piled up in the second and third cars as well. Passengers were decapitated, left without limbs, mangled beyond recognition. Survivors pulled themselves from the wreckage and tried to find their way out of the tunnel in the darkness. They brushed up against the train's power source and were electrocuted.

Ninety-three people were dead and many more were injured. From the city's press and politicians and ordinary people came one simple question: How could this have happened?[1]

Al Smith had been saying for weeks that the Public Service Commission, which regulated the BRT, was not doing its job under Governor Whitman, that private companies operating public utilities were able to do whatever they wanted without so much as a glare of disapproval from the governor's own commissioners. Companies effectively nullified the regulatory protocols put in place while Smith was in the state legislature in Albany, turning back the clock to the days when government thought it best to stay aloof and let men of business sort out their own problems.

That very night, Smith spoke in Brooklyn and excoriated Whitman for allowing the powers of the Public Service Commission to wither at the behest of the companies it regulated. He never mentioned the accident explicitly (it is possible he did not know the extent of the tragedy). But when he accused the governor of refusing to "strengthen the hands" of the commission, when he asked, "What has Governor Whitman to say about all this?" surely some of his listeners knew. They knew what had happened the day before and they knew that there were shattered bodies in burlap sacks in the Kings County morgue that might never be identified, and those bodies were there because a company regulated by the state had put an untrained man in charge of five wooden subway cars.[2]

The election was just days away. Smith stepped up his attacks on Whitman and the status quo even as he introduced himself to an entirely new group of voters: women. They would be voting for the first time in New York, and Smith happened to have on his side a woman who would prove to be one of the state's shrewdest political minds, Belle Moskowitz. The daughter of immigrants from Prussia, Moskowitz grew up in Harlem, attended the prestigious Horace Mann School, and spent a year at Columbia University's Teachers College before becoming absorbed in social work and government reform. She married an architect in 1903, had three children while working as a union activist and good-government advocate, and then found herself alone with those children when her husband, Charles H. Israels, died in 1911. She married a fellow social reformer, Henry Moskowitz, in 1914, but it was Belle, not Henry, who plunged wholeheartedly into the arena. She was a tireless organizer, a ferocious advocate, and, as time passed, she proved to be a brilliant political strategist.

She was an anomaly in the testosterone-filled world of early twentieth-century politics, and she turned that into an advantage. "Because I am a woman, I have certain intuitions, certain powers of sensing reactions on the part of others that men lack," she once said. A later generation of feminists might well recoil from Moskowitz's formulation—women's intuition?—but Al Smith embraced it. "She had the greatest brain of anybody I ever knew," Smith would say. Not the greatest brain among the women he knew. The greatest brain of anybody he knew.[3]

As the election neared, Belle Moskowitz persuaded Smith to speak to small groups of women, to talk to them as equals, to treat them as informed voters who knew their interests, even if they had never cast a ballot before. Tell them about what you've done to improve the lives of working women, she told Smith. Talk to them as voters. He did, and it worked. He shared stages with women active in the textile workers unions, women who taught in the city's public schools, women who had campaigned for years for the right to vote. He spoke to them as Belle Moskowitz instructed him to, and it was then that he realized what a brain this child of immigrants had.

In the final days of the campaign, Smith was unable to avail himself of Franklin Roosevelt's offer to leave Washington and speak on his behalf in New York City. Roosevelt's dreadful autumn became even worse when he returned to work at the Navy Department in late October, for within a matter of days he, his five children, and several servants came down with the flu. The pandemic continued to take a dreadful toll: Thousands in Washington were bedridden, and nearly four thousand died in the fall of 1918, with the worst yet to come. More than 675,000 Americans died of influenza in 1918 and 1919. But all the Roosevelts and their servants recovered, nursed back to health by Eleanor, who did not fall ill, and a doctor who visited the patients twice a day.

Franklin was well enough in early November to arrange for friendly newspapers to publish a story about his plans to resign as assistant secretary and take his place in the navy on active duty. "I think I shall get into the Navy without question," he wrote a friend, Lathrop Brown. But the war ended before he could do what cousin Teddy had done a generation earlier: get out from behind a desk and put on a uniform.[4]

Election Day, 1918, was like none other in the history of New York. The backrooms of Tammany Hall and the Republican state committee were covered in thicker clouds of smoke than usual as bosses and ward heelers waited on results, wondering how hundreds of thousands of new voters—women—would respond to their first election. The press paid special attention to the wives of the two candidates for governor, Olive Whitman and Katie Smith, as they cast their votes on a gray, wet day in New York City. The Whitmans voted together in midmorning at a polling place near the Plaza Hotel in midtown Manhattan. Katie Smith, however, decided she couldn't wait for her dawdling husband. She beat him to the polling place at PS 1 on Oliver and Henry Streets by two hours.

Equally eager to get to the polls was Catherine Smith, Al's mother.

Dressed in a long overcoat, wearing a colorful hat, and peering out from behind large round glasses, Catherine Smith, now nearly seventy years old, made her way to the polling station in Brooklyn and handed her paper ballot to a burly man wearing a vest and a moustache. Catherine Smith had vehemently opposed women's suffrage; politics was a man's world, she believed, and nothing good would come of allowing women into the process. She told her son she would never, ever cast a vote, even if the men were foolish enough to allow it.[5]

When the time came, however, she put on her fine hat and marched to the polls, later pointing out that she was the first woman in the history of the state of New York to vote for her son for governor.

It was a long day, the longest of Al Smith's life. The polls closed in the evening and Smith followed the returns in the Biltmore Hotel, headquarters of the independent committee formed to support Smith. Early counting showed him way ahead, but the votes were from Manhattan and Brooklyn, the source of his strength. Old friends, not as savvy as the political professionals in the hotel's raucous ballroom, gathered around Smith and shook his hand and started calling him governor. "Wait now!" he said. "Wait 'til we hear from some of the small cities and villages upstate." Smith knew, as his friends did not, that the numbers were about to change and not in his favor.[6]

And so they did. The clock turned past midnight and shirts began to show signs of sweat and clouds of smoke thickened over desks where frowning men hunched over papers and shook their heads. Smith was not getting the votes he needed to tamp down Whitman's support upstate. More smoke, more sweat, more shaking of heads. Catherine Smith left the Biltmore at three o'clock in the morning, exhausted and on the verge of bitter disappointment. The morning newspapers reported that Whitman was leading with results still unaccounted for upstate.

As the sky began to brighten and the city shook off sleep, Al Smith met with two of his former roommates in Albany, state senators Robert Wagner and Jimmy Walker. The election was slipping through their fingers. The Republican organizations upstate were just as capable as Tammany

Hall was said to be at stealing elections. Bleary eyed, hoarse, and bone tired, they decided to board a train from Grand Central to Syracuse in central New York, where they could be closer to the upstate vote count.

It took another two days of careful counting before Al Smith could breathe a little easier. He won by a little more than fourteen thousand votes out of about two million cast. Significantly, Smith won Brooklyn, site of the horrific train crash just days earlier, by seventy-seven thousand votes. Whitman himself conceded that the accident and its aftermath helped turn the tide for Smith.[7]

He was too tired to give a victory statement. The governor-elect needed sleep, fresh clothes, a bath, and a return ticket from Syracuse to Grand Central. But his old mentor, Tom Foley—the man who gave him his first job in politics and then sent him on his way to the assembly—summed up what so many were thinking. "I do feel pleased . . . to think that one of our own people is elected governor," Foley wrote to an up-and-coming young political operative in Rockland County, James A. Farley.[8]

In the days after Christmas, as Al Smith prepared to pack up his family—including a beloved Great Dane named Caesar—for the move from their flat on Oliver Street to the executive mansion on Eagle Street in Albany, Franklin Roosevelt was packing up as well. He and Eleanor were headed to Europe to supervise demobilization of the navy, a job he had demanded and received ahead of the navy's top uniformed officers. The trip across the Atlantic meant that he would have to decline a personal invitation from Al Smith to attend his inauguration on January 1. Roosevelt wrote to Smith with his apologies, saying he was quite sorry to miss the occasion. But as long as he had the governor-elect's ear, he had a slight favor to ask.

"I won't bother you with many suggestions" for jobs, Roosevelt told Smith in a letter dated December 27, "but I do want to make an exception in the case of William Gorham Rice. I really believe it would be good politics and good efficiency to retain him on the Civil Service Commission."[9]

William Gorham Rice, who could trace his lineage to the founding of the Massachusetts Bay Colony, was a good-government reformer who started his political career as a private secretary for James Roosevelt's friend and favorite Democrat, the ponderous and cautious Grover Cleveland. Some years later, Rice had taken the place of none other than Theodore Roosevelt on the U.S. Civil Service Commission, and since then he had only added luster to his already golden reputation as the ideal public servant, a man who had no interests other than the common good, a man of refinement and breeding.

The politicians pretty much hated him. He was a symbol of the last century's politics, when government was led by what the newsroom philosophers called the "best men," the graduates of colleges from the northeastern portion of the country. When politicians like Al Smith were elected to high office, men like William Gorham Rice generally found themselves on the outside looking in and not particularly enamored of the view.

Asking Al Smith to retain a man like William Gorham Rice was inconceivable—they were on opposite sides of most public issues—and Smith gently indicated as much in his response to Roosevelt. Retaining Rice, Smith said, "is quite a problem."[10]

But retain him he did, to the astonishment of the press, which had been assuring readers that Tammany boss Charles Francis Murphy was in residence in Albany and was in possession of the state payroll, performing unspeakable atrocities upon the public treasury and subverting the civil service rules that people like Rice had sworn to preserve and protect. The *New York Times*, amazed that a Tammany man would find a place for somebody like Rice, declared that Smith was "a rare find among politicians."[11]

That particular revelation was old news to Murphy, and he was determined to make sure that the newspapers would continue to sing Al Smith's praises. Not long after Election Day, Murphy summoned Smith to his vacation home in Good Ground, Long Island. The boss's property was expansive enough to include a nine-hole golf course, and perhaps not co-incidentally, Al Smith was learning how to play the game, something the neighbors on Oliver Street surely found amusing.

The two men sat on the front porch of Murphy's home, enjoying a sunny fall afternoon, and spoke of the future and the pressures that Smith would face from old friends and new allies. Indeed, Murphy himself would have favors to bring to the new governor's attention. "I shall be asking you for things, Al," Murphy said. "But I want to say this to you. You understand these things better than I do. If I ever ask you to do any-thing which you think would impair your record as a great governor, just tell me so and that will be the end of it."[12]

Franklin Roosevelt had heard the buzz about Al Smith. As time ran out on the Wilson administration, Roosevelt's thoughts turned to what might come next, what opportunities might be there for him in New York. So it was no accident that the squire of Hyde Park was eager to keep in touch with the favorite son of Oliver Street. Letters were sent and invita-tions extended. Would Smith care to join Roosevelt for the commission-ing of a new battleship, the USS *Tennessee*, in Boston? Alas, Al couldn't make it, but he was grateful for the thought. Al invited Frank to the news-paper correspondents' annual show in Albany and to then spend the night in the executive mansion—there was plenty of room, even with Katie and the five kids and the Great Dane and other animals Smith was beginning to accumulate. Roosevelt replied that he would be delighted to be Al's guest, and he looked forward to spending private time with the new gover-nor. It was a fine plan until Roosevelt got sick again in the spring of 1919. But just so there was no mistaking his intent, Roosevelt sent trusty Louis Howe in his place.[13]

Slowly, carefully, but ever so surely, Frank and Al began to talk to each other, and each friendly word, each pleasant exchange was a step across a chasm that nobody had quite been able to bridge. Patricians and pols gen-erally had nothing to say to each other. City and country Democrats had little in common save for their party registration. Elite progressives and urban liberals never saw each other as potential allies. Until now.

It seemed as though everybody on the Lower East Side took a train to Albany to watch one of their own, Al Smith, take the oath of office as governor on New Year's Day, 1919. A new crowd was in charge of state government: When a distinguished-looking man named John Dix presented himself at the main entrance to the capitol to attend Smith's inauguration, he was turned away. The man had been governor of New York just eight years before. Nobody knew who he was.[14]

As the new governor settled in, he remembered how much he admired a lobbyist he had met nearly a decade ago, a young woman who had an idea for a fifty-four-hour workweek for women and children, and who simply did not give up until the legislature came to see the wisdom of her idea.

Frances Perkins would make for a fine addition to the state's moribund Industrial Commission, designed to be a check on the exploitation of workers but, after four years of a Republican administration, now was nothing more than a patsy for factory owners. Smith asked Perkins to come to Albany for a talk in his second-floor office in the capitol. After an exchange of pleasantries, Smith got to the point: "I ought to bring women in to the political picture in my administration," he said. "I thought about you."

Perkins thought Smith wanted to talk about legislation, not a job. No woman had ever served as a prominent, paid adviser to the governor of New York. But that's what Smith was offering.

"I know a lot of women," he said. "Most of them in the Democratic Party are the wives and sisters of political leaders. They're all right. They're nice women, but they don't know anything about things like this. They don't know anything about government. I didn't want to appoint somebody's sister or wife. That's kind of an insult to women."

Perkins didn't know what to say. She asked if she could first discuss the offer with her mentor, Florence Kelley, one of the nation's most prominent voices on behalf of workers and women.

"What an idea!" Smith replied. "She'll say, 'Glory be!'"

Perkins went back to New York City, met with Kelley, and told her about Smith's offer. Kelley burst into tears. She never thought somebody she had trained, somebody who wanted to do right by women, by workers, by children, would ever be offered a job as an adviser to the governor of New York. Take the job, she told Perkins.

For good measure, she added an exclamation: "Glory be!"[15]

Al Smith began to bring to Albany men and women whose careers would have an extraordinary impact not only on the state and the nation but also on the relationship he was beginning to build with Franklin Roosevelt. In addition to Perkins, who would go on to become Roosevelt's labor secretary and the nation's first female cabinet officer, Smith hired a young political operative named Edward Flynn, destined to become one of Roosevelt's chief political advisers; James Farley, who would manage Roosevelt's first two presidential campaigns; and Samuel Rosenman, who wrote speeches for Smith and then was loaned to Roosevelt to bolster his own ambitions.

Their careers and service would become inextricably connected to Franklin Roosevelt. But it was Al Smith who gave them their start, something he never forgot even when it seemed to him that they did.

Franklin and Eleanor Roosevelt were aboard the USS *George Washington* when they heard the sad news: Theodore Roosevelt had died in his sleep in the predawn hours of January 7, 1919, at age sixty. Although he had been in poor health, although he was grief-stricken over the death of his youngest son, Quentin, shot out of the sky by German fire over the fields of France six months earlier, he seemed vital and energetic. His death shocked the nation and the world.

Franklin and Eleanor could not change their plans to attend the funeral. Nor could the former president's two other sons, Lieutenant Colonel Theodore Roosevelt Jr. and Captain Kermit Roosevelt, both of whom still were in France, where Franklin and Eleanor were headed.

Theodore Roosevelt was buried on January 8 in Oyster Bay, New York. The stock exchanges of New York City cut short the trading day, closing at 12:30, half an hour before the funeral began. The city's stores and markets, the courts, and the schools stopped for a minute of silence at one o'clock when the ceremonies got underway on Long Island. Among the solemn-faced men and women gathered in the church, still decorated for Christmas, was the governor of New York, Alfred E. Smith. He did not speak. He would not have been asked, and certainly would not have expected such an invitation. He was not a member of the fraternity of the high and the mighty who turned out to bid the colonel farewell. But he held the very office Roosevelt himself once held, and the Vanderbilts and the Winthrops and the Lodges would have noted the incongruity of a Tammany man at the funeral of the great reformer.

Smith followed the crowd to a gravesite on a quiet knoll off Oyster Bay. The cemetery was covered in a light snow, and a chilling wind off the bay made the final rituals even more of an ordeal for family and friends. And there Alfred E. Smith, representing the people of the state of New York, paid one final tribute to his indomitable predecessor.

The end of the world war that cost Teddy Roosevelt a son gave way to bitter conflict at home over working conditions, race, and the very foundations of American society and government. Hundreds were killed in race riots in more than thirty American cities, including Washington, DC, where army reservists patrolled the streets to keep order. Millions of workers went on strike and employers grew fearful that the growing power of unions was a sign that the United States was following the path of Russia, now in the hands of the Bolsheviks. Radicals saw no solution to the nation's ills short of revolution.

Smith himself intervened in several tense labor disputes in the turbulent summer and fall of 1919, confident that by his combination of charm and street smarts he could persuade management and labor that they were not bitter enemies, as the radicals claimed they were. Smith knew full well how the other half lived, but he rejected the notion that the haves and have-nots were engaged in a great ideological conflict from which there could be only one winner. He sought common ground, not a field of battle, as he dealt with unhappy workers and recalcitrant capitalists throughout his first term. In the fall of 1919, teamsters in New York City—men who trucked milk to stores and markets, men very much like his father—threatened to walk off their jobs over pay and working conditions. Smith caught wind of an impending strike vote on a Sunday night when he happened to be in New York City for his weekly supper with his mother. He rushed to an enormous meeting hall uptown and burst in, asking to be heard, seeing in the faces of these hard-working men with broad shoulders and thick forearms a trace of his long-dead father. The truckers, nine thousand of them, cheered when he appeared on stage, and somebody yelled out, "Hello, Al!" He had his audience where he wanted them, simply by being Al Smith.

"It doesn't seem so long ago to me when I worked in the Fulton Fish Market, and there are many of the old men now there who can remember when I used to work for Feeney and Baker," he said.

"I contend there is no disorder—social, political or labor—so great that it cannot be settled," Smith said, his foghorn voice cutting through the haze of resentment and grievance. "Now, you men can settle your troubles. You have the ability and the intelligence to do it in an orderly, peaceful manner, if you will follow your leaders. If you will follow your leaders, I will go with them. I'll put all my strength into it to see that you get an absolutely fair, square deal, both personally and as governor." The truckers decided not to strike after all, and in the press the following morning, headlines said that the governor's "eloquence" had turned the tide.[16]

For Al Smith, graduate of the Fulton Fish Market School of Labor Relations, no conflict was inevitable, no gulf too wide, no river unbridgeable. And while the nation panicked over the specter of radicals lurking around the corner or under the bed, Smith insisted there was nothing to fear. Five socialists were elected to the state legislature in 1919 (as was a distinctly nonsocialist candidate, Theodore Roosevelt Jr., hailed as his father's heir and a future leader of the state's Republican Party). The presence of radicals in the halls of the state legislature was, for some, a sure sign that the very fabric of American society was unraveling. Smith, on the other hand, saw democracy in action. The state assembly's leaders prevented the socialists from taking their seats in the chamber in January 1920, and were prepared to expel them. Theodore Roosevelt Jr. devoted his maiden speech as an elected official to demand that the socialists get a "square deal." But Republicans and Democrats alike argued for expulsion, the sooner, the better.[17]

Al Smith sent a message not only to the assembly but the entire state and the nation itself when he invited the socialists to a reception in the executive mansion. He then announced that the socialists should be recognized as the duly elected representatives of the people who chose them, saying that it was "inconceivable" that a minority party should be suppressed simply because the majority found its views abhorrent. The assembly speaker, an upstate Republican named Thaddeus Sweet, had a ready response to Smith's argument. "They have no right to be called a political party," he said of the socialists. "They have as little right to be a political party as the followers of Mohammad have to call themselves a political party."[18]

The legislature expelled the socialists despite Smith's plea. And as law-enforcement officials continued to warn of left-wing plots against the nation, lawmakers in New York passed a series of bills designed to keep socialists and other radicals out of civic life—barring them from taking elective office and authorizing the firing of public school teachers deemed to be disloyal. Smith vetoed the bills, named for their author, a state senator named Clayton Lusk, in a series of messages that appealed to the nation's founding principles of free speech, free thought, and free elections. "The clash of conflicting opinions, from which progress arises more than from any other source, would be abolished by law, tolerance and intellectual freedom destroyed, and an intellectual autocracy imposed upon the people," Smith's veto message read.[19]

Smith's was a lonely voice in the hysteria of the immediate postwar

years. Red-hunting was a bipartisan sport in which players and spectators alike were loud and energetic and determined to crush the enemy by
means fair and foul. Nearly six hundred people deemed to be national
security threats were deported. Thousands were arrested during Justice
Department raids in late 1919 and early 1920. The urge to suppress, arrest,
deport, and crush dissenters extended to the nation's armed services, including the navy. Assembly Speaker Sweet claimed that socialists were
hard at work trying to undermine the service and the nation's defenses,
or so he was told by an unnamed navy official. This navy man, Sweet said,
insisted that "if the American people realized how much the Navy was
permeated with socialist ideas they would not sleep until every vestige of
such an idea was eradicated."[20]

In Washington, the assistant secretary of the navy found these and
other reports puzzling. Franklin Roosevelt shared Al Smith's belief that if
some voters were buying socialism's pie in the sky, it was not government's
job to void the sale. Nor, for that matter, should institutions devoted to
education and the free expression of ideas attempt to place limits on what
might be discussed and by whom. Roosevelt quietly ignored fervent appeals from Harvard alumni to join in a campaign to purge suspected radicals from the university's faculty. He admonished an admiral who fired
three machinists from a navy yard in Boston because they were suspected
of being socialists. "My dear admiral," he wrote, "neither you nor I can fire
a man because he happens to be a Socialist. It so happens that the Socialist
party has a place on the official ballot in almost every state in the union."[21]

Franklin Roosevelt and Al Smith had no reason to consult with each
other about the panic that seemed to overtake so many of their colleagues.
But in their calm faith in the democratic process and their willingness to
uphold their values even in the face of widespread opposition, the two
New Yorkers from very different places were not on opposite sides after all.

New York politics at the dawn of the Roaring Twenties featured the names
of officials grand and minor who would be well-remembered in histories

of the twentieth century. There were the big names, the stars: Al Smith, Franklin Roosevelt, Frances Perkins, Robert Wagner. There was a supporting cast: James Farley, Edward Flynn, Belle Moskowitz. And there were the understudies: Robert Moses, Theodore Roosevelt Jr., Jimmy Walker, and a young congressman named Fiorello La Guardia, who in 1919 was elected to Smith's old position as president of the New York City Board of Aldermen.

But one prominent New Yorker was absent from the inner councils of political decision making, and he knew it and couldn't stand it. Newspaper publisher William Randolph Hearst was more famous than anybody in New York politics save perhaps for Smith, and yet his dreams of becoming president were rapidly fading. He was years removed from his two terms in Congress, and his attempts to become mayor of New York City and governor of New York had failed miserably. He was nearing sixty now and was building a castle for himself and his mistress, Marion Davies, in California while keeping a residence on Riverside Drive in New York, home of the two newspapers, the *New York Evening Journal* and the *New York American*, that gave him his power and his leverage.

Hearst's newspapers supported Smith in his campaign for governor, and in an election as close as the Smith–Whitman contest was, every influence-peddler who supported the victor could claim to have delivered the margin of victory. Hearst's support certainly helped Smith, and he was not shy about collecting on the debt he believed Smith owed him. Hearst decided he had an ideal candidate for a job as a state Supreme Court justice and sent his name to Smith, who promptly ignored the request and nominated somebody else.

It was then that Hearst's newspapers decided that Al Smith was to blame for the deaths of babies and children. His newspapers had devoted thousands of words to flaws in the supply of milk to New York City, and to illustrate the point, literally, they printed pictures of skeletal children, alive and dead, said to be the victims of greedy dairymen and distributors who charged exorbitant prices in the city. The images very likely were not of children from the Lower East Side but from atrocities in Europe, but it didn't much matter: Hearst set his attack dogs on Smith and blamed him for standing by while greedy capitalists denied milk to poor children. Letters poured into the governor's office in Albany: How could Al Smith, the son of the sidewalks of New York, stand idly by while children were dying because milk suppliers wanted to squeeze more money from their poor parents?[22]

The price of milk and the methods of its distribution were not new issues in New York politics. But Hearst upped the ante when he ordered his papers to attack Smith personally, to argue, day after day, that there were dead babies in New York City who might have lived were it not for Alfred E. Smith, tool of the Milk Trust.

Smith was enraged as he had never been before. He challenged Hearst to a debate in Carnegie Hall, adding, cryptically, that the publisher could ask him any question about his public or private life "if he will let me do the same." That was Smith's way of letting Hearst know that this was more than a typical dispute between a political figure and a newspaper publisher. This was personal: the governor of New York knew all about Hearst's private life—the mistress, the castle, the broken marriage. Smith could, and would, ruin Hearst if he went too far.[23]

On the morning of October 29, a Wednesday, the mayor of New York, John Hylan, walked his daughter down the aisle of Our Lady of Good Counsel Church in Brooklyn. The pews on both sides of the church were filled with government officials, for the groom was the mayor's personal secretary, the son of the city's tax commissioner. Seated near the front of the church, to the left of the center aisle, was William Randolph Hearst and his wife, Millicent, playing the role of dutiful spouse. Three pews away was Governor Alfred E. Smith. The two men ignored each other.

Later on that night, after the grand wedding reception in the Waldorf Astoria, Al Smith made his way to Carnegie Hall for his debate with his fellow wedding guest, Hearst. Four thousand people showed up, but Hearst did not. He sent word that he would not be appearing alongside a "public plunderer."[24]

So Al Smith had the stage to himself, and not just any stage but the stage in Carnegie Hall. He gave the audience what it wanted: a performance nobody would soon forget.

"I am alone," he told the crowd. "I knew I would be, because I knew the man to whom I issued the challenge, and I know that he has not got a drop of clean, good red blood in his body."

He went on, speaking without notes, gesturing to the audience. He defended his actions in the milk controversy, accused Hearst of seeking revenge because Smith wouldn't appoint a crony of his to the state Supreme Court, and pointed out that this tribune of the people spent most of his time in California and Palm Beach. How to explain Hearst's campaign against him? "It has got to be envy, it has got to be hatred or it has got to be something that nobody understands," Smith said. It was time, he said, to "get rid of this pestilence that walks in the darkness."[25]

Smith left the Carnegie stage to cheers. Years later, journalist Claude Bowers would write that "a great actor was lost when Smith went into politics." His speech was front-page news the following day: Nobody had ever challenged Hearst so publicly. Nobody had dissected him so brilliantly.[26]

It was the beginning of a bitter and prolonged feud, but neither man could imagine on that October evening how their hatred for each other would affect politics on a grand scale, and how it would one day benefit Al Smith's new friend in Washington, Franklin Roosevelt.

nine

DEFEAT

ON THE COLD, SNOW-COVERED morning of January 17, 1920, the *New York Times* reported on page one that John Barleycorn had died peacefully hours earlier, at the stroke of midnight. The death had been widely expected; indeed, it was not a natural death at all but a government-ordered execution. Restaurants around the country brought out black tablecloths in a show of grief.

John Barleycorn was a euphemism, brought to American shores from Ireland, for alcohol. And as of January 17, 1920, the manufacture, sale, and transportation of alcohol was expressly forbidden in accordance with the Eighteenth Amendment to the U.S. Constitution. A noble experiment, in the words of Herbert Hoover, was about to begin, with enormous implications for Al Smith, Franklin Roosevelt, and other politicians from urbanized, industrialized, religiously diverse states that did not share the dusty heartland's obsession with the power of intoxicating spirits.

Smith and his friends in Tammany Hall viewed the anti-saloon movement as just another outbreak of feverish anti-immigrant, anti-urban sentiment of the sort that had been plaguing the nation's body politic for decades. The drys, as they were called, tended to live in the south, the plains states, the mountain west, where everybody was native born, white, and Protestant. The wets invariably were, well, they were Al Smith: they lived in cities, they were not Protestant, and their parents or grandparents called another country home. Oh, the drys were well-meaning all right, and you couldn't grow up in the old neighborhood without hearing about lives ruined thanks to demon rum. But on the Lower East Side and wherever immigrants and their sons and daughters lived, the drys sounded a lot like the zealous reformers of the previous century who saw poverty as evidence of vice and a lack of self-discipline. Alcohol consumption was for the weak of will, and it led to immorality, and everybody knew what the consequences of immorality could be. The prohibitionists believed they could legislate morality and use the police power of the state to enforce it. And Al Smith believed they were terribly misguided.

If nothing else, though, at least the issue was settled as the presidential campaign of 1920 neared. The prohibitionists had gotten their way; the ban on alcohol was quite literally the law of the land. A battle that had been raging in state capitals for decades finally was over, and the prohibitionists had won. But even still, John Barleycorn's gravediggers and pallbearers remained alert to the possibility of a resurrection. The governor of New York with his city mannerisms and loud clothes and, most of all, his nonconforming ethnic and religious persuasions seemed just the sort who might yet breathe life into the corpse of immoral drunkenness.

They were watching Al Smith, watching to see how he would enforce Prohibition, how zealously he would deploy the resources of the state to deny his people their now-illicit pleasure. They watched and they did not like what they saw. An official with the state's Anti-Saloon League complained of the "scandal" that was unfolding as New Yorkers blithely paid no attention to the law of the land.[1]

Smith made little attempt to disguise his own private consumption of alcohol—he had a stash in his office on the second floor of the capitol and was anything but shy about making good use of it. He certainly had no concerns about reporters lurking about, for they had a tendency to indulge as well.

Not every visitor to Smith's office, however, could be counted on to ignore bottles or glasses scattered about. One day Franklin Roosevelt's boss, Navy Secretary Josephus Daniels, showed up at the capitol quite early for an appointment with Smith. Daniels was drier than dust and adamantly so: early on in his tenure at the Navy Department, he banned alcohol from the navy's bases and all the ships at sea, a move that did nothing for his popularity with the rank and file.

Daniels's arrival at the capitol set off a frenzy in the governor's office, for Smith and his aides were in the midst of settling the state's problems over a few cocktails. Smith summoned his young aide Edward Flynn and told him to rush downstairs and do his best to keep Secretary Daniels occupied while other aides scurried about to gather up beer mugs and highball glasses.

Flynn showed why he was considered such a promising political operative. Without giving off a trace of his own indulgence, he chatted amiably with Secretary Daniels for several minutes—the weather was always a good topic of conversation in Albany. Finally, when he judged the coast to be clear, he escorted the secretary of the navy to the governor's office, where the two men then carried out their business with all due sobriety.[2]

The obvious hypocrisy of it all bothered Smith, but as the elections of 1920 approached, he chose to keep his remarks to himself, paying lip service to the amendment and to the law establishing enforcement, the Volstead Act. He was running for reelection in November, so there was no reason to unnecessarily antagonize the substantial dry vote upstate.

The Democratic Party gathered in San Francisco for its national convention in 1920, and in the years to come, the hard shell of famed journalist H. L. Mencken would melt away as he recalled the pleasures of that convention and the hospitality offered to delegates and reporters alike. Booze, and good booze at that—fine bourbon and not the cheap bathtub gin that sustained so many thirsty working people—flowed to his heart's content in hotels, caucus rooms, press lounges, and speakeasies. The brazen display of an outlawed substance plus the presence of women delegates attending their first convention turned Mencken into a downright sentimentalist. San Francisco, he wrote, was a place where the police acted as "if there were no laws against honest joy."[3]

And that was a good thing, for nobody in San Francisco was filled with more honest joy than Al Smith. It had been arranged that he would be nominated for president along with a handful of other candidates, and while it was only a tactical maneuver—Smith would be among several candidates nominated as "favorite sons" to allow their state delegations room to cut a deal with the more serious candidates—it was an honor all the same.

Smith and his wife and family joined Tammany boss Murphy and their friends aboard the Overland Limited from Chicago to San Francisco, traveling first class in their own private car. Smith saw sights he had only heard about—the salt flats of Utah, the snow-peaked mountains of the Sierra Nevada, the vast open spaces of the heartland. It was all very beautiful, but nothing he saw compared to the view of the Brooklyn Bridge from his old apartment on South Street.

Smith, Murphy, and the whole New York delegation had a treat awaiting them once they arrived in San Francisco and unpacked their bags at the St. Francis Hotel. A fellow delegate from New York, the assistant secretary of the navy, had used his influence to arrange for a special reception aboard a battleship newly assigned to the Pacific fleet, the USS New York. Franklin Roosevelt, tall, handsome, and eager, shook the hands of his fellow New Yorkers as he welcomed them aboard. Al Smith joined the party with his teenage daughter Emily, who nearly blushed as she was introduced to their host with his impeccable manners and fabulous smile. He was so debonair, so unlike anybody she knew back on Oliver Street. She listened as her father and Roosevelt chatted amiably on the quarterdeck about Albany, the old days, the old friends. They smiled and laughed and managed to convey good cheer and fellowship.

Swept up in the moment, Al Smith grabbed hold of Roosevelt and asked him a favor: he needed somebody to second his nomination, somebody who would be willing to follow Congressman William Bourke Cockran, a silver-tongued native of Ireland known for his baroque turns of phrase. Nobody ever wanted to follow Cockran on a stage, but somebody had to second the nomination. Would Roosevelt consider it?

He most certainly would, he told Smith. The deal was done with a handshake.[4]

It was all for show, this side deal between Roosevelt and Smith. Roosevelt didn't actually support Al Smith for president—he was backing his friend William Gibbs McAdoo, the treasury secretary and son-in-law of President Wilson. Practically speaking, Al Smith didn't even back Al Smith for president. He was a placeholder, and he knew it, a pawn to be traded when Tammany boss Murphy was ready to conduct business with one of the serious candidates. But the theatrics were not entirely pointless: the name of Al Smith, New Yorker, wet, Catholic, city dweller, would be placed on the record as a candidate for president, and that was something. And now Al Smith was giving Franklin Roosevelt a chance to shine in front of thousands of delegates and reporters, and that was something, too. He needed the attention. He had a plan for the convention: he hoped to be nominated as vice president, just like his late and lamented cousin Teddy.

The nomination process, scripted and tedious, began on the morning of June 30, the convention's third day. Each of the ten candidates required not only a long nominating speech but one or two seconding speeches of lesser length but equally fulsome. The speeches would then prompt a noisy demonstration of love and affection for the candidate, complete with music and chants and banners as the gimlet-eyed press attempted to gauge the seriousness of candidates based on the level of enthusiasm on the convention floor. Women would feature prominently in the seconding speeches, for they were about to cast votes for president for the first time, and each party was eager to display its acceptance of this cultural and political revolution in 1920. This courtship, however, often seemed as awkward as a parish hall dance: when a distinguished, gray-haired woman from Massachusetts, Susan Fitzgerald, stepped forward to second the nomination of Senator Robert Owen of Oklahoma, the house band struck up a ditty called "Oh, You Beautiful Doll."[5]

Cockran took the podium midway through the session and recounted, for the many who did not know, Al Smith's rise from the sidewalks of

New York, his accomplishments as a legislator, his humility, his human-ity. He called him "Al" and made sure his listeners understood why. "He is the only one I ever knew, who, in high office, could be called by a diminu-tive appellation of friendship without abasing in some degree the dignity of his office," he said, sounding very much like the Victorian Irishman he was. A voice from the floor shouted, "That is wonderful!"

On he went, describing Smith as an "orphan," talking about the re-spect Smith had earned and the love his neighbors had for him. "I think it only fair and proper to tell you now that New York reluctantly offers her governor as the candidate of the convention for the presidency," Cockran concluded, "but if the convention thinks differently, then New York will claim the right to take her favorite son back to her own borders, and there, as a candidate for governor, ensure the vote of the state for the candidate of this convention."[6]

As Cockran finished, the New York delegation waved its banners and a band struck up Tammany Hall's anthem, which was neither the wisest nor the best-known tune it might have conjured, and then, sensing the crowd's displeasure, it launched into a more familiar tune called "The Sidewalks of New York."

East Side, West Side
All around the town . . .
We'll trip the lights fantastic on
The sidewalks of New York

And suddenly the mood changed, and men and women began waltzing on the convention floor while others marched behind placards decorated with Al Smith's smiling face. The band kept playing, moving on to Irish-American songs like "Sweet Rosie O'Grady" and then to American stan-dards that had nothing to do with Al Smith like "A Bicycle Built for Two," and now even the shy ones were on their feet, dancing with strangers. Stationed with the professional skeptics in the press room, even the cur-mudgeonly Mencken allowed himself a smile.

Franklin Roosevelt waited at his place with the New York delegation, waiting for the singing and dancing to subside so he could follow
Cockran's speech with a short one of his own. One thing was certain: back
in the day, when he was organizing meetings of sober, righteous, and
right-thinking reformers, he had never seen anything like this. These
people were having *fun*. Such an interesting concept at a political gathering.

It went on and on, half an hour, forty-five minutes, an hour. Then Roosevelt saw his chance. The band was tapering off, exhausted. Sweaty men
and women were heading back to their seats. But the aisles were clogged
in ways that no fire marshal would ever allow and for a moment there
seemed no clear path to the podium. Roosevelt had no choice but to vault
over a row of chairs and then make an undignified beeline for the front
of the auditorium. From her place with the New Yorkers, an amused Frances Perkins watched with delight. Roosevelt no longer seemed to be the
effete snob she remembered from his Albany days, his nose stuck in the
air as he observed his social inferiors from a distance. Older now, more
mature, he seemed even better looking and certainly much friendlier—
he quite literally slapped the backs of his fellow delegates and chatted
away about nothing and everything. He was becoming quite the politician, and as Perkins knew from her experience with Al Smith, that was
not such a bad thing.[7]

Roosevelt's speech, the first he ever gave at a national convention, was
mercifully shorter than Cockran's but no less effusive. "I love him as
a friend," he said of Smith. "I look up to him as a man; I am with him as a
Democrat. . . . In the Navy we shoot fast and straight. Governor Smith,
in that respect, is a Navy man."[8]

There were cheers for Roosevelt, and as he retreated from the podium
after his two minutes in the spotlight, Frances Perkins reckoned that while
his speech was short, it was well-delivered and well-received. Still, in the
end, it was a performance given for the sake of performance, because Al
Smith was not a serious candidate for president. Everybody knew that,
even two women who worked for the New York Police Department back

in Manhattan. While the Democrats were gathered on the West Coast, the two policewomen were busy tracking down and confronting a suspected con artist named Annie Criswell, thought to be running an illegal fortune-telling operation from her room in the Hotel Arlington in midtown Manhattan. The day after Cockran placed Smith's name in nomination, the two women, posing as eager customers, visited Criswell and asked her to foretell their futures. She took the measure of them, perhaps poring over their palms. Finally, she announced that one of them would marry a wealthy widower and would receive a raise at her job. The other, she predicted, would soon receive a diamond ring. But then, overcome by the clarity of her visions, Criswell added a bonus fortune: Al Smith, she said, would receive the Democratic Party's nomination for president. This was too much hokum. Predictions involving rich husbands and diamond rings were a dime a dozen, but Al Smith for president? The policewomen arrested Criswell on the spot and hauled her over to the Jefferson Market jail.[9]

Annie Criswell was proved a poor fortune teller indeed after eight ballots in San Francisco, when Tammany boss Charlie Murphy moved the majority of his delegation from its favorite son, Smith, to the candidacy of Ohio's James Cox. The short presidential candidacy of Alfred E. Smith came to an abrupt end, but the *New York Times* said all that marching and all the music and all the good will had transformed him "into a figure of national prominence."[10]

Franklin Roosevelt's man, McAdoo, battled Cox on the floor and in the backrooms for days until finally surrendering, exhausted, after forty-four ballots. Murphy had picked a winner: James Cox. And Cox returned the favor by choosing a member of Murphy's New York delegation to be his vice president: Franklin Roosevelt. Protocol demanded that Cox ask for Murphy's approval, and it was quick in coming. If you want him, Murphy told Cox, take him. He's all yours.

The deal was done. The new star of the party, Al Smith, was asked to deliver a seconding speech for the man who had seconded his own nomination. He announced that he "heartily" seconded Franklin Roosevelt's nomination, describing him as "a leader in local legislative reform . . . and a man who has held a position of great power and importance in a governmental department." It wasn't exactly an extravagant endorsement; Smith resisted the urge to reciprocate Roosevelt's profession of his love for him. Still, the symmetry was downright poetic.[11]

On the morning of August 9, 1920, Smith and his wife left the relative comfort of summer in Albany for an eighty-mile journey south to Hyde Park, where it was hotter—temperatures in the Hudson Valley were in the unbearable upper eighties—and much more humid. Katie dressed for the weather in a light summery outfit, but the governor wore a sober dark suit and a jaunty bow tie. They were on their way to Springwood for their first visit to the residence of Franklin Roosevelt.

The Smiths received one of fifteen thousand invitations dispatched to prominent politicians, various Hudson Valley potentates, and Hyde Park neighbors, all of whom seemed to arrive by automobile. Great columns of dry August dust rose from the tree-lined driveway as car after car pulled into the estate from the Albany Post Road.

The occasion was yet another bit of political theatrics, the formal notification to a candidate that he had been chosen at his party's convention for a place on the national ticket. The ceremony was a relic of the days before modern communication, but it was a tradition after all, and it was obeyed. So Franklin Roosevelt arranged for thousands of his friends to be on hand when the chairman of the Democratic National Committee informed him of what had been decided in San Francisco a month earlier. Roosevelt was expected to be charming and delighted but there was no need for him to feign surprise. This was, after all, 1920.

Al and Katie Smith took their places with the guests of honor, including Cox, William Gibbs McAdoo, Navy Secretary Josephus Daniels, and Roosevelt's friend and Hudson Valley neighbor Henry Morgenthau, who managed the gigantic affair. Smith and Roosevelt stood together for several minutes as the crowd burst into applause for the two New Yorkers whose names would appear on the ballot in November.[12]

Smith's career had taken him to places he could not have imagined, but few sights compared to this—here he was, he and Katie, guests of honor on the property of one of the most famous families in America, on an estate that seemed large enough to fit the entire population of the Fourth Ward, standing outside a manor house that made the governor's residence look like a beach cottage at Coney Island.

The campaign began in earnest not long after everybody piled back into their cars, kicked up more dust, and left Hyde Park to its own version of normalcy. Cox and Roosevelt had their work cut out for them, for the Republican ticket of Warren Harding and Calvin Coolidge was promising a return to the way things were before the war, before Woodrow Wilson tried to sell the country on a League of Nations, before anybody thought it was a good idea to send American boys to the Old World to fight in a war to end wars. The country had rejected Wilson's vision, leaving him a broken man, and it now seemed prepared to reject everything else about Wilson, including those who campaigned on his legacy.

One Republican in particular was determined to make sure that Franklin Roosevelt was defeated in 1920. Theodore Roosevelt Jr., the freshman assemblyman from Oyster Bay, was appalled by the prospect of Franklin becoming the next great Roosevelt. Cousin Franklin was a lightweight, a usurper, a man who stayed behind a desk during the war rather than serve in uniform, as he had—wounded in his leg, he would walk with a limp for the rest of his life—and as his father had. Young Teddy traveled out west to campaign for the Harding-Coolidge ticket, never mind that Harding's blandness and conservatism surely would have infuriated his father. Franklin Roosevelt, Theodore Roosevelt Jr. declared, "does not have the brand of our family." The blow stung.[13]

The voters' foul mood figured to have an impact on Smith's chances for reelection, never mind that his term seemed to be a success. He once again mobilized not only the Tammany Democratic machine in all its glory but a separate committee of reformers, progressives, and good-government advocates. Even Samuel Seabury, the cantankerous reformer who made such a show of not voting for Smith as the party's nominee for governor in 1918, joined the independent committee for Smith.

Republicans chose a former state judge named Nathan Miller to oppose Smith. Miller was an inspired choice, for he had no record that the
feisty Smith could attack. He had served in no public office save for the
judiciary and was able to campaign as an outsider in a year when voters
were restive and cranky. And scared: they were scared of Bolsheviks at
home and abroad, scared of the changes unfolding in the streets of their
cities, scared of globalists who sought to drag the United States into the
League of Nations. They wanted it like it was, like they remembered it,
before the war, before all the changes, before the government thought it
fitting and proper to attend to their health and welfare in some small
degree.

Smith and Roosevelt campaigned together at a rally in Madison Square
Garden in late October, although it was Al Smith's show from begin-
ning to end. Roosevelt spoke first, and briefly, talking confidently about
victory before passing on the show to "our own Al Smith." Thousands
of city people rose from their seats and sang "The Sidewalks of New
York" when Smith began to speak. He smiled and wisely let them finish.
And then they sang another song in tribute to their favorite son, "The
Bowery":

> *The Bowery, the Bowery!*
> *They say such things,*
> *And they do strange things*
> *On the Bowery! The Bowery!*

He knew the song and he joined in, his voice hoarse and gruffer than ever
after delivering speech after speech for weeks on end.

"I am very much afraid that there is very little kick in Al tonight," he
told his listeners once they finished singing and settled in their seats. "After
a solid month of campaigning I feel as though I could scarcely speak."
Everybody laughed and cheered. Off in the wings somewhere, Franklin
Roosevelt watched a master in his element. Scarcely speak? Smith launched
into a lengthy speech based, as always, on a few notes scrawled on the

backs of envelopes. That was all he ever needed, that and his wonderful memory and his actor's sense of timing and delivery, and he soon had his audience cheering his achievements as governor and roaring back disapproval at the very mention of his opponent. He talked about the laws he supported to help mothers and children, about the plan he had to harness the power of the St. Lawrence River to create cheap electricity, about how Republicans were trying to dilute the state's law requiring employers to give workers a day off every seven days.[14]

Ten thousand New Yorkers filed out of the Garden happy and perhaps even confident on that Saturday night, with the election just three days away. Smith and Roosevelt assured them of victory, but as the candidates themselves surely knew, it was all just so much theater. They were about to get shellacked.

Election Day in New York was dreary, wet, and cold, an omen for what the night would bring Democrats across the nation. Franklin Roosevelt's place on the national ticket did little to help deliver the state's forty-five electoral votes to the Democrats. For a while, though, it appeared that Al Smith might survive the Republican deluge. "Congratulations, governor," a voice rang out as Smith worked his way through the lobby of the Biltmore Hotel, heading downtown to Tammany Hall. Smith said nothing in return.

Ninety miles up the river in Springwood, Franklin Roosevelt waited on the defeat he knew was coming, seemingly philosophical about it all. Just as well, for the Republican landslide of 1920 was historic. Harding and Coolidge won 61 percent of the popular vote and 404 electoral votes, with the Democrats settling for 127 electoral votes, with nary a one above the Mason-Dixon Line. Democrats around the country were swept away.

And that included Al Smith. He followed the returns with Tammany boss Charlie Murphy, secluded in a conference room while hundreds of supporters dragged on their cigarettes and chewed on cigars as Smith's early lead evaporated. He lost by seventy-four thousand votes out of two and a half million cast. It was actually something of a personal victory, to lose by so little when Cox and Roosevelt were pummeled so badly at the top of the ticket. But it was a loss all the same.

It was the first electoral defeat of Al Smith's career. For Franklin Roosevelt, the Democratic disaster was his second straight electoral embarrassment, coming six years after his devastating defeat in the 1914 primary for the U.S. Senate. Smith was forty-six years old; Roosevelt, thirty-eight. They were in the prime of life, as energetic as they were when they were twenty years younger but a good deal wiser. There was nothing to suggest that these defeats would mean the end of their public careers.

But it certainly felt that way for Al Smith. He had been in office since 1904, and he had risen beyond anybody's expectations. But he had little to show for his efforts other than the glory, and that didn't pay the bills for his five children. He made $10,000 a year as governor, but save for his lucrative two years as sheriff of New York County, he had never made any kind of money. Perhaps his loss was a signal that it was time to get out of the government racket and go make some money. He had friends, and they would be happy to find him something.

Less than a week after the election, looking for somebody with whom to commiserate, Smith dashed off a letter to perhaps the only other person in New York who understood how he felt: Franklin Roosevelt, another victim of the 1920 Republican landslide.

"Maybe it is for the best," he wrote, trying his best to sound philosophical but clearly letting the pain show. "The people of this country, in no uncertain terms, gave responsibility to the Republican party. Probably it is but right that they not be handicapped to even the slightest degree."

The letter was already on its way to Hyde Park as Roosevelt was writing a letter of his own to Smith. Roosevelt, too, tried to put the best face on his defeat, but his disappointment was equally impossible to mask.

"Now that the smoke has cleared away it all seems in many ways for the best," Roosevelt wrote. The two of them, he said, "will in all probability not run for state office" again.

But they mustn't give up, he said. There were votes to be had upstate, in the rural areas, far from the cities that were the party's base. "I feel that you and I have about as broad an insight into the affairs of upstate as any two people," he told Smith. The two of them needed to talk about how to win the upstaters, how to expand the party's reach beyond the cities. They needed to lead a reorganization of the party so it could emerge renewed in two years when there would be another race for governor.[15]

They soon found new jobs in the private sector, Smith as president of a trucking company, Roosevelt as a vice president with a financial firm in lower Manhattan, Fidelity & Deposit. He told Smith he would be back in touch so they could hash out a plan to rescue the Democratic Party in New York.

Nine months later, the task of building a new, vibrant Democratic Party with Al Smith became next to impossible for Franklin Roosevelt.

He couldn't move his legs.

ten

RESURRECTION

HE WENT FOR A SWIM with his children in the icy waters off Campobello Island one August afternoon in 1921, and when he woke up the following morning he could barely stand. Soon he could not stand at all.

Franklin Roosevelt would never again take an unaided step, and even those halting efforts were not really steps at all but the well-rehearsed motions of a performer pretending that he had control over muscles that had long since atrophied. But he would not retire to the peace and quiet of Hyde Park and spend his life playing the role of a river squire, wheeling himself from the dinner table to the parlor to the veranda as his mother wished. Perhaps to his own surprise, he told her that he could not bear such a life.

He would get better. That's what he told his friends as news of his illness made its way into the newspapers and into the conversations of men who spoke clinically rather than sentimentally about those who might lead civic affairs in the 1920s and beyond. They would conclude that Franklin Roosevelt was finished, for not only was he a two-time loser at the ballot box but now he could not walk. Perhaps somebody would take pity on him and appoint him to a high-minded commission or department someday. But there was no reason for unsentimental men to spend time thinking about Franklin Roosevelt's future political prospects because they did not exist.

Although there were moments of depression and despair in the weeks and months after his diagnosis, Roosevelt did not dwell on negative thoughts, for there was too much to do: exercises, hours and hours every day; correspondence; the newspapers; new hobbies to cultivate—model ships rather than golf. He had Louis Howe on one side, to tend to his political alliances, and Eleanor on the other, administering support because it was needed and affection because it seemed a suitable substitute for love. They took him by the arms, gripping him tightly, guiding him gently. He could not move on his own, but move he did.

He circulated the fiction that his illness was nothing more than a bit of a bother. "I'm glad to say that I am still getting on well and making noticeable improvement every week," he told his old friend from his Wilson days, William Gibbs McAdoo, in August 1922. He was far more interested in talking politics than in dwelling on his health. In an earlier letter to McAdoo, he dissected the results of a recent special congressional election in upstate New York, where a Democrat running on an explicitly anti-Prohibition platform nearly beat his Republican opponent in a heavily Republican and very dry district. Roosevelt read the returns with the eyes of a professional: he noticed rural voters did not come out for the Republican candidate, but Democrats in the district's cities and towns showed up in impressive numbers for a candidate Roosevelt described as an "out and out wet." It was hard to know exactly what the numbers meant for Democrats in general, Roosevelt told McAdoo, but "it at least shows that the [Republican] tidal wave has subsided . . . and that we are 'back to normalcy' in a way not exactly meant by President Harding."[1]

McAdoo filed away this small but perhaps significant bit of intelligence from his friend. He had failed to win his party's nomination in 1920, but he would try again in 1924 when, he hoped, Harding's profound mediocrity would offer opportunities for a good progressive Democrat like himself. McAdoo moved from New York, a place he had grown to hate, to California in the spring of 1922, but he knew he could rely on his friend Roosevelt to keep him informed about politics in the nation's most powerful state. "I find the Administration is extremely unpopular throughout the West," McAdoo told Roosevelt shortly after his move. "If this keeps up, the Democrats will have a real chance in 1924."[2]

Roosevelt relished that thought and perhaps it gave him something to focus on as the hard work of rehabilitation began in earnest. "As to my legs," he told his friend and law partner, Langdon Marvin, "the doctors say that there is no question that I will get their use back again."[3]

He kept out of sight so that few except his family and Howe knew the true extent of his illness. His long and growing list of correspondents could detect nothing amiss other than a damned nuisance that was keeping him off the golf course—for the time being—and away from political meetings—for the time being. A prominent upstate Democrat, Neal Brewster of Syracuse, invited him to a conference to discuss the party's prospects as New York's gubernatorial election of 1922 approached. Roosevelt parried the issue of his health in explaining why he couldn't attend. He really couldn't do much in the way of speechmaking at the moment, he explained, but he took the opportunity to offer Brewster some unasked-for advice about a possible candidate for governor that year. "We have in our Party an individual who not only stands (and has always stood) for Progressive Democracy of the best type, but has also, through years of experience in various positions of trust in the State, acquired a reputation for honest and vigorous efficiency," he wrote. "It is almost unnecessary for me to add that my own personal conviction is that the Democracy of the State of New York should again call upon Governor Alfred E. Smith to lead us in the coming campaign."[4]

Roosevelt's letter was read aloud to the upstate Democrats gathered in Syracuse, and while they might have agreed with the sentiments, they also knew that Al Smith had given no indication that he wanted back in. And that was the problem.

He was, by all accounts, thoroughly enjoying life as a private citizen. He was making an enormous salary—$50,000—as chairman and chief operating officer of the New York–based U.S. Trucking Company. He was living the American dream and quite pleased with himself, thank you very much.

Still, there were those who looked at prosperous Al Smith and saw a man who was dying to get back into the game, never mind what he was saying. After Roosevelt sent his letter to the Democrats in Syracuse, he dispatched a private letter to Smith discussing what he had done and why he had done it, suggesting that it had been carefully orchestrated. "I realize full well the extremely difficult position you are in and I was very careful in my letter to the Syracuse Convention not to call upon you for any kind of statement," he told Smith. But he gave Smith a bit of a prod, gentle, but a prod all the same. The time for some kind of statement might be coming, he suggested, noting slyly his concern that if Smith didn't declare himself soon, somebody else might. "As a matter of fact," he wrote, "I am frankly a little worried about the Hearst drive."

Hearst. The mere mention of the man, Roosevelt knew, should be enough to get Al thinking hard and long about another term in Albany. He invited Al and Katie to "pack as many children as possible into a car any Saturday or Sunday and come up and lunch with us." There was, after all, much to discuss.[5]

New York Democrats who were not privy to these discussions were beginning to wonder aloud if they had no choice but to embrace the ambitious publisher. Whatever his flaws, Hearst had money, people knew who he was, and he certainly was no stranger to politics. From his home in California, Hearst—still technically a resident of New York—sent a telegram informing New York Democrats that he had no interest in running for governor. "I am a rancher, enjoying life on the high hills overlooking the broad Pacific," he wrote. "I have no ambition to get into politics unless there be some special reason, and I don't see any special reason."[6]

It was then that Democrats realized that a man they distrusted and feared was not only interested but most likely desperate to run for office again. They knew this because he said the opposite.

The U.S. Trucking Company's office on Canal Street was just a few minutes' walk from Oliver Street. It was a walk Smith seldom made alone, especially in the early evening when the office shut down for the day and the man everybody called by his former title made his way home to Katie and their children. Smith had money now, money enough to leave the old neighborhood and St. James parish for less gritty surroundings. The thought might never have crossed his mind. He walked home every night, the sun setting behind him as he passed the five-floor walkups lining Canal Street, headed for the marvelous arch and colonnade decorating the newest East River miracle, the Manhattan Bridge, turned into the Bowery, where the ghosts of his boyhood gathered in the shadows cast by the Third Avenue El, and then turned left toward the river, to the apartment on Oliver Street. Along the way he saw a hundred people he knew or who claimed to know him. Hands would be shaken, backs would be slapped, and there would be promises of a lunch and jokes about the need for some sort of refreshment stronger than lemonade or iced tea.

One of his regular companions was a tall young man who had written the bible of the short-lived Smith administration, the ponderously titled *Report of the Reconstruction Commission to Governor Alfred E. Smith on Retrenchment and Reorganization in the State Government*. Neither Smith nor the report's author, Robert Moses, were in power long enough to achieve the sort of retrenchment and reorganization they had hoped for, but even Smith's successor, Nathan Miller, occasionally made some noise about similar goals, so perhaps the whole thing wasn't in vain after all.

They walked together, Smith and Moses, and they talked about how government might function better, and soon the conversation ended not on the sidewalk but inside the apartment on Oliver Street, over the dinner Katie had prepared, where the well-dressed young man with a doctorate in public administration eagerly absorbed the stories and lessons Al Smith shared with him. He heard things his professors had not told him in the seminar rooms of Columbia and Oxford universities because they had never stood at the bar rail with Tom Foley, they had never been invited for a private dinner at Delmonico's with Charles Francis Murphy, they had never had their arms twisted by Frances Perkins, they had never picked the magnificent political brain of Belle Moskowitz.

But all of this talk—what did it mean if Al Smith was out of the political game for good?

He returned to the state assembly chamber in Albany to deliver a speech in favor of ambitious plans to begin building bridges and tunnels connecting New York and New Jersey. The work would be undertaken by an agency Smith had helped create, a bi-state organization called the Port of New York Authority. The chamber was packed when Smith began his speech, and he held his audience spellbound with visions of a modern port whisking people and goods to and from the city thanks to modern engineering marvels that would be paid for through bond issues and maintained through toll collections. He talked about cabbage, and how much effort it took to get the humble vegetable from a farm in Rockland County to a dinner table in Manhattan. He pointed to a map of the lower half of the state and showed how the Port Authority's bridges and tunnels would make the journey so much easier. "Now," he said, "when that cabbage gets to Oliver Street by our route, it will be worth eating!"[7]

The papers were filled with praise for Smith's performance and his continued place in New York's civic life. Everybody loved Al. Why in the world would he return to a job that paid a measly ten grand a year, where every day brought criticism and condemnation rather than handshakes on Canal Street and high praise in the city's newspapers?

Why? The answer, it became clear, could be summed up in a word: Hearst.

He had never forgiven the publisher for telling hundreds of thousands of newspaper readers that he was to blame for the deaths of babies deprived of milk in 1919. "I cannot think of a more contemptible man," he had said that night in Carnegie Hall when Hearst refused to debate him. "Any man that leads you to believe that your lot in life is not all right, any man that conjures up for you a fancied grievance against your government or against the man at the head of it to help himself is breeding the seeds of an anarchy and a dissatisfaction more disastrous to the welfare of the community than any other teaching that I can think of." Radicals, he said, at least had the virtue of being sincere, and so William Randolph Hearst could not be the radical he pretended to be.[8]

Hearst's allies were organizing upstate with the state nominating convention just weeks away. Their confidence was such that one of the publisher's allies, William Conners, sent a message to Smith through the newspapers that Hearst would be delighted if Smith would run for the U.S. Senate in 1922 so that the Democratic Party could feature its two most popular candidates on the same ticket, William Randolph Hearst and Alfred E. Smith. The thick-necked Conners, his graying hair slicked back and obedient, was a formidable character from Buffalo, where he rose from stevedore to wealthy gangster to political powerhouse. He was known by the nickname of "Fingy," in honor of his left thumb, missing in action since childhood when one of his playmates hacked it off with a cleaver on a dare.

Fingy Conners told the newspapers that Al Smith was obliged to heed Hearst's offer. "No man is bigger than his party," Conners said. Smith issued a terse statement in reply, saying that he had no intention of discussing politics, at least not at the moment. Privately, though, he fumed. "Do you think I haven't any self-respect?" he snapped to a friend who urged him to take Hearst's offer.[9]

If Smith wasn't in the mood to talk publicly about the governor's race with the state nominating convention less than two months away, somebody else—a new voice—was more than happy to fill the void. "The women of New York state are incensed at Governor Miller's attitude on welfare legislation and his cynical indifference to the perils of long working hours for women and children," proclaimed a new member of the Women's Division of the Democratic State Committee, Eleanor Roosevelt.[10]

With her husband's political activities restricted to writing letters, Eleanor became the public face of the Democratic Roosevelts in 1922. She was not a natural, and she knew it, but with the encouragement of friends who were involved in Democratic politics and under the tutelage of the inevitable Louis Howe, she became not simply a substitute for her missing husband but an active and vocal presence in the state party. Her withering criticism of Miller came on the very day that Fingy Conners was boasting about Hearst's gubernatorial prospects and lecturing Al Smith about his duty to run for Senate on the Hearst ticket.

On August 14, less than a week after Eleanor's statement, Franklin Roosevelt released a public letter addressed to Al Smith but meant for other Democrats who feared the prospect of Hearst running for governor. It had all the earmarks of an arrangement, for nobody with an ounce of political brains would risk making such a public appeal without knowing what the answer would be. "I have been in touch with men and women voters from almost every upstate county and there is no question that the rank and file Democrats want you to run," Roosevelt's letter read. "I am asking you personally and publicly to accede to the wishes of so many of your fellow-citizens."[11]

Until this moment, Al Smith's reemergence seemed far from certain. He had steadfastly declined to engage in any public conversation and was careful to be at his summer home in the swanky Sea Gate section of Coney Island when Roosevelt's letter hit the newspapers. From Hearst's operatives in the state, there was only stunned silence. Fingy Conners was nowhere to be found.

Al Smith replied in a "Dear Frank" letter on August 15. He dearly wished to remain in business, he said, but if the party was calling him to leadership, well, what sort of man would he be to put personal interest ahead of his civic duty? He was careful to note, though, that whatever his wishes might be, delegates to the state convention would have the final say. "If a majority of them desire me to accept the nomination for Governor and lead the party in this State to what seems to me to be a certain victory," he told FDR and the entire literate population of the state of New York, "I am entirely willing to accept this honor from their hands and battle for them with all the energy and vigor that I possess."[12]

Charles Francis Murphy, meeting with other members of the executive committee of Tammany Hall, was spotted with a smile on his face when Smith's letter was released to the newspapers. On the other hand, the mayor of New York City, John Hylan, who had taken up residence in

Hearst's hip pocket, seemed even more puzzled than usual. Asked for his reaction to the exciting news, the mayor said, "I read Al's letter, but I can't figure out who Frank Roosevelt represents."[13]

Roosevelt's friend in California, William Gibbs McAdoo, was delighted to hear of his reemergence in public life, at least through the public prints. "I think you have rendered the Party a genuine service by getting Smith into the race again," McAdoo wrote. He said he was prepared to come back east to campaign for Smith if he were asked.[14]

Al Smith couldn't walk. The doctors said he was suffering from neuritis, an inflammation of the central nervous system, and it left Smith virtually, though not literally, paralyzed. The state convention in Syracuse was about to begin and the outcome was still uncertain: how would the party deal with the rivalry between the former governor and the formidable publisher?

Smith was flat on his back in his hotel room on the eighth floor of the Onondaga Hotel. He'd have to rely on Belle Moskowitz and other trusted aides to keep him up to date on the drama in the convention hall, the hotel lobbies, and even in adjacent rooms. An acquaintance from Smith's first campaign for governor, James Farley, made himself particularly useful. Friendly, outgoing, and eager, the thirty-four-year-old Farley was given the task of buttonholing delegates and reciting the virtues of Al Smith and the vices of William Randolph Hearst. Farley made the most of the opportunity, for he was as ambitious as he was convivial. "I was like a duck who had been searching for water all his life and finally found it," Farley later wrote of this crucial moment in his career.[15]

The Hearst forces quickly realized that they couldn't beat Al Smith, so as the convention opened, they offered a deal: Hearst would be delighted to accept the convention's nomination as a U.S. senator rather than challenge Smith for the nomination for governor. It was, it seemed, a perfect solution.

Charlie Murphy, saloonkeeper and political boss, knew a good transaction when he saw one. He dispatched emissaries to Smith to inform him of Hearst's offer. He was a shrewd politician, Murphy, but in this case he misjudged the man he had mentored for more than a decade. Smith sent Belle Moskowitz to the lobby of the Onondaga Hotel to make an announcement: "Alfred E. Smith will never consent to join with Mr. Hearst," she said. "But he will be nominated just the same, and he will be elected."[16]

This was not the result Murphy was expecting. Hearst's intermediaries met with the boss and with one of Smith's young aides, Edward Flynn, now being groomed as one of Murphy's lieutenants, and together they breathed nothing but tobacco smoke as they sought some kind of accommodation. Men were sent to Al Smith's hotel room, and from his bed or from a chair, he said the same thing: no. "If the party is going for Hearst," he said, "then I'm through." He told Murphy's emissaries there was no point in negotiating. He wouldn't share a taxi with Hearst, never mind a ticket. He wouldn't do it, not even for Charlie Murphy's sake.[17]

Hearst was now officially, politically, a dead man. Murphy caved in—given a choice between Smith and Hearst, there really was no choice. Hearst's supporters skulked out of town, boarding trains bound for home before Jimmy Walker delivered the convention's opening speech. An editorial in the *New York Evening Post*, a reliable guide to liberal thought in New York City (and whose shareholders included Franklin Roosevelt), bore the headline "Al Smith Saves the Day."

"He was not fighting for himself; he was fighting the battle of the decent element of his party," the editorial said of Smith. "In such a struggle there could be no compromise. . . . As a result, he has won a victory that will hearten the forces of decent politics everywhere."[18]

When the inevitable was made official, with Al Smith winning renomination by acclamation, Eleanor Roosevelt leaped from her seat with the Dutchess County delegation and took part in a victory parade around the hall, carrying the county's banner with her neighbor, Henry Morgenthau. Louis Howe, watching with pride as his latest project, Eleanor, reveled in the glory of politics, dispatched a telegram to Hyde Park: "Al nominated with great enthusiasm."[19]

Miraculously, although perhaps not coincidentally, the pain in Smith's legs and back disappeared when William Randolph Hearst's scowling men left Syracuse. His own journey home may as well have been on clouds.

He took a moment to drop a quick line to Franklin Roosevelt, letting him know how much he appreciated Eleanor's support. And he had a thought for Franklin, too: "[Take] care of yourself—there is another day coming." And with that last phrase, Al Smith unwittingly summed up precisely what Franklin Roosevelt was thinking, and it was a thought that got him through every day of his confinement, every day when others looked at his braces and his crutches and his withering legs and saw only the faded promise of yesterday.[20]

Franklin Roosevelt followed Smith's campaign from his listening post in Hyde Park, and not all of his information came via letters or the newspapers. Some of it was delivered in person, by his wife. Eleanor continued to find her voice in politics through the Women's Division of the state party, making lifelong friends and allies as she worked the political luncheon crowd, teaching herself to speak in public without a nervous, self-conscious giggle.

In mid-October, Eleanor's husband dictated a long letter to Smith filled with his unrequested analysis of the campaign as it neared its final few weeks. More and more New Yorkers, Roosevelt said, were no longer casting their votes merely from custom. They were voting from conviction. And those voters, he told Smith, would deliver him back to Albany.

"You, in your whole public career, have shown a true understanding of the needs and desires of the average American man, woman, and child," Roosevelt told Smith. "Your attitude has been one of belief in progress, and you have not opposed measures of relief and improvement merely because they were new. In other words, you have been essentially human, for it is human to want to better conditions and to seek new things. That point of view is what has made America."[21]

Al Smith won in a landslide so large it seemed to render him speechless on election night, November 8, as he followed the results in Tam-many Hall. "Wonderful, wonderful," he muttered, over and over again, bewildered over a show of support the likes of which he could never have expected. More than 1.4 million people voted for him, the most votes any candidate for governor in New York had ever received. That gave him nearly 57 percent of all votes cast, 386,000 more than Miller. In his wake, the state senate flipped from Republican to Democrat, and the new leader of the senate would be Smith's eternally boyish protégé, Jimmy Walker.[22]

Franklin Roosevelt took more than mere satisfaction in Al Smith's comeback. He took credit for it, sort of. "I had quite a tussle in New York to keep our friend Hearst off the ticket and to get Al to run," he wrote to a friend who might have heard the soft thumping sound of a man patting his own back. But Roosevelt had a right to be pleased, for he was back in the game. As far as the public was concerned, Franklin Roosevelt had single-handedly transformed the gubernatorial race of 1922 with his plea to Smith to come out of retirement and to save the state from William Randolph Hearst. He could not move his legs, but he proved that he could exercise power and influence. And that was something. That was worth a pat on the back.[23]

eleven

THE DARNED OLD LIQUOR QUESTION

ON NEW YEAR'S DAY, 1923, Albany was bathed in rivers of icy rain that felt like so many needles on those who were gathered to witness Al Smith's return to the governor's office. Even the tough troops from the 69th Regiment—the Fighting 69th, known for its conspicuous gallantry and its equally conspicuous Celtic makeup—were sagging at the shoulders as they waited to escort Smith and the outgoing governor, Nathan Miller, from the executive mansion to the capitol. In an act that could only be described as one of great humanitarianism, Smith canceled the parade and dismissed the escort. He and Miller, he said, could manage to find the capitol on their own.

The assembly chamber erupted when Smith made his appearance. Somebody in the room yelled, "Our next president!" Miller turned to Smith with a smile. "They seem to prefer your politics to mine," he said.[1]

Smith seemed surprisingly serious and single-minded in his formal attire, walking slowly to the front of the splendid chamber he knew so well. Voices from the galleries above chanted his name. "Who's all right?" shouted a voice in the crowd. "Al Smith," came the reply from dozens throughout the chamber.[2]

His inaugural speech was short and gracious—he'd save the details for the annual State of the State message to the legislature, which he chose to deliver several days later in person, something no governor had ever done before. He wished to continue the agenda that was so rudely interrupted by voters in 1920: He offered proposals for an eight-hour day for women and children, for minimum wages, for a stronger workers' compensation system. He demanded a repeal of the Lusk Laws, especially the measure requiring teachers to take a loyalty oath or risk being fired; repeal of laws censoring motion pictures; state development of hydropower; exemptions from the state income tax on incomes of less than $5,000 a year; continuation of rent regulations; a state constitutional amendment giving cities more power over their own affairs and budgets; and municipal ownership of public utilities.

These proposals were ambitious and important. But another issue, unspoken in Smith's address, cast a shadow over everything else he proposed. In a letter to Smith, Franklin Roosevelt called it the "darned old liquor question."[3]

New Yorkers knew when they returned Al Smith to Albany that they were voting for a man who had no time for the national mania over the evils of drink. It was hardly a secret that like so many millions of his countrymen, the governor of New York did not consider himself bound by the Eighteenth Amendment.

Smith's sentiments were put to the test in May, five months into his new term, when the legislature passed a bill designed to get the state out of the business of enforcing Prohibition. The assembly and senate voted to repeal a law, called the Mullan-Gage Act after its two legislative sponsors, authorizing the state police and other local law enforcement officials to uphold the national ban on booze. The law was never popular, and now lawmakers were eager to stop trying to enforce the unenforceable. The assembly passed the repeal bill by a single vote, and the new senate majority leader, Jimmy Walker, guided it through his chamber. It was sent to the office of the governor, where it received the sort of greeting a federal revenue agent might have gotten when he knocked on the door of a speakeasy.

Al Smith wanted no part of it.

Yes, he despised the hypocrisy of Prohibition. But he intended to run for president in 1924, and this time it would be for real.

The plan was already in the works. Murphy was using his influence as the most powerful Democrat in the most important state in the union to bring the Democratic National Convention to New York City, where it had not been held since 1868. Back then, in the first national elections since the end of the Civil War, the nation's Democrats had assembled in Tammany Hall itself, the very building on 14th Street where Charlie Murphy was scheming and plotting in 1923. The delegates were so taken with New York hospitality that they nominated New York governor Horatio Seymour as their candidate to face the unbeatable war hero Ulysses Grant. Seymour lost, but it was a triumph all the same for New York Democrats and for Tammany Hall. Charlie Murphy was hoping for a repeat performance in 1924.

But now there was this liquor question threatening to spoil Smith's ambitions and Murphy's careful plans. There was no more bitter divide and no wider gulf in American society than liquor, and the Mullan-Gage repealer meant that there was no way for Al Smith to bridge the two sides. The party's dry forces—the aging voice of the party's evangelical heartland, William Jennings Bryan, and the ambitious son-in-law of Woodrow Wilson, William Gibbs McAdoo—would hold it against him in 1924 if he signed the repealer. And if he didn't, his wet friends and allies would consider him a traitor and a hypocrite—worse yet, a man who could not be trusted.

Smith's dilemma was no mere local story. The eyes of the nation surely were upon him: Harvard law professor and future U.S. Supreme Court justice Felix Frankfurter summarized the stakes for Smith in a letter to Belle Moskowitz's husband, Henry. "This disposition of the Mullan-Gage repeal bill will show the mettle of the man," Frankfurter said. "If he vetoes the repeal, he will be damned for a comparatively brief time . . . if he signs it, he would be damned for good."[4]

He had thirty days to make up his mind. Great heaps of mail landed at the capitol every day, reminding him that one way or the other he was about to make enemies. His reliable voters demanded that he sign the repeal bill and put an end to New York's complicity in enforcing a law so many people despised. But the other side was equally adamant: Prohibition was the law of the land. It was in the United States Constitution. It was, therefore, sacred. New York had a duty to enforce it. To do otherwise was almost treason.

Franklin Roosevelt understood how high the stakes were for Al Smith. As he continued his regimen of exercise and therapy, as he continued to assure friends that he was getting better by the day, Roosevelt sought to come up with some sort of clever compromise that would extricate Al Smith from his dilemma. He was in touch with other Democrats from around the country, and they told him what everybody else was saying. If Smith signed the repeal bill, he was finished.

As the deadline for a decision neared and the nation's press descended on Albany to see what New York's governor would decide, Roosevelt dispatched a letter to Smith offering a shrewd scheme. "Frankly," Roosevelt told Smith, "it is going to hurt you nationally a whole lot to sign the Repealer Bill. This information comes from people who like you a lot and admire you a lot. . . . On the other hand I well realize that the vote in all the cities of this state will shriek to heaven if you veto the Bill."

Roosevelt's proposed solution reflected an appreciation for the sausage-making of legislative politics that he so conspicuously lacked a decade earlier. He advised the governor to veto the repeal bill, meaning that Smith would side with Prohibition supporters. He should tell the voters that "the State of New York is . . . bound, morally, to assist the federal government in enforcing the legislation." But, Roosevelt added, Smith should remind the voters that he was "not in sympathy with the Mullan-Gage law, that it is unworkable." He should call the legislature into a special session and twist the arms of lawmakers until they passed a new law saying that the state would actively enforce Prohibition only—*only*—when requested to do so by the federal government. Without such a request, state law enforcement would turn a blind eye to the making, distribution, and selling of liquor in the state of New York.[5]

It was quite brilliant and possibly doable. Most of the state's practical politicians regardless of party wanted the issue to simply go away. If they went along with Roosevelt's plan and passed a law that didn't exactly nullify Prohibition but didn't exactly commit the state to its enforcement, well, the damage to Al Smith's presidential prospects figured to be minimal. The great dry crusader of Democratic conventions past, William Jennings Bryan, could never condemn Al Smith with obscure biblical passages for signing a bill that nullified the law of the land. At the same time, the nation's drinkers would see Roosevelt's proposal as a step—at least in theory—toward repeal of the hated Eighteenth Amendment.

But there was a problem with Franklin Roosevelt's compromise, and it came in the form of the formidable Charles Francis Murphy. The Tammany boss was not in the mood to consider compromise, no matter how clever, because he believed Al Smith's voters demanded that he be true to them and to himself. The issue was straightforward: the people of New York hated Prohibition, and they wanted the state out of the business of enforcing it. Murphy invited Smith to join him in the Hamptons for a chat.

Smith arrived at Murphy's favorite spot, the magnificent Canoe Place Inn near the Shinnecock Canal, to find that the boss had also invited along one of his new protégés, Edward Flynn, the young lawyer who started his career with Smith several years earlier. Flynn was now a man on the rise, Murphy's choice to become the county leader of the Democratic Party in the Bronx.

The three men settled in: Murphy, inscrutable as always; Smith, anxious and ready for a fight if one were necessary; Flynn, young, quiet, and out of place, a card Murphy played to unsettle his old friend Smith. Murphy got down to business.

"Al," he said, "you must sign this bill."

Smith looked at his old friend and mentor and told him that he would do no such thing. Perhaps he was influenced by Franklin Roosevelt's proposed compromise. Perhaps he thought that after forcing Murphy to jettison Hearst several months earlier, he was in a position to dictate to the boss again. Perhaps he thought this was the time and place to declare his independence from Tammany. Whatever his thinking, he made it clear to

Murphy—in language that became louder and more colorful as the argument went on—that he would veto the repeal bill. If he signed it, he said, he would never be president

And with that, Charlie Murphy had heard enough. He stared through his round spectacles at the man he had helped send on his way to power and fame, the man who was now telling him no on an issue that mattered to him, to the Tammany organization, and to its voters.

"Al," he said, "you will either sign this bill or I will never support you again, either for the presidency or for the governorship."[6]

He stared for a moment to allow the threat to sink in, then turned and left the room and did not return. Smith was stunned, alone, save for the unwanted company of young Ed Flynn, who thought it better to say nothing.

The governor left without speaking again to Murphy. On the long journey back from Long Island, as he passed country roads and small villages destined to be transformed into suburban housing tracts, he had time to think about Murphy's cold-blooded warning.

He returned to Albany and scheduled a hearing for May 31 in the assembly chamber and invited the citizens of New York to come before him and speak their peace. They came in droves, some bringing along a brown-bag lunch in anticipation of a long afternoon. The speakers addressed themselves directly to the governor, pleading their case and seeking to appeal to his better angels. The most prominent advocate for the dry cause was not a Bible-thumper from upstate but the U.S. attorney for Manhattan and famous war hero, William Hayward, who spoke with passion about the rule of law and the sanctity of the Constitution, and he reminded Smith—as if he did not know—that the nation was watching.

"They are wondering, governor, how big you are, how brave you are, whether you, like they, believe in, love, and uphold the Constitution," he said.

One of the few Republican legislators who supported the repeal demanded to be heard although he was not scheduled to speak. He lashed out at the drys and their spokesmen. "Those on the other side have been claiming a 100 percent mortgage on law and order and Americanism," and yet he had voted for repeal and had done so as an American, he said. The other side had portrayed people like him to be little more than secessionists willing to divide the union for the cause of a cocktail. And with that, state senator Thomas Douglas Robinson, nephew of Theodore Roosevelt, turned and left the chamber. Another Roosevelt, telling Al Smith how to do his job! There was no escaping them.[7]

Smith sat through five hours of pleas and demands, trying his best to seem open-minded and engaged. When the last speaker was finished, he declared the hearing adjourned and said nothing else, offering not the slightest hint of his decision.

At six o'clock the following evening, reporters gathered in the governor's office, where they found a very serious, even dour, Al Smith seated behind his desk. Reporters loved Al Smith because he was quick-witted, entertaining, and accessible. On this occasion he was anything but. Without saying a word, he reached for a pen and signed the bill that repealed the Mullan-Gage law. At that moment, New York officially and unequivocally withdrew from the enforcement of the Eighteenth Amendment to the U.S. Constitution. The federal government was free to act as it saw fit in New York, but its police officers, state troopers, and other law-enforcement officials would no longer expend time and resources in pursuit of rum-runners, bootleggers, and the proprietors of speakeasies.

The reaction was just as Franklin Roosevelt and Felix Frankfurter and so many others had predicted. He was denounced as an apostate, as a threat to the Constitution itself. The various officers of the powerful Anti-Saloon League issued separate statements expressing their fury and accusing Smith of nullifying federal law. And then came the ringing voice of evangelical temperance, the leader of the Democratic Party's prairie populists, William Jennings Bryan. It took him more than a week to compose a proper response to Smith's action, but when he did, it was national news. "[When] the Governor of the largest state in the Union boldly raised the black flag and offers to lead the representatives of an outlawed traffic in their assault upon the nation's honor and the people's welfare, he must expect resistance from the defenders of the home, the school and the Church," he thundered in an essay published in the *New York Times* and quoted throughout the nation. "Governor Smith has simply dishonored his office and disgraced himself: he cannot lead the nation back to wallow in the mire."[8]

Bryan had been a national figure for more than a generation, a three-time failed candidate for president, the silver-throated voice of pious Democrats in the West and the South. In 1923 he was sixty-three years old and still a striking presence on the political stage, dressed in a white shirt and dark bow tie and vest, his bald head often covered in a skull-cap, his voice still capable of bringing the pious to their knees.

Smith, however, was undaunted. His withering response called out "fa-natical" drys and their "narrow and bigoted" agenda and assailed Bryan personally. Whenever Bryan ran for office, Smith wrote, a "wise and dis-criminating electorate usually takes care to see that Mr. Bryan stays at home."[9]

The bitter exchange between Bryan and Smith suggested that the Democratic Party would enter the presidential year of 1924 divided by geo-graphy, by ideology, by culture—by just about everything, enough so that it was fair to wonder how it could be considered a party in the first place. Reading the war of words between the man from the sidewalks of New York and the man from the prairies of the Midwest (newly decamped to the lowlands of Florida), Franklin Roosevelt saw the need for an intervention.

He quickly sent off a letter to Bryan, imploring him to not simply dis-miss New York as a hotbed of hard drinkers, regardless of what Al Smith said. "New York State is not nearly as wet a State as some Democrats try to make out," Roosevelt wrote, although he conceded that the party was filled with "hopeful idiots" who wished to bring about an end to Prohibition. He led Bryan to believe that he was on his side: "[As] you doubtless know, cer-tain reactionary forces are working more or less together with the idea that even if they cannot nominate their own man and write their own platform, they will have enough votes in the convention to prevent the nomination of a real progressive Democrat or an outspoken dry candidate."[10]

It sounded as though Franklin Roosevelt was referring to the forces lining up behind Al Smith and that surely is how Bryan would have interpreted it. The leading candidate for the party's nomination was their old colleague from the Wilson days, William Gibbs McAdoo, the man Roosevelt supported in 1920 after he was finished pretending that he was for Smith during the early ballots. McAdoo was every thinking person's idea of a real progressive. He was as dry as the deserts in his new home state of California and had only contempt for the big-city machines that plagued his party in the North and Midwest. He was the kind of progressive that somebody like Franklin Roosevelt would be expected to support, just as he had in 1920.

Nearly two years into his ordeal, Roosevelt certainly had improved since those terror-stricken days and nights of late summer 1921, but it was becoming clear that he could and would improve only so much, despite his formidable willpower, access to first-rate healthcare, and dedication to an exhausting exercise regimen. He had returned to his position as a vice president at Fidelity & Deposit in late 1922, and in his first appearance there since his illness, he crashed to the floor of the building's lobby as he sought to perform his "walk" in public for the first time after hours and hours of practice on the gravel driveway in Hyde Park. Onlookers were horrified but Roosevelt seemed unshaken. Several months later, Roosevelt's old running mate from 1920, James Cox, visited him aboard a houseboat in the Florida Keys. Cox nearly burst into tears when he saw Roosevelt and his withered legs, even though Roosevelt insisted he had never felt better save for the nuisance of his leg braces. "From that day on," Roosevelt wrote, "Jim always shook his head when my name was mentioned and said in sorrow that I was a hopeless invalid."[11]

Although few people actually set eyes on him, Roosevelt seemed a constant presence in New York society and politics thanks in part to Louis Howe's flair for publicity. His name appeared in newspaper headlines chronicling his work as the national chairman of the Woodrow Wilson Foundation and his appointment as chairman of the American Construction Council, where, it was reported, he would supervise the nation's building industry just as Kenesaw Mountain Landis was watching over baseball and Will Hayes was monitoring the motion picture industry. The construction council was a special project of the nation's secretary of commerce, Herbert Hoover. The New York press took note when he and Eleanor entertained Al Smith and his family at Springwood in the late summer of 1923, as gossip about the governor's possible presidential campaign began to make the rounds.[12]

Roosevelt was determined to play a role, to be part of the action, in the coming campaign. He thought, as his friend McAdoo and others did, that Warren Harding was eminently beatable in 1924. The Senate was investigating the administration's leasing of public lands for oil development in places like the Teapot Dome field in Wyoming, and the prospect of a first-rate election-year scandal heartened Democrats who might otherwise have been willing to concede the election to the incumbent. But Harding died of a cerebral hemorrhage in August 1923 while on a tour of the West. His presidency was about to be tarnished as one of the worst in American history, but death did him the favor of taking him away before he could see his reputation reduced to ruins. The public mourned and the politicians calculated. "I cannot help feeling that Harding's unfortunate taking off has helped . . . the Democratic Party," Roosevelt wrote. The new president, Calvin Coolidge, "is no world beater. . . . He will be considered, of course, a Conservative, and that means that we must nominate a Progressive without fail."[13]

The leading progressive in the field was McAdoo, whose claim to be Woodrow Wilson's heir became more poignant when the former president died in early 1924. Roosevelt was frequently in touch with one of McAdoo's chief supporters, Daniel Roper, and was sending would-be McAdoo supporters to see Roper. But in late January, the *New York Evening Post* reported that several McAdoo supporters were abandoning their man and switching to Smith. "One of these who, according to the *Evening Post*'s informant, have quit the McAdoo camp and joined that of Smith is Franklin D. Roosevelt, ex-Assistant Secretary of the Navy."[14]

The report sent Roosevelt into an uncharacteristic rage. He dashed off an angry letter to the newspaper's publisher, H. J. Adamson, protesting the story's assertion that he was a McAdoo man in the first place. Why, he had always been for Smith, he wrote. "I am horrified to see by your story that I have 'switched' from McAdoo to Smith," he wrote. "Where and when did you get the idea that I had deserted Al for McAdoo? I have always supposed that if I went to the next Convention I would, in common with the rest of the delegation, be for Al. Please don't accuse me again of shifts or changes of heart."[15]

All of this surely came as a shock to Roper. Only a few months earlier he had written to Roosevelt to ask for his help in rounding up "friendly delegates" for "our mutual friend, Honorable W.G. McAdoo." And on January 21, two days before the *Post* accused Roosevelt of dumping McAdoo for Smith, Roper had written Roosevelt with an upbeat note about the McAdoo campaign, saying that he would be sending along another McAdoo supporter to see Roosevelt about setting up an organization and raising money. If Roosevelt always was for Smith, Roper had been played for a fool. Or perhaps he had always been for McAdoo *and* Smith, depending on his audience.[16]

While Roosevelt was trying to cover his tracks, the apparent inevitability of McAdoo's nomination became doubtful if not improbable when his name surfaced in the growing Teapot Dome scandal. One of the key figures in the scandal, oilman Edward Doheny, revealed that he had kept McAdoo on retainer for $50,000 a year for several years. There was no suggestion that McAdoo was involved in helping Doheny get one of the tainted leases of oil-rich public land, but his attachment to one of the nation's leading villains damaged his reputation and emboldened other Democrats. The *New York Times* reported that Democrats were saying Al Smith's chances for the nomination were "greatly improved."[17]

New York's Democrats assembled for a state convention in Albany in mid-April to tend to some party business and to make plans for the coming national convention. They were a happy and confident lot, filling the lobby of the Ten Eyck Hotel with the loud optimism of a Roaring Twenties springtime and the boozy laughter of a city that did not consider Prohibition to be an impediment to a good time. But the matter at hand was serious, and it took a woman's voice to tell the party's male leaders that whatever they thought of the Eighteenth Amendment, they would do well to take the Nineteenth Amendment—which gave women the right to vote—more seriously. Eleanor Roosevelt, one of the leaders of the party's Women's Division, addressed a dinner at the Ten Eyck on the eve of the state convention and declared that women, not men, should appoint the four women who would attend the national convention as delegates at-large. "It is always disagreeable to take stands," Roosevelt told the crowd. "It was always easier to compromise, always easier to let things go." Now, however, was the time for confrontation, she said. The men gave in. The women nominated their delegates at-large without seeking approval from the party boss, Charles Murphy.[18]

Then it was on to more pleasant business at the state convention itself, held just up the hill from the Ten Eyck in a three-tiered auditorium named for another descendant of the city's Dutch founders, Harmanus Bleecker. With Murphy's assent, delegates selected Franklin Roosevelt as one of the state's male at-large delegates (Eleanor Roosevelt's friend and a future member of Congress, Caroline O'Day, was named as one of the female at-large delegates). Eleanor Roosevelt appeared on stage to read a resolution pledging that the New York delegation to the national convention would vote for Governor Alfred E. Smith as the party's presidential nominee. The hall exploded in cheers and whoops, and somewhere in the galleries men and women began singing "The Sidewalks of New York." Eleanor left the stage with a big toothy Teddy-like smile, and then Al Smith himself appeared, telling the delegates what they wanted to hear: he was a candidate for president of the United States.[19]

And so it was official, this plan that he and Charlie Murphy had been working on for years. Al Smith, child of the sidewalks of New York, was about to seek the nation's highest office, and it was something no Roman Catholic had ever done.

At a time when the country, and certainly Washington, DC, seemed satisfied with the status quo, Al Smith was shaking up Albany, cutting deals and twisting the arms of Republicans who controlled the state assembly and dispatching Robert Moses to help Jimmy Walker push bills through the senate, which Democrats controlled by a single vote. It was a remarkably successful combination. The state's infamous Lusk Laws were now off the books, so teachers no longer could be fired if they were suspected of something less than 100 percent Americanism. The state's Labor Department, which monitored workplace safety, was revived. Money was allocated for public health programs in rural counties, for new conservation programs and the creation of new state parks, for child welfare programs, for new laboratories for the state Health Department, and for a Housing Board to help finance slum clearance and the construction of new housing. Laws regulating rents, passed as an emergency measure during the world war, were continued (and do continue, more than a century later). Perhaps even more remarkably, Smith managed to cut the state income tax by 25 percent in March 1924, about a month before officially declaring his presidential candidacy. He could afford to do so because he had begun the tedious and decidedly unexciting work of overhauling the state's sprawling bureaucracy of nearly two hundred departments, a task that would take several more years and one that would make Albany more efficient and more accountable to the governor. It was one of his greatest achievements.

The Democratic National Convention was scheduled to begin on June 24, and it would be held in Madison Square Garden in New York City, thanks in part to Murphy's lobbying. The old boss showed up on Roosevelt's doorstep in early 1924 to ask for the younger man's help in recruiting national support for Smith. Roosevelt was cordial as always, but he was not entirely optimistic. He later said that he spent a good portion of the meeting analyzing, for Murphy's benefit, the strength of Smith's support in various states. Murphy no doubt was beside himself with delight as the young man who once called him a "noxious weed" offered him advice about strategy and tactics for the coming convention.

In late April, not long after receiving his diploma from the Franklin Roosevelt School of Practical Politics, Murphy traveled to Albany to meet with Smith and talk over how they would proceed during the two months before the convention opened. McAdoo, they knew, already had more than 140 pledged delegates, but that was nowhere near the two-thirds majority, some 732 votes, that he or any successful nominee would need at the convention. Deals would be done in backrooms, as they always were at conventions, and there was nobody better in those rooms than Charles Francis Murphy.

But there was one issue that no backroom deal could resolve. Among the nearly eleven hundred delegates who would soon be boarding trains for the journey to New York City were hundreds of avowed members of the Ku Klux Klan. If they had formed a caucus of their own, the Klan would have been the largest delegation at the 1924 Democratic National Convention. They would arrive in plainclothes, their robes and hoods left behind, but their loathing of Al Smith was undisguised. He was a Catholic, a wet, a product of an urban political machine, a threat to the party, the presidency, and the republic itself. They would block Al Smith. They would not leave New York until they arranged, by whatever means necessary, his defeat. When Franklin Roosevelt warned Williams Jennings Bryan of certain "reactionary" forces that sought to block the nomination of an unfriendly candidate, he seemed to be referring to the urban bosses that Bryan loathed. Roosevelt chose not to acknowledge the truly reactionary forces that were preparing for battle in Madison Square Garden.

The Klan's revival in the 1920s came about as people like Al Smith— Catholics and Jews, city people, immigrants or the descendants of immigrants, consumers of demon rum—were coming of age politically. The two developments were not coincidental. A U.S. senator from Alabama,

James "Cotton Tom" Heflin, said of the Klan, "God has raised up this great patriotic organization to unmask popery." The Klan was part of a revived anti-immigrant campaign that was on the verge of passing new restrictions designed to keep out immigrants in general and people from eastern and southern Europe in particular. Nearly twenty million immigrants had crossed the nation's threshold between 1890 and the start of World War I, and the coming of peace brought efforts to staunch the flow of new arrivals, so many of them Catholics and Jews. The Immigration Act of 1924, enacted in May of that year, imposed new quotas that favored immigration from northern European countries, but the more general intent was to let dust gather on the floor of the waiting room on Ellis Island. The urban machines in the North bitterly opposed the bill, with one Tammany-backed congressman saying that the legislation was an "insult to the origin of a great number of Americans who gave their sons and wealth to keep America American and not British or Nordic." The nation didn't want to hear that argument. The immigration restrictions passed overwhelmingly.[20]

The Klan of the 1920s was a sprawling enterprise, its geographic reach moving beyond the borders of the old Confederacy to terrorize immigrant-filled cities in the North. There were chapters in Chicago, Detroit, and Buffalo. Klan members had helped to elect governors not only in Georgia and Alabama, but California and Oregon as well. Many congressmen owed their elections to Klan support, and many no doubt owned a set of robes and a hood of their own.

It was called the "invisible empire," but by 1924, Klansmen saw no need to hide themselves, not even above the Mason–Dixon Line. They fired into a crowd protesting their presence in Pennsylvania in April 1924, killing four people and wounding more than a dozen. Klan supporters elected mayors in two small cities in Maine, Saco and Rockland. A dozen men in Klan robes held a demonstration in the city of Binghamton in upstate New York. And on Long Island, ten thousand Klansmen and their families gathered in a field to hear one of the Klan's national leaders warn that six million Klan members were prepared to vote against Al Smith if the Democrats were foolish enough to nominate him.[21]

Murphy, Smith, and their mostly Irish Catholic colleagues from the cities of the North and the Midwest had no intention of allowing the Klan to hijack the coming convention. They supported a resolution calling on delegates to condemn the Klan by name, an issue that could only lead to a civil war within the party. It was likely their intent. The Klan, in the meantime, was rallying sympathetic delegates around the candidate they believed best suited to stop Smith—William Gibbs McAdoo.

Murphy and Smith knew there would be no negotiating away the Klan, no splitting the difference, no mutual back-scratching. They were counting on the strength of their people, the tenement dwellers and factory workers, the stitchers of shirtwaists and the haulers of produce, to rally against those who despised them.

As he left Albany after a meeting with Smith, Charles Francis Murphy seemed prepared for the coming struggle. He had the same round spectacles he always had, and the shape suited the rest of him, thanks to his regular dinners at Delmonico's. At the age of sixty-five, he was at the peak of his power, easily the longest-tenured boss Tammany Hall ever had or ever would have, and among the urban bosses who were gaining influence in the national party he was the acknowledged senior statesman. The convention would be in his city. His protégé would be one of the leading candidates for the nomination, and Murphy himself would serve as Smith's campaign manager. It had been a long and remarkable journey for the son of an Irish immigrant, for a child of New York who went to work on the city's streetcars as a teenager and now was the maker of governors and senators and perhaps even a president.

Charlie Murphy worked past dinnertime in Tammany Hall on the night of April 24, 1924, a Thursday, discussing Al Smith's prospects with a visitor from Buffalo, Norman Mack, who was a member of the party's national committee. He left the building at 7:30, patting his belly and muttering about his indigestion, and made the short three-block journey to his townhouse on 17th Street. It had been a long day and he was off to bed early. The following morning brought no relief from the indigestion, so he asked the family maid to send for a doctor, who immediately ordered the boss to bed.

He didn't put up a fight, and he died just after nine o'clock in the morning. The newspapers reported that he died of acute indigestion, although it was more likely a heart attack.[22]

Al Smith heard the news in Albany at eleven o'clock. He didn't believe it at first, not until he called down to the city and a friend assured him, sadly, that it was quite true. He was in tears, dabbing at his eyes with a handkerchief, as he spoke with reporters in the state capitol. "It's awful," he said. "No one had a better friend."[23]

Charles Francis Murphy's funeral took place in St. Patrick's Cathedral in Midtown Manhattan on the morning of April 28, 1924. Sixty thousand people lined Fifth Avenue as Al Smith and New York mayor John Hylan, each dressed in silk top hats and dark cutaway jackets, led the procession into and out of the cathedral. On an ordinary day, the buildings of Fifth Avenue near the cathedral flew American flags and all kinds of colorful banners. But on this day, the flags and banners were put away, the streetscape somehow grayer and sad in quiet tribute to the dead boss of Tammany Hall.

Hours after Murphy was placed in his grave in Calvary Cemetery in Queens, Al Smith's advisers gathered to discuss how the governor's presidential campaign would move forward without its chairman. There was no question that two of Smith's closest allies would handle the grunt work of organizing and publicizing the campaign: Belle Moskowitz, whose modest title of director of publicity for the state Democratic Party did no justice to her influence over state government, and Joseph Proskauer, the Alabama-born lawyer who had put together independent campaign committees for all three of Smith's gubernatorial races. But they needed a chairman

Moskowitz and Proskauer had an idea: What about Franklin Roosevelt?

twelve

THE HAPPY WARRIOR

NOBODY WAS SAYING that Franklin Roosevelt was going to be the next Charlie Murphy, and that was the point. Belle Moskowitz was nothing if not cold-blooded when she said that Murphy's death was the best thing to happen to Al Smith's presidential campaign, never mind the tears that streamed down the governor's face when he talked about his old friend and mentor. With Murphy gone, Moskowitz knew, the Democrats in the South and West, the Klansmen, the evangelicals, the farmers, and the Anti-Saloon Leaguers could no longer say that Alfred E. Smith was a puppet of a corrupt boss.

Moskowitz and Proskauer paid a visit to Roosevelt at his home on East 65th Street to offer him the post. They acknowledged Roosevelt's disability but told him that it needn't prevent him from serving as chairman. They would handle the bulk of the grunt work that came with organizing a national campaign, and by "they" the two Smith allies really meant Moskowitz, because Proskauer was now a justice on New York's state Supreme Court and so could not overtly participate in a political campaign. But Moskowitz had enough energy for two people, perhaps more, when it came to advancing the career of Alfred E. Smith.

And so Roosevelt agreed. The announcement was made just days after Murphy was buried, and the press said that it was a masterful bit of politics. Roosevelt's appointment, wrote the *New York Herald-Tribune*, showed that Al Smith was looking to "lift his campaign above the rough and tumble Tammany style. . . . What the campaign has lost in practical political ability through the death of Murphy it has now compensated for in prestige and principles." Prestige and principles—that's why you hired a Roosevelt.[1]

He brought something else, too, something that Moskowitz and Proskauer did not anticipate. He brought energy and enthusiasm, because Al Smith gave him an opportunity to show politicians and reporters that he was not an object of pity.

The Smith campaign would work out of its headquarters in the Prudence Building on Madison Avenue; Roosevelt would work out of his townhouse on East 65th Street on the Upper East Side. He told the press that the campaign's official headquarters would be on East 65th Street; he referred to the offices at the Prudence Building as a "workshop." Moskowitz bit her tongue and got on with the work at hand.[2]

Roosevelt and Louis Howe operated on their own, sending out letters to delegates they had been cultivating for their own reasons for years, assuring them that Smith was exactly what they wanted—a true progressive with an impressive record as governor. Roosevelt told his friends from the farming states that Al Smith was a great supporter of a complicated farm relief bill under discussion in Washington (Smith likely did not know of its existence, and in any case, Roosevelt himself opposed it). He told friends who still worshipped the late Woodrow Wilson that Smith was a firm internationalist, which was true only in the sense that as a resident of the Lower East Side these many years he had crossed paths with people from many nations. There was no need to go into too many details.

And then there were those who didn't need to hear platitudes about farm policy or foreign affairs, those who might respond to Al Smith for reasons that had little to do with policy and everything to do with Al Smith being Al Smith. Roosevelt reached out to one such possible supporter, a man who had been raised in an orphanage and who knew what it was like to be poor as well as what it was like to be talented, ambitious, and lucky enough to escape the streets. Roosevelt wrote to Babe Ruth, just beginning a season that would see him lead the major leagues with forty-six home runs, and asked him if he would support Al Smith for president. The slugger wrote back immediately—he would be delighted to support Smith, he said. "There was one thing about your letter, Mr. Roosevelt, that went across with me good and strong," Ruth wrote, "[and] that was the talk about the humble beginning of Governor Smith. . . . I wasn't fed with a gold spoon when I was a kid. No poor boy can go any too high in this world to suit me."[3]

When one of Roosevelt's contacts insisted that Smith's election would be impossible because he was Catholic, he fired off a "my dear fellow" letter, saying that "any talk of injecting religion into the campaign is coming from the states where the Klan is notoriously strong, and you and I as good Americans cannot afford to stand for anything that would destroy the fundamentals of our government."

Roosevelt's ascension to the top spot in the Smith campaign did not win universal praise. "Thousands feel you are a black mark on the name you bear—a disgrace [to] the former President of the U.S. by that name," read one of the many letters that arrived at FDR's townhouse on East 65th Street. "What is the matter with you? Keep the Pope out of the U.S. He is bad enough where he is." It was signed, simply, KKK.[4]

Not all of the letters arriving at the Roosevelt residence were filled with such vitriol. He heard from plenty of Smith enthusiasts as well, including one who passed along a suggestion for a new campaign song.

March boys march for Liberty . . .
By the Stars and Stripes we'll fight
For we know you Al and you're Al right

Roosevelt thanked the songwriter but made no commitments. Charlie Murphy would have been proud.[5]

Meanwhile, in the campaign "workshop" in the Prudence Building, ripe with the smell of the governor's ever-present cigar, Belle Moskowitz and other top aides realized that the convention was shaping up to be like none in the party's history. The imperial wizard of the Ku Klux Klan,

Hiram Evans, announced that he would take leave of his day job as a dentist and make the journey from Texas to New York to personally supervise and coordinate the efforts of hundreds of Klansmen heading to the city for the convention. The Klan claimed to have a majority in at least twelve delegations, including the non-southern states of Iowa, Michigan, and Ohio, and had infiltrated states like Indiana.

Smith and his allies in northern cities continued to demand that the convention's platform committee include a plank, or clause, in the platform condemning the KKK by name. Asking the Democratic National Convention to condemn the Klan was like asking Republicans to condemn big business. It was a blow aimed at a core constituency, and it was bound to inspire fierce resistance from the sons and grandsons of Confederate veterans.

Al Smith decided it was time to strike that blow.

He had an unlikely ally in Alabama's Oscar Underwood, a moon-faced sixty-two-year-old veteran of the U.S. Senate with sleepy eyes and slicked-back brown hair. Underwood had been engaging in his own personal war of words with the Klan for several years, declaring that it was a twentieth-century version of the anti-immigrant Know Nothing movement that swept the nation in the 1850s. He noted that the Democratic Party had formally rebuked the Know Nothings in its party platform in 1856 and said it should do the same to the Klan in 1924. His fellow senator from Alabama, Cotton Tom Heflin, had a rather different view of the Klan—he thought it was an upholder of American values and culture, and he would order his set of sheets and a hood by the end of the decade, while he still was a member of the U.S. Senate.

The Klan may have despised Smith but it reserved a special sort of hatred for Underwood, for he was an apostate, a white southerner who declared that the Klan was un-American. Underwood was hardly a voice for racial justice, for he joined other southern Democrats in a filibuster that blocked passage of a Republican-sponsored anti-lynching bill in 1922. But the Klan offended him and he said so, a position that required no small amount of courage in the Deep South in 1924. "It is all right to have fraternal organizations and civic clubs," he told a crowd in Texas, "but when men have secret organizations for the purpose of governing, then they are striking at the very principles of government." He didn't mention the Klan by name but nobody missed the reference. The Klansmen in Texas announced that they would support former treasury secretary William Gibbs McAdoo, born in Cobb County, Georgia, in 1863, the year before General Sherman arrived.[6]

McAdoo, still lean and ambitious at age sixty, was preparing to make the long rail journey from his new home in Los Angeles to New York, the city he had come to loathe during his years there as a lawyer. He was far ahead in committed delegates, claiming the support of nearly 300, with 732—a two-thirds majority—required for the nomination. He brushed aside critics who noted that a good many of his supporters spent their evenings gathered around burning crosses and speaking ill of those who did not look like them, sound like them, and worship like them. A friend pleaded with him to renounce his Klan supporters, saying, "I don't think you get the seriousness of the KKK matter, especially with Al Smith in the race."[7]

McAdoo ignored that advice, but he did seem to understand that the Klan issue could prove embarrassing after he won the nomination and had to make peace with Smith and his friends from the cities. So he recruited a former senator from California and onetime mayor of San Francisco, James Phelan, to deliver his nominating speech. Phelan happened to be Catholic, the son of an Irish immigrant who struck it rich during the gold rush. He also happened to be a virulent anti-Japanese racist who campaigned for reelection to the Senate in 1920 with the promise to "keep California white." (He was defeated.)

Al Smith also had a decision to make about the man who would place his name in nomination. It was no small matter, for great speeches had been known to sway a convention and even, in the case of William Jennings Bryan and his Cross of Gold speech in 1896, make history and create a legend.

There was little doubt who Smith would have wanted: the Irish-born orator William Bourke Cockran, the man who nominated him in 1920. But Cockran, alas, had died two years earlier.

His friend Joseph Proskauer had a suggestion, and it was the same suggestion he and Belle Moskowitz made when Smith needed a new campaign manager after Murphy died: Franklin Roosevelt.

Smith was not struck by the genius of it all, to put it mildly. He narrowed his eyes when Proskauer mentioned Roosevelt's name. As Proskauer would recall many years later, Smith may have grown fond of Roosevelt, but he still couldn't help but think of him as a lightweight, an amateur.

"For God's sake, why?" he asked.

"Because you're a Bowery mick," Proskauer said, "and he's a Protestant patrician and he'd take some of the curse off you."[8]

Roosevelt it would be. For the second time in fewer than two months, Franklin Roosevelt, Protestant patrician, would take the place of a dead Irishman. First Murphy, now Cockran.

The two of them went to see Roosevelt to ask him if he'd do it. He'd love to, he said, but there was an edge to his apparent eagerness. He was a busy man—the work of a campaign manager never ended. He didn't have time to write a speech, he said. Then, turning to Proskauer, he said, "Joe, will you write a speech for me?"

Proskauer already had one written—he came prepared. He thought it was a good speech, especially its poetic flourish, in which he called Al Smith "the happy warrior of the political battlefield." Roosevelt read it over and recognized the "happy warrior" reference from a poem by William Wordsworth. What sort of fool would quote poetry in a hall filled with two-bit cigar-smoking politicians? The speech did nothing for Roosevelt, and that line about the happy warrior—that was the worst. Quite suddenly it occurred to Roosevelt that perhaps he was not so busy after all. The weekend was coming, when even campaign managers had some time to themselves, so he asked Smith and Proskauer if they would give him a few days to write a speech of his own.

He retreated to Hyde Park and dictated a speech to his new personal assistant, Marguerite "Missy" LeHand. There would be no poetry in this speech, that much was certain. He was so pleased with himself and his new assignment that he even told the household staff that he was writing Al Smith's nomination speech, although he was careful not to offer a preview of it.

He and Proskauer met again a few days later, without Smith. They read each other's work and grunted and winced. The situation called for a mediator, and they agreed on a well-known journalist, Herbert Bayard Swope, winner of the first ever Pulitzer Prize for reporting. Swope, an urbane and witty man and an accomplished poker player, was friendly with power brokers of all sorts in New York. He agreed to read both speeches in their presence, without knowing who wrote what, and would then deliver his Solomon-like decision.

He read Roosevelt's first. It was, he said, "the goddamnedest, rottenest speech I've ever read."

He then read Proskauer's and his face brightened. This was the one, he said. Roosevelt refused to accept Swope's judgment, for he was still stuck on the happy warrior reference. The delegates wouldn't get it, he insisted.

"Frank," Proskauer said, "I have enough authority from the governor to tell you that you're either going to make that speech or you're not going to make any."

Roosevelt could have stuck to principle and told Proskauer to tell Smith to find some other Protestant patrician to do his work. But he didn't. He gave in but he made sure Proskauer and Smith were put on notice that they would soon see that he was right all along.

"All right," he said, "I'll make the goddamned speech but it will be a flop."[9]

A flop—an interesting choice of words. Franklin Roosevelt would survive if his speech was a flop. But he could not survive an actual flop, like the spill he took in the lobby of the Fidelity & Deposit building back in 1922 when he tried to make a show of returning to work and a normal life. He had to figure out how to get himself to and from the podium without taking a flop. And he had just a few weeks to do it.

There was a spacious library on the second floor of his townhouse on East 65th Street, room enough to practice the arduous art of pretending to walk while flashing a smile that betrayed none of the effort he was making and none of the fear he was feeling. The smile would confirm all of the fiction he had been circulating about how he was improving and it was just a matter of time before he got better.

He knew exactly how far he would have to "walk" from his seat on the convention's floor to the podium. He measured the distance in the library and he practiced, hour after hour, day after day, using the power of his upper body to pivot and swivel to get his legs, encased in braces, in front of him, step by excruciating step. He held onto the arm of his sixteen-year-old son James with his left hand while he used a crutch under his right arm. Close friends like Marion Dickerman, educator, political activist, and friend of Eleanor, watched with equal parts fascination, admiration, and anxiety as the tall man with the useless legs tried over and over again to get it right and to make it seem like it was nothing extraordinary. "Nobody knows how that man worked. . . . Oh, he struggled," Dickerman would say years later.[10]

People who knew Franklin Roosevelt only from a distance often underestimated him and would continue to do so. Had the skeptics been in Roosevelt's library in the early weeks of June 1924, had they caught even a glimpse of the sweating, grimacing figure in the middle of the room gripping his son's arm while leaning on a crutch, stiff-legged, thrusting his shoulders and hips forward, falling, sprawling, stretching out his arms for help, insisting on trying again and again until he got it right—had they witnessed this scene, they would never again doubt the man's tenacity, ambition, character, and courage. It was breathtaking to behold.

William Gibbs McAdoo arrived at Pennsylvania Station in New York on June 19 wearing a double-breasted pinstripe suit and a stiff, high collar.

ABOVE: From Albany, Smith followed the 1928 presidential convention in Houston via radio. The new medium did not serve him well, but his successor as governor, Franklin Roosevelt, mastered it. (MUSEUM OF THE CITY OF NEW YORK)

OPPOSITE TOP: Franklin Roosevelt, second from left, on crutches, welcomes Democratic presidential nominee John W. Davis and Al Smith to Springwood in 1924. (FRANKLIN D. ROOSEVELT PRESIDENTIAL LIBRARY AND MUSEUM)

OPPOSITE BOTTOM: Eleanor Roosevelt helped organize women on behalf of Al Smith, and in so doing found the confidence to become a public figure. Here, she is barely visible, upper left, as she and her colleagues prepare to campaign for Smith and against her cousin, Theodore Roosevelt Jr., in the 1924 race for governor. That's Katie Smith, Al's wife, in the large hat standing almost directly in front of Eleanor. Anna Roosevelt, daughter of Franklin and Eleanor, is in the front row, right. (FRANKLIN D. ROOSEVELT PRESIDENTIAL LIBRARY AND MUSEUM)

ABOVE: Smith, wearing his trademark brown derby, with the man who defeated him in 1928, Herbert Hoover, shortly after the election. (MUSEUM OF THE CITY OF NEW YORK)

LEFT: With the bottom of his heavy leg braces visible, Franklin Roosevelt greets Al Smith, his predecessor as governor of New York. (FRANKLIN D. ROOSEVELT PRESIDENTIAL LIBRARY AND MUSEUM)

LEFT: Franklin Roosevelt enters the gubernatorial ball to celebrate the beginning of his second term as governor on New Year's Day, 1931. Eleanor Roosevelt is to the right. (FRANKLIN D. ROOSEVELT PRESIDENTIAL LIBRARY AND MUSEUM)

BELOW: Al Smith remained a highly public figure after losing the 1932 presidential nomination to Franklin Roosevelt. Here, he belts out a song during a national radio appearance. (MUSEUM OF THE CITY OF NEW YORK)

Franklin Roosevelt signs the Social Security Act in 1935 in the company of two old friends from his Albany days, Senator Robert Wagner, left, and Secretary of Labor Frances Perkins, center. Meanwhile, another member of the old Albany crowd, Al Smith, was attacking the New Deal.
(FRANKLIN D. ROOSEVELT PRESIDENTIAL LIBRARY AND MUSEUM)

Al Smith, brash as ever. (MUSEUM OF THE CITY OF NEW YORK)

The last photograph of Franklin Roosevelt, taken on April 11, 1945, the day before he died. (Franklin D. Roosevelt Presidential Library and Museum)

His wife, Edith, was on his arm, dressed in a black hat and black dress, still mourning for her dead father, Woodrow Wilson. McAdoo waved his hat and announced that he was prepared to make his stand against "sinister, unscrupulous, invisible government," by which he meant New York City's ruling Democratic Party faction, Tammany Hall, and not the invisible empire of the KKK, which had placed its members in high positions of government north and south. Then, to further ingratiate himself with his hosts upon his arrival, he attacked the city's newspapers, which he said were out to get him with their lies and slanders. He told his supporters not to believe anything they read in the New York papers, for they refused to give him a "square deal." He passed up an invitation to attend an enormous dinner for all eleven hundred delegates, claiming the event had been "stacked" with Smith supporters. Instead, he chose to dine privately with publisher William Randolph Hearst, the closest thing Al Smith ever had to a blood enemy.[11]

The other candidates made their entrances in the days before the convention opened, the favorite sons and the darkest of dark horses, a dozen of them, but none with the strength that McAdoo and Smith had.

Hundreds of delegates began to assemble midmorning outside Madison Square Garden on Tuesday, June 24, for the routine and tiresome business of declaring the convention open for business. There was far more excitement in the air above the Garden's thirty-two-story tower, where a squadron of army airplanes circled in formation and drew gasps and pointing fingers from the visitors, some of whom no doubt had never seen a flying machine. The Garden itself was draped in red, white, and blue bunting inside and out.

It was brutally hot that afternoon—almost eighty-five degrees—and it was even worse inside the Garden, where it became apparent that while the Ringling Bros. and Barnum & Bailey Circus had cleared out of the building several weeks earlier, the lions and elephants and gorillas had left behind a scent that overpowered even the odor of a thousand lit cigars.

The most exciting moment of the convention's opening day came when Babe Ruth himself made a brief appearance before heading north to the

Bronx for a game with the Senators. The Babe also called on his favorite candidate, Al Smith, at the candidate's headquarters in the Manhattan Club, just across the street from the Garden, and presented the governor with a bat, saying it would help Smith "knock out a nomination."[12]

The following day was set aside for beginning the long process of nominating the various and sundry candidates, many of them merely placeholders waiting to strike a deal with one of the real contenders. The Garden air once again was heavy with the smells of circus animals, tobacco, and human sweat. Alabama, first in line by alphabetical order, dispatched a young lawyer named Forney Johnston to place the name of Senator Oscar Underwood in nomination. Johnston spoke at length of the senator's many fine qualities, chief among them the fact that he was a staunch defender of religious liberty. At a convention in which a Roman Catholic was a serious contender for the presidency for the first time in the nation's history, this was no insignificant claim.

Toward the end of his speech, Johnston announced that at the request of the candidate for whom he spoke—custom had it that the candidate's name was not mentioned until the end, the better to keep up the profound suspense—he would read a resolution that the candidate believed delegates should vote on and pass:

> Resolved, that we do . . . condemn as un-American and un-democratic political action by secret or quasi-secret organizations in furtherance of any political objective whatsoever, and in particular do we condemn such action for the purpose of prescribing the political rights and privileges of citizens of the United States, as is now proposed, practiced and publicly acknowledged by the organization known as the Ku Klux Klan.[13]

Johnston had barely finished saying those three strange and frightening words when Jimmy Walker grabbed the New York delegation's banner and began marching in the aisles, gesturing and leading his fellow New Yorkers in a parade around the convention floor. Franklin Roosevelt had maneuvered his way to his seat on an aisle hours earlier, and he remained there, smiling, while the marchers stepped carefully past him. He was seated in a heavy chair, braced against the possibility that somebody might get out of hand, brush up against him, and send him sprawling to the floor.

Other states were joining in the march—not just Smith's supporters, but Underwood's as well. They filed past state delegations of fellow Democrats from Georgia, Texas, the Carolinas, Kentucky, Florida, and even Wyoming, Nevada, Idaho, and Oregon, states where the Klan had taken over the delegations outright or had a significant presence. The northerners pointed at them, shouting, telling them to stand up and march, which of course they refused to do. They sat, sullen, furious, as these Catholics and Jews and their friends called them "Kleagles" and other names that the newspapers declined to print.

It went on for fifteen minutes, ending only when a woman appeared on stage and began singing "The Star-Spangled Banner." Those listening to the chaos on the radio, including President Calvin Coolidge, might well have concluded that this was a convention on the verge of anarchy. The thought might have even inspired a smile from the famously dour president.

The nominations continued after order was restored, and California was delighted to present its adopted son, William Gibbs McAdoo, for consideration as the convention's nominee. If McAdoo hoped that the presence and eloquence, not to mention the ethnicity and religion, of his speaker, James Phelan, might capture the hearts of skeptics in the crowd, he was disappointed. Phelan's speech was boring and tedious, and while these qualities were not especially unique to Phelan's oratory, he had the bad luck to speak after three o'clock in the afternoon, and it was steaming hot in the Garden and delegates had not had lunch. They wandered through the aisles in search of some sort of relief while Phelan portrayed McAdoo as the second coming of Andrew Jackson. When, at last, he was finished, the McAdoo delegates and the Klansmen who supported him erupted as the anti-Klan delegates had earlier, shouting their man's

slogan—"Mc'll Do!" The governor of Colorado grabbed the state's banner and joined the McAdoo parade, but he had to fend off the state's Smith
delegates as they tried to rip the banner from his hands. Police were called
in to separate the Democrats from Colorado. Voices from the upstairs gallery, filled with Smith supporters, began chanting "Ku, Ku, McAdoo." It
was all bedlam, again, until convention chairman Thomas Walsh gaveled
the session to a merciful close.[14]

Franklin Roosevelt was scheduled to speak at noon on June 26, but he arrived at the Garden hours earlier, hanging on to the arm of his son James
on his left, a crutch under his right arm, walking that stiff-legged walk he
had practiced in his library. Spectators in the galleries and other delegates
broke out in applause in tribute to the man's evident courage.

Al Smith, as was the custom of the time, was not in the hall. Like so
many others, he was listening to the radio, to the live sounds of Walsh calling for order, the band music in the background, the murmur of crowds. It
was like being there.

It was nearly noon. Showtime. The star and his sidekick rose from their
places with the New York delegation and made their way toward the
podium. Slowly. Slowly. Just like they practiced. And twelve thousand
mouths grew quiet and twelve thousand throats grew dry. Slowly. Stiffly.
With a smile they walked, as if out for a stroll, a very slow and awkward
stroll. James Roosevelt seemed to be enjoying his role as helper so the
crowd had no idea that his father's fingers were digging into his arm.
Like pincers, he would later recall.[15]

A step and then another. For the one and only time during the convention it was quiet in the hall. Nearly everybody save for a chosen
few were seeing Roosevelt for the first time since 1920. He did not hide
the fact that he was not the man he once was. What he was hiding was
the fact that there was no way on earth he ought to be trying to walk in
front of twelve thousand people.

Father and son neared the back of the flag-draped stage, where they halted and Roosevelt was overcome for a moment with doubt. The podium! He would need to grasp it with both hands to keep himself upright. Was it sturdy enough?

He asked a national committeeman from Pennsylvania who happened to be on stage to give the podium—the pulpit, he called it—a test. The committeeman dutifully gave it a shake, leaned on it, and nodded. It was strong enough.[16]

And then off he went, by himself now, with two crutches to keep him balanced and upright. And he smiled all the while so nobody would ever guess that his shirt was soaked through with sweat. He reached the podium, threw back his head, and began speaking. He was flawless. He pointed to Smith's record, his achievements as a legislator and governor, the progressive reforms he authored, supported, and signed—laws against child labor, pensions for widows with children, programs to promote public health, workmen's compensation, labor boards, highway construction, increases in state support for public schools. "This is progressive," he said, over and over again, repeating it because there were men and women in the hall who thought of progressivism as something else, who thought of it as a series of moral judgments about the character of the poor rather than a package of practical reforms designed to help them. He was telling William Jennings Bryan and Josephus Daniels and William Gibbs McAdoo and all the others he knew from his Wilson days that progressive politics could not be defined simply as opposition to drink or to cities or to immigrants and it surely could not be defined by men who burned crosses in the fields of the South or even in the cities of the North.

"The masses of labor look to him as a protector and good friend," he said of Smith. "He has the personality that carries to every hearer not only the sincerity but the righteousness of what he says." It was all pitch-perfect, and then it was time to deliver the line he was certain nobody would understand.

"He has a power to strike at error and wrongdoing that make his adversaries quail before him. He has a personality that carries to every hearer not only the sincerity but the righteousness of what he says. He is the

'Happy Warrior' of the political battlefield." Did the delegates on the floor and spectators in the galleries get the reference? Of course not. He was right about that. They didn't know William Wordsworth but they knew Al Smith, most of them, and they knew there was no better description of him. The Happy Warrior. The place went wild.[17]

Roosevelt wasn't finished. There was more, until finally, after about thirty-five minutes, he declared that he was placing in nomination the name of Alfred E. . . . .

If he managed to finish the sentence, if he managed to say his candidate's last name, it was not heard. This was the moment the spectators in the galleries were waiting for, and they erupted with noise and sirens and cheering the likes of which few had ever heard and even fewer wished to hear again. The band struck up "The Sidewalks of New York." Smith delegates marched through the aisles, carrying their state's banners and huge posters decorated with Al Smith's face. It was a fantastic display of joy and chaos and sound, so much so that one of the delegates from Kentucky, D. W. Griffith, director of the Klan-friendly film *The Birth of a Nation*, stood on a chair and watched scenes he could not have imagined on a movie set. On it went, and as it did, Frances Perkins left her seat and made her way up to the stage to attend to something she knew the male politicians hadn't considered: how to get Franklin Roosevelt safely off the stage. All those "fat slob politicians—men," she said. "I knew they wouldn't think of it." She and several other women gathered around Roosevelt as a screen while he moved to the back of the stage, where a wheelchair awaited him. Nobody saw it, nobody noticed.[18]

Order was restored after an hour, and the convention proceeded with more nominations and more speeches, but it was all an anticlimax. The convention's energy was spent. Privately, McAdoo's forces were furious over the length and volume of the Smith demonstration. They began to whisper that the convention was rigged.[19]

Later that evening, Roosevelt saw Marion Dickerman, Eleanor's friend who had witnessed so much of the practice and rehearsal leading up to this day. He was tired and he looked it, but he threw out his arms. "I did it!" he said.[20]

It was a personal triumph, but it was so much more. In making Al Smith's cause his own, Roosevelt bridged a chasm between the party's elite progressives and its working-class liberals, between Hyde Park and the Lower East Side, Springwood and Oliver Street, and between the party of Grover Cleveland, who thought it improper to spend public money on a statue in New York Harbor, and the party of Al Smith, whose life story might as well have been written on the statue's pedestal.

He did it.

thirteen

UNCIVIL WAR

LETTERS OF CONGRATULATIONS POURED into campaign headquarters, and even the hard-bitten newspaper correspondents found themselves putting aside their practiced cynicism to take note of the man's courage, his delivery, his smile, his enthusiasm. "No matter whether Governor Smith wins or loses, Franklin D. Roosevelt stands out as the real hero of the Democratic Convention of 1924," the *New York World* wrote. A rare dissenting vote came from humorist Will Rogers, who said in his newspaper column that Roosevelt ought to have kept his speech simpler. All he needed to say, Rogers wrote, was this: "Delegates, I put in nomination Alfred Smith. Try and find out something against him."[1]

As for the line in the speech that Roosevelt hated, the line he was certain would mark him as an effete elitist in a hall filled with cigar-chomping pols—the description of Al Smith as the Happy Warrior of the political battlefield—it was cited in headlines across the country. It was attached to Smith for the rest of his political career and then, as luck would have it, it was often used to describe Roosevelt himself in his later years.

Franklin Roosevelt's speech would be remembered as the best moment of the 1924 Democratic National Convention. It was a turning point in the party's history. But within twenty-four hours, all the good feelings inspired by Roosevelt's courage and all of the historic implications of his speech were put aside as the party declared war on itself. The raucous, violent, passionate debate that followed, over the course of two weeks, through 103 exhausting ballots before a nominee was chosen, was nothing less than a shouting match over what it meant to be an American and a Democrat in the still-maturing twentieth century.

It started with the Klan.

Behind the scenes and a few blocks to the north of Madison Square Garden, the convention's platform committee was meeting in a restaurant, called the Rose Room, in the Waldorf Astoria Hotel. There were several prickly issues, not least of which was a statement about the enforcement of Prohibition, but the Klan was proving to be the most intractable. Smith's forces demanded a statement condemning the Klan by name; Underwood's supporters pushed for his resolution likening the Klan to the Know Nothing movement of the nineteenth century, and McAdoo's backers were adamant that the party should settle for a general condemnation of secret societies—no need to be specific. The Klan had already signaled that it would accept such a generic resolution, so why not compromise? The Smith and Underwood forces would have none of it. They worked through lunches and dinners and sometimes into the early morning to no avail, filling the Rose Room with the stench of tobacco smoke. They were at an impasse at dawn on Saturday, June 28, when the great and venerable William Jennings Bryan brought the committee's membership together in a sweaty huddle and suggested that they pray together for the Almighty's guidance. He asked a Roman Catholic delegate to recite the Lord's Prayer, which Christians believe to be the words of Jesus Christ. The delegate recited the well-memorized phrases, the assembled politicians muttered their amens, but as they raised their heads to return to the business at hand, Bryan raised his voice in a spontaneous prayer of his own, perhaps believing that the words of Jesus himself were insufficiently dramatic for the occasion. "Cleanse our minds of all unworthy thoughts and purge our hearts of all evil desires," he prayed aloud, his sweaty face looking skyward while other committee members, not used to the evangelical's fervor, very likely kept their heads down and their comments to themselves. "So guide and direct us in our work today that the people of our party and of our country and of the world may be better for our coming together in this convention and this committee."[2]

After another chorus of amens, Bryan did something unexpected: he asked, begged really, for a compromise, and one that must have seemed tempting to the anti-Klan committee members. He suggested that the committee agree on a resolution that condemned the Klan by name, which was what the Smith and Underwood forces said they wanted, and then bring that resolution to the floor for a vote. But if it passed, it would not be included in the party's official platform.

Not good enough, Smith's people said. For the anti-Klan delegates, a resolution was nothing more than empty words unless it was part of the party's official statement of principles. It was time to take a stand, they said. The anti-Klan committee members refused Bryan's compromise. And so the full committee voted then and there, just after dawn, to recommend a generic condemnation of secret societies with no mention of the Klan, and the Smith and Underwood forces vowed to offer their own resolution on the floor later that afternoon.

At Smith headquarters in the Manhattan Club, one voice recommended compromise over confrontation: Franklin Roosevelt. He knew the McAdoo people. He had worked with the man himself and with Bryan. Unlike Smith and his team, he had contacts with Democrats throughout the country, in the South, the Midwest, the far West, Democrats who were bone dry, who were evangelical Christians, who surely knew men who owned a hood and sheets. Why alienate them? Why provoke them? But Belle Moskowitz and Joseph Proskauer and other Smith allies, like Frank Hague, mayor of Jersey City, and George Brennan, the boss of Cook County in Illinois, were in no mood to hear about the inherent good nature of men who refused to see the Klan for what it was and what it stood for. Democrats had to take a stand, now.

The debate on the dueling resolutions—one condemning generic secret societies, the other singling out the Klan as un-American—started just after eight o'clock on Saturday night. The governor of North Carolina, Cameron Morrison, tried his hand at defending the Klan, asking if the convention truly was prepared to "try, condemn and execute more than a million men who are professed believers of the Lord Jesus Christ?" Senator Robert Owen of Oklahoma suggested that most Klansmen were decent folk, although he conceded the organization, like any other, had some troublemakers. "I assume it is true, to some extent at least, that members wearing the mask and indulging in midnight frolics with their nighties on have been guilty occasionally of depredation on their neighbors," he said as some delegations broke into knowing laughter. "That is probably true. It is also true that there are other lunatics in the country who do not wear the shroud."[3]

The Klan's foes were much more aggressive and passionate, taking advantage of the defenders' evident discomfort and defensiveness. Among the first to speak against the Klan was a politician from Maine named William R. Pattangall, chosen in part because he was neither Catholic nor Jewish. He told the crowd that he could not be content to name and condemn the Klan at the convention. "I want to name it all over the United States. I want the gospel of democracy to be preached alike in Maine, in Colorado, in Texas and in Pennsylvania, wherever the gospel of democracy is preached at all." A voice from high in the galleries, filled with men with connections to Tammany Hall, hollered, "Attaboy!" The Klan delegations hissed and shook their fists.

Three consecutive speakers went to the podium to urge delegates to join with them in voting for the anti-Klan resolution. "I have no sympathy with a group of gentleman who move only in the dead of night, only in the deep disguises of pillow cases and flying shrouds," thundered New York's Bainbridge Colby, a former secretary of state. Senator David Walsh of Massachusetts summoned fresh memories of American troops in the fields of France during the world war: "No soldier fighting and dying for you and me asked his buddy whether he was black or white, Jew or gentile, Catholic or Protestant." Edmond Moore of Ohio, a member of the party's national committee, noted that he was not a Catholic, not a Jew, not foreign-born, and not an orator. Nevertheless, he asked the delegates to consider this: "Think of the proposition when religious bigots . . . can come into a Democratic convention and control its action."

Now it was the Klan's turn as Georgia's Andrew Erwin, the son of a Confederate army officer, a true son of the South, was summoned to the podium. He said how proud he was to be a Georgian, and this prompted smiles from the state's delegation and all of the Klansmen scattered among a dozen or more delegations.

But he surprised them. He announced that any convention that failed to condemn the Klan by name was destined for "an ignominious defeat."

The galleries exploded with delight; the Klansmen shouted, "No, no!" He continued, shouting now above the noise:

> The constitution of every state in the Union preserves to each individual the right to freedom of conscience. The Ku Klux Klan makes a direct attack on these vital principles of our fundamental law. The insidious activities have spread discord and distrust through this land of peace and harmony. . . . Let us show to the world that no American worthy of the name will bend his knee to this un-American and un-Christian thing.

The galleries exploded again, and the Smith and Underwood delegates leaped from their seats and paraded around the floor carrying their signs and banners. A group of burly delegates joyfully seized hold of Erwin as he left the podium, placing him on their shoulders and carrying him around the floor and away from his fellow southerners, seated, shocked, seemingly ready for murder. The house band searched for an appropriate tune and came up with "Marching Through Georgia," and that only made matters worse: the song was a celebration of Sherman's march of conquest through the state, and there were delegates in the hall who had living memories of scorched earth and burned-out homes. William Gibbs McAdoo himself was an infant when Sherman's men visited his native state.

Treason fled before us, for resistance was in vain
While we were marching through Georgia.

Once again order was restored only when a singer was brought out to perform a hasty rendition of "The Star-Spangled Banner." Then it was time for one last speech, this one by William Jennings Bryan, a star at every Democratic National Convention since 1896, the nominee three times, still revered by delegates of a certain age who heard from him the grievances of men who worked the land or sold dry goods in small towns, of decent folk whose fear of God was surpassed by their fear of those who worshipped Him in deviant ways. The "booboisie," a sneering Mencken called them. Mindless middle-class conformists, as Sinclair Lewis described them in *Main Street* and *Babbit*. They stood and cheered when the magnificent Bryan came to the podium, introduced as "that revered Democrat." He was sixty-five years old now and he looked every day of it, for he had been up all night with the platform committee. Irreverent spectators in the galleries joined their more respectable party members on the floor in according Bryan silence and respect as he grasped the podium. But the silence, and even the respect, lasted only a few minutes, until he railed against Democrats who were so willing to split the party over three words. And then he said those words, Ku Klux Klan, and quiet and respect gave way to jeers and loathing as the New Yorkers in the gallery let him have it. William Jennings Bryan, revered Democrat, was booed without mercy at a Democratic National Convention.

It was time for the Democrats of 1924 to choose: would they support a condemnation of the Ku Klux Klan as part of their official platform, or would they support the generic slap on the wrist directed at unnamed secret societies? Balloting took two hours, stretching into the early morning hours of Sunday. Fights broke out on the floor and in the galleries. A thousand police officers were called in to reinforce those already breaking up brawls and grabbing spectators by the neck and tossing them into the street. The state-by-state roll call proceeded in fits and starts, making it difficult to follow which plank was winning. All of the chaos and the shouting and the hatred were transmitted from the Garden to listeners in the heartland, in the West, the South, and the North. They had never heard anything like this in their lives. Nor had anyone else.

Chairman Walsh announced the result at two o'clock in the morning. The generic plank won by a single vote. To put it another way, at this moment in the history of the party and the nation, the Democratic National Convention declined to condemn a racist, nativist, terrorist organization. And as a result, the party was bitterly and perhaps fatally divided.

Sitting amid the ruins, Franklin Roosevelt raised his voice and asked for immediate adjournment. Enraged Smith supporters were demanding a recount of the Klan vote, convinced that during the two hours of chaos ballots were either counted mistakenly or were stolen outright by menacing Klansmen in plainclothes stalking the convention floor. Roosevelt saw only further disaster in a recount. He told Hague and Brennan that they had to move forward, that the ultimate prize—the nomination—was still attainable, that a Smith victory on the floor would wipe away the memory of the Klan vote. For once, the patrician prevailed over the bosses. Hours later Roosevelt released a statement on Smith's behalf, saying that the governor respected the vote and hoped for fair play from "our Southern and Western brothers."[4]

As the exhausted thousands streamed out of the Garden into the post-midnight darkness, a thousand men dressed in white hoods and robes lit up the sky in Perth Amboy, New Jersey, to commemorate the induction of 150 new members into their chapter of the KKK. Five crosses, each thirty feet high, were put to the torch in strategic locations throughout the small industrial city about thirty miles from the Garden. The Klansmen announced they would gather again in less than a week to celebrate Independence Day.[5]

A rambling letter arrived at Roosevelt's townhouse several days later. "[The] U.S. is only a Protestant Country and we don't want any Catholics in any part of political life a Jew either. . . . The K.K.K. are fine good people not like a lot of Irish Catholics with no brains. No Irish bum or even if they have a drop of Irish blood in them is going to be president of the U.S."[6]

It was hard to believe, but the convention was only just beginning, even though according to the schedule, Monday, June 30, was supposed to be the day everybody went home.

Al Smith knew that with a little less than 250 delegates pledged to him, he was far behind McAdoo's 430 or so. Still, they were both far from the 732 required for the nomination. The next few days could change everything. Letters addressed to Smith's campaign poured into Roosevelt's townhouse on East 65th Street, deeply personal letters—most of them from women with Irish last names. A Mrs. M. G. McCarthy of West 155th Street sent Smith a four-leaf clover. Miss Catherine T. Calvin from Brooklyn sent him a Sacred Heart badge to wear and said she was praying for him during novenas. Mrs. Maria McKaigney, also from Brooklyn, sent a miraculous medal.[7]

What Roosevelt made of these letters and tokens of Catholic devotion is hard to know. But he knew that Smith would need a lot of luck once the balloting began. That four-leaf clover might come in handy—not to mention the miraculous medal.

The roll call began with Alabama. While delegates and the press and the radio audience would always associate the voice of Franklin Roosevelt and his Happy Warrior speech with the drama at the Garden, there was another voice and another phrase from the convention of 1924 they would remember, although perhaps not as fondly. It was the drawl of Governor William Brandon, chairman of the Alabama delegation, announcing with no particular sense of urgency that "Alabama casts twenty-four votes for Oscar W. Underwood." It was destined to be repeated, over and over again.

And so it began. The first ballot had McAdoo with 431½ votes, Smith with 241, and twelve other candidates splitting the rest (Underwood added only a handful besides his home state, finishing with 42½ votes—in some instances, certain delegates cast fractional votes). McAdoo seemed to have a few more votes than expected; that was because some Smith delegates strategically cast their initial vote for McAdoo. When the balloting got serious, they would switch to Smith, leaving the impression that McAdoo was running out of steam and Smith was gaining.

They voted fourteen more times that day with nothing to show for it save a stalemate. They voted fifteen times the next day. The same, save for one notable ballot—a single delegate from Florida voted for Smith. It was to be the only vote he received from the old Confederacy.

The smells, the stalemate, the growing bitterness and hatred were getting to delegates. More pragmatically, so were the expenses: they had been in New York for a week already and there was no end in sight. A hundred delegates left; alternates took their place.

On July 3, in the midst of the thirty-eighth roll call, William Jennings Bryan asked for permission to address the convention. The galleries shouted, "No!" The convention chairman said he heard no objections and allowed Bryan to speak.

He said the party had many great men from which to choose, and he listed them, and conspicuous by its absence was the name of Al Smith. He made the case for McAdoo, extolling his progressivism. The galleries chanted "Oil! Oil! Oil!," a reference to McAdoo's tangential connection to Teapot Dome. Bryan, sweating and pale, pointed up at the galleries, trembling. "You do not represent the future of this country!" he told the New Yorkers in the gallery. Somebody set off a siren, hoping to force Bryan to give up. Franklin Roosevelt, who had been reading a newspaper during the tumult, scribbled a note and motioned for an usher. "Dear Siren Man," Roosevelt wrote, "Cut out the siren. No more today."[8]

Bryan continued to ramble but finally won cheers when he said this would probably be his last convention. "Don't applaud," he snarled. "I may change my mind."[9]

Franklin Roosevelt turned to other delegates seated near him in the New York delegation. "Mr. Bryan has killed poor McAdoo," he said, "and he hasn't done himself any good."[10]

The roll was called nineteen times that day to no avail. Smith had made some headway but seemed stuck at just over three hundred votes, still very far from the more than seven hundred required. McAdoo had just over five hundred but had made no real breakthrough. The *New York Herald-Tribune* reported that delegates were looking desperately for somebody else, somebody who might be able to bridge the differences between McAdoo and Smith. If the delegates were released from their commitments, the paper reported, "everybody would vote for Roosevelt and he would be nominated."[11]

The president of a local Democratic club in Brooklyn sent a telegram to Smith. "It looks as though our bigoted opponents will prevent your nomination," the telegram read. "If you feel the same way why not have Franklin Roosevelt take your place if his health permits."[12]

There was no response from the Smith campaign.

Al Smith was aware by Independence Day that his chances of winning the nomination were remote at best. But as he chewed on his cigars in his strategy room in the Manhattan Club, he made one thing clear to his campaign team: William Gibbs McAdoo must not be the nominee. He would block McAdoo even if it took until Christmas, he said. But there were no alternatives for Smith supporters. The only other overtly anti-Klan candidate, Alabama's Oscar Underwood, had picked up no momentum—he started every roll call with twenty-four votes but finished with only a handful more.

They voted all day and into the evening on July 4 with no result, and once again frustrated delegates filed out of the Garden in the dark of night, and once again, Klansmen were gathering in New Jersey—four thousand of them, along with sixteen thousand family members and supporters—as a show of force meant for Al Smith and his friends at the convention. The Klansmen created an effigy of the Catholic candidate for president with a whiskey bottle tucked under his arm. Men, women, and children were invited to fire baseballs at Smith, five cents for three tosses. It was a memorable and fun-filled Independence Day for the Klansmen of New Jersey.[13]

July 5, July 6, July 7: more roll calls, more deadlock, more frustration. The Smith campaign sent Roosevelt to the podium to make an announcement, asking that the convention suspend its rules and allow his candidate, Smith, the opportunity to speak to the delegates. It was an extraordinary request and, perhaps not without reason, the McAdoo people sensed a trap. They conferred in sweaty groups and whispered and gestured as they came to the conclusion that this was the moment Roosevelt and Smith had been plotting—Smith would be brought forward to give a fiery speech followed by a huge, prearranged explosion of enthusiasm, followed by a quick roll call that would give Smith either the nomination outright or the momentum he needed. In fact, the plan was for Smith to publicly withdraw from the race on the proviso that McAdoo would do likewise. But the McAdoo forces blocked Smith from speaking. The gesture was never made. The balloting would go on.

There were signs of despair even in the New York delegation, the heart of Al Smith's crusade. As the convention's chairman, Walsh, droned on with another roll call, Jimmy Walker, the skinny-as-a-lamppost state senator who spent a year as Al Smith's roommate years earlier, made a beeline for Franklin Roosevelt, seated as usual in an aisle seat near the front. Walker wanted Roosevelt's permission to suggest him as a compromise candidate for president. It was too late now for Smith, Walker said, and McAdoo would never win the nomination—the New Yorkers would make sure of that.

"Frank, you are the only man who can be nominated now with any hope," Walker told him. "The Smith people can't object to you, and you are the only one who will be acceptable to the McAdoo crowd."

Roosevelt smiled that brilliant smile. He was flattered, of course. But he couldn't do it. His legs, of course. And besides, he was with Al, and he'd be with Al until the end.[14]

They paused for a moment, these battling Democrats, on the afternoon of July 7 when the convention's chairman announced sad news: Calvin Coolidge Jr., the son of the president of the United States, had died of sepsis in Walter Reed Hospital at the age of sixteen. Coolidge would later write that the power and majesty of the White House ended for him when he watched his son take his last breath.

The delegates were hushed and the Garden was quiet for an ever so brief moment. And then the battle continued, roll call by roll call. Roosevelt again lurched his way to the podium on July 8, after the ninety-third roll call. Smith had actually leaped ahead of McAdoo in the vote count, with 350 votes to McAdoo's 314. The Smith campaign seemingly had achieved its mission: McAdoo was clearly finished. Roosevelt, acting on Smith's orders, announced that the governor would withdraw from the race—as long as McAdoo did the same. But if McAdoo hung on, Roosevelt added, "I can say that Governor Smith's supporters will continue to vote for Governor Smith." The governor himself was sequestered in his strategy room in the Manhattan Club, seated near a radio, listening to a man conquer a medium. All the other voices making their way through the airwaves from New York were hoarse and loud and churlish, but Franklin Roosevelt's was resonant and strangely melodic, a calming voice, a determined voice, a voice that prompted cheers and affection.[15]

Roosevelt made it clear that even after more than ninety ballots and after two weeks, he and his candidate Smith were not budging, not until William Gibbs McAdoo, the chosen candidate of the Ku Klux Klan, gave up first.

It finally ended on July 9, after McAdoo gave up and Smith did the same. Smith offered Underwood's name as a compromise but McAdoo would have none of it. They agreed instead on John W. Davis of West Virginia, now a lawyer in New York who had the benefit of having almost no public record and therefore almost no enemies. He was nominated on the 103rd ballot. To appease William Jennings Bryan, the party nominated his brother, Charles, the governor of Nebraska, as vice president.

The convention had been a disaster. "The two factions lost everything that they had fought for," wrote H. L. Mencken. Another defeat, this one in November, seemed inevitable.[16]

Lost amid the recriminations was the historic victory won on the convention's floor and in the hall's backrooms and in hotel suites near the

Garden: the emerging leaders of the new Democratic Party, led by Al Smith of the Fulton Fish Market and supported by the patrician progressive Franklin Roosevelt, had blocked the nomination of a candidate supported by the Ku Klux Klan. Achieving that goal required courage and determination and a certain degree of recklessness, because the easy course of action would have been to accept compromise, to back down in the interest of unity, to put aside the unpleasant task of confrontation.

Something else of historic significance emerged from the convention: the public partnership of Al Smith and Franklin Roosevelt. One Smith loyalist, an insurance broker and onetime state legislator named James Hoey, summed it up: "An electric fixture minus the bulb would be Smith without Roosevelt."[17]

After the bedraggled Democrats left New York in the summer of 1924 and Al Smith decided to run for reelection as governor in the fall, the state's Republican Party shrewdly chose one of its rising stars to oppose him—thirty-seven-year-old Theodore Roosevelt Jr. The party was counting on some of that old Roosevelt magic to deny Al Smith something no New York governor had achieved in a century: a third two-year term.

Once again, the life of Al Smith was destined to intersect with that of a Roosevelt, this one from the Oyster Bay branch of the family. Like his cousin Franklin years ago, young Teddy was an amateur in a field that professionals like Smith dominated. Sure, he had served a couple of years in the state assembly and seemed honorable and decent. But like cousin Franklin, he left Albany quickly and abruptly when he was offered a job in Washington—assistant secretary of the navy. The position apparently had become a Roosevelt heirloom, and it was strange that few considered this to be disturbing, dangerous, and undemocratic. If the Tammany crowd ever attempted such a thing, the reformers and newspapers would have screamed to the high heavens.

Smith was delighted to have this new Roosevelt in his life. He was an easy target for a pro like Smith, who would later say that he was never so confident of victory than he was when he learned that Teddy Jr. stood in the way of a third term in Albany. Voters, he was certain, would see beyond the famous last name and decide that this was no time to throw out an old pro and put in place a rank, if well-meaning, amateur.[18]

Roosevelt resigned from his position as assistant secretary of the navy so that he could devote his full resources to the campaign. To find his replacement, President Calvin Coolidge surveyed the immense amount of talent available to him for this critical job and concluded that the most qualified person in the country was New York state senator Theodore Douglas Robinson, young Teddy's cousin, President Theodore Roosevelt's nephew. It was a fortunate thing, indeed, that members of the Roosevelt family had always been strong supporters of the merit system in the hiring of government employees. Otherwise the positions they coveted might have been doled out to less-qualified people based only on their political connections.

The emergence of another Roosevelt in New York turned Al Smith's reelection campaign into a family drama whose lead player was not Franklin Roosevelt but Eleanor, Teddy Jr.'s first cousin. She was still new to politics, still uncomfortable as a public speaker, but she was learning the trade under the watchful eye of her husband's faithful servant, Louis Howe. And she saw Al Smith's 1924 reelection campaign as the right moment to emerge as a political force in her own right as she traveled throughout the state on behalf of the man her husband called the Happy Warrior.

Doing so, of course, meant that she actively, enthusiastically, and somewhat underhandedly campaigned against her own family. She seemed to love every minute of it, indulging in a playful—some might say cruel—prank on young Teddy by seizing on a tangential connection to the Teapot Dome scandal. As assistant navy secretary, young Teddy had overseen the transfer of navy property in Wyoming to the Interior Department, and those properties were then leased without bidding to the principals in the scandal. Eleanor would later admit that her cousin had nothing to do with the scandal itself, but in the fall of 1924, she and her friends stalked

Teddy Jr.'s campaign appearances with a car that carried a giant teapot on its roof, rigged to spew steam as it traveled through the roads and lanes of upstate New York. She told audiences that her cousin was a "nice young man whose public service record shows him willing to do the bidding of his friends."[19]

Franklin played no role in these shenanigans. He was hundreds of miles away, in a place called Warm Springs in Georgia, where he was literally testing the waters to see if, as a friend suggested, it might help restore his leg muscles. He was delighted with the result and saw possibilities in what was a ramshackle old southern spa. But as the election neared, he issued a statement about the man who shared his last name and who had campaigned against him when he ran for vice president in 1920, telling the nation that he did not share the "family brand."

Of young Teddy, Franklin said, "He is indeed a 'promising' young man . . . [but] his promises make very little difference—the accomplishments are the real thing and will be left in the competent charge of Governor Smith for the next two years." And he couldn't help but point out that he and young Teddy both held the same job in the Navy Department. The difference, he said, was that he had presided over a "splendid, honest, and economical purchasing system," while his cousin had "a record in public service which is wretched."[20]

With friends like the Roosevelts attacking his opponent named Roosevelt, Al Smith didn't have to exhaust himself on the campaign trail. His opponent gave multiple speeches a day, barnstorming across the state by rail. Smith limited himself to one major speech a day.

He won reelection by 108,000 votes even as the national Democratic ticket of John Davis and Charles Bryan lost in a landslide. Eleanor Roosevelt sent a letter to Smith not long after his smashing victory. "Permit me to take this occasion to add my congratulations on the splendid way in which you handled our bewildered Republican brethren," she wrote.[21]

Theodore Roosevelt Jr. never ran for office again.

_____

fourteen

THE CHALLENGE OF NEW AMERICA

NEWLY REELECTED, AL SMITH UNDERSTOOD that he might never again have the power and prestige that was his in the spring of 1925. He was serving a third term as governor, and none of the legendary governors in whose shadow he operated—Teddy Roosevelt, Grover Cleveland, Samuel Tilden (presidential candidates, each of them)—had served even two terms in Albany. He was now widely thought of as the leader of New York's Democrats as the old bosses passed from the scene—Charlie Murphy was a year into his eternal rest as Smith began his third term, and Smith's earliest mentor and friend, Tom Foley, died in January 1925. They left a power vacuum that Smith was ready and eager to fill.

He started in New York City, where the mayor, the ineffectual John Hylan, took his orders from Smith's archenemy William Randolph Hearst. It was time to declare that arrangement null and void. Smith conferred with the new boss of Tammany Hall, an ally of his named George Olvaney, and the young boss of the Bronx, Ed Flynn—who broke into politics working for Smith during his first term—and they agreed on a candidate to unseat Hylan: state senator Jimmy Walker. He was smart—he could lead an argument on the senate floor even after a long night spent in violation of the Eighteenth Amendment—he had a progressive record, and he was, for better and worse, a perfect symbol of New York in the Roaring Twenties.

And so it was agreed, but there would be no deal before Smith had a long talk with his wayward protégé, the skinny, dashing man who called him "Algie." The Smith apartment on Oliver Street had always been open to Walker and his wife, such was the relationship between the two very different men. But the invitations ceased when Walker began squiring his young, English-born mistress, Betty Compton, all around the town. Al Smith most certainly did not approve, nor would he sign off on, Walker's candidacy until Walker promised to change his ways. They had what Smith believed to be a heart-to-heart talk one afternoon, with Walker passing up Smith's offer of bootleg whiskey and asking with practiced sincerity for a glass of soda water. He was not the man he used to be, he said. "We all grow up sometime," he said, his famously blue eyes wide and earnest. That was good enough for Smith. He endorsed Walker, and that was good enough for most of New York City's voters. Walker defeated Hylan in a Democratic primary and then easily won the general election, prompting Franklin Roosevelt to invite him to a celebratory supper on East 65th Street. As for Hylan's patron, Hearst, he once again found himself outmaneuvered by the man from the Fulton Fish Market. The *New York Times* proclaimed that "Alfred E. Smith today is the most powerful leader the Democratic Party has ever had in the greatest State of the Union."[1]

As he sought to change the political dynamic in New York, Smith turned to the village of Hyde Park for assistance. He was tired of seeing his ideas rejected in the legislature or revised so radically that he could barely recognize them. The state assembly was up for reelection in 1925, and Al Smith reached out to Franklin Roosevelt, among others, to help recruit and campaign for Democrats outside the party's power base of New York City. In a "Dear Frank" letter in June 1925, Smith asked Roosevelt to join a four-person committee that would attempt to strengthen the party in the lower Hudson Valley, a Republican bastion. "At no time in my public career has there been greater reason for a change in the complexion of the Legislature," he told Roosevelt. Also on the committee,

Smith noted, was the shrewd and affable James Farley, one of the many young Democrats who had attached themselves to Al Smith in the 1920s. In addition to Farley and the Bronx leader Ed Flynn, those young Democrats included the financier and philanthropist Herbert Lehman, who was vice chairman of Tammany Hall's finance committee, and Sam Rosenman, a former assemblyman who was now a speechwriter for Smith.[2]

Roosevelt was already performing another task Smith had assigned him, serving as chairman of a commission that oversaw Taconic State Park, a lovely tract of land to the northeast of Hyde Park near New York's border with Connecticut and Massachusetts. The assignment drew on his lifelong interests in conservation and in the region's natural beauty and history, and it also offered him an opportunity to plan something big and grand: a beautiful parkway that would connect lower Westchester County with the Hudson Valley and eventually Albany. The chairmanship was no mere ceremonial position, and it was quickly made clear to Roosevelt that he would be treated no differently than any other bureaucrat. When he sought to find a place on the commission's payroll for his long-suffering aide Louis Howe, Robert Moses, the head of the park system, refused to make any such accommodation. If Roosevelt wanted a "secretary or a valet," Moses said, he'd have to dig into his own pocket to pay for one. Moses chose his words carefully—describing Howe as a valet and reminding Roosevelt that he required the services of one, well, that was a double insult and it was deliberate. (Privately, Moses soon began referring to Roosevelt as a "poor excuse for a man.") Louis Howe never forgot the way in which Robert Moses so imperiously dismissed him, and he certainly made sure that Roosevelt never forgot, either.[3]

Regardless of how they felt about each other, Roosevelt and Moses were members of the same team, and as the months passed, it became clear that they all had one goal in mind. Roosevelt expressed it in a letter to Smith in the summer of 1926, writing, "You will be a candidate in 1928 whether you like it or not." Roosevelt was not talking about yet another term in Albany. He was talking about putting Al Smith in the White House.[4]

But there was no need for Roosevelt's stern language. Al Smith liked the idea. He liked it a lot.

Al Smith chose Franklin Roosevelt to deliver the keynote speech at the state Democratic convention in 1926, when Smith was nominated for a fourth term as governor after another extraordinary two years, during which he began to rebuild the state's prison and hospital systems, continued to consolidate state agencies, developed a state housing bank to finance affordable housing, expanded state spending on education and parks, and still managed to cut taxes. Even the oldest New Yorkers could not remember a more popular governor, although some of them saw Smith as others did beyond the Hudson River, as a symbol of the new America that was threatening the values and culture of the old. Delegations from New York's Ku Klux Klan chapters gathered on Long Island to celebrate Independence Day in 1926, and several weeks later eleven thousand Klansmen lit up three huge crosses near the upstate city of Rochester. Even in New York, there were Americans who felt threatened by people who acted, worshipped, and thought like Al Smith.[5]

In his address to the state nominating convention, Franklin Roosevelt portrayed Smith as a figure of historic proportions. "Some day in the distant future men will raise statues to the memory of a great American by the name of Smith, and when they do, I hope that instead of a list of his titles to fame, they will carve the simple words: 'He taught us to think— and to think straight,'" Roosevelt said. As for the governor's record, well, there was no need to recite all his achievements, Roosevelt said, just as there was no reason to point out the virtues of the Ten Commandments. Both were obvious.[6]

Smith easily defeated his opponent, a wealthy congressman from the Hudson Valley named Ogden Reid. While the Smith landslide was not enough to break the Republican hold on the state legislature, it helped to elect his old roommate Robert Wagner, the German-born son of a janitor, to the U.S. Senate, another symbol of New America gaining entrance to one of Old America's most exclusive clubs.

Al Smith was sworn in for a fourth time on January 1, 1927, before the usual record crowd jammed into the assembly chamber. "I have no idea what the future has in store for me," he said during his short inaugural speech. "Everyone else in the United States has some notion about it except myself." He did concede, however, that he was "receptive" to the idea of running for "the greatest position the world has to give to anyone."[7]

This pose as a demure, duty-bound candidate may have seemed honorable to Smith, but it drove Franklin Roosevelt crazy. He wanted Smith to get out of New York and meet with influential Democrats around the country, and he offered to put him in touch with far-flung friends who wanted to get to know this exotic man from the sidewalks of New York.

Roosevelt was now spending months at a time in Warm Springs, far from the action in Albany but never out of touch. Throughout the mid-1920s, he wrote to Smith often, generally in the manner of a man looking to ingratiate himself with a powerful elder. Smith, not much of a man for putting thoughts on paper, replied almost by rote but with occasional flashes of affection. They were not, to be sure, the best of friends: at one point in the spring of 1926, Smith wrote with some surprise that he had only just realized that Roosevelt's daughter, Anna, and his daughter, Emily, were getting married on the same day in a few weeks' time. "I guess we are getting old," Smith wrote, "and while we may not feel it, the evidence is beyond dispute." Obviously neither man had invited the other for the great occasion, but there was no sense of embarrassment when the coincidence was discovered.[8]

Roosevelt invited Smith and his wife to Springwood for lunch and, on another occasion, to join him at the Dutchess County Fair. Letters spoke of private meetings called to talk over state politics. "I hope to have a chance to have a long talk with you about a lot of things," Roosevelt wrote Smith from Warm Springs in the spring of 1925. "The old legs are improving a lot. If I could only drop my business and stay here for a whole

year I am convinced that I would be able to get around without crutches."
Smith occasionally solicited the younger man's advice, never mind that
aides like Moses and Moskowitz continued to think of Roosevelt as a
lightweight and made little attempt to disguise their opinion. "I am anxious to have a talk with you when you return [from Warm Springs]," Smith
wrote to Roosevelt in the spring of 1926. Roosevelt was just as anxious to
have a talk with Smith, inviting him down to Warm Springs not only for
conversation but for the cure as well. The governor continued to suffer
from bouts of the neuritis that left him unable to walk at the 1922 state
convention in Syracuse. "If you could spend two or three weeks bathing
in a warm pool, it is the finest thing in the world for the nerves, and by
that time the golf course will be opened," Roosevelt wrote to Smith,
using the governor's favorite nonpolitical hobby as a lure. "You would be
entirely free from politicians and it might be a novelty for you to visit the
south without it being said that you were starting a campaign!" Smith
declined. There were amendments to the state constitution under debate,
and, well, his presence was required in Albany.[9]

Undaunted, Roosevelt encouraged Smith to take his message beyond
New York's borders, to talk about issues like the forty-eight-hour workweek, child welfare laws, reforming state institutions like prisons and
schools—issues that spoke to Smith's genuine achievements in New York
and that had made him a reputation in national politics. He even hinted,
gently, that perhaps Smith might take a stab at national issues from the
point of view of a governor. Why not issue a statement about flood prevention in the Mississippi Valley? Eventually, Roosevelt told Smith, the
country would use the water from the region's great rivers to develop
hydropower, one of Smith's signature issues in New York.

Smith always seemed to have something else to do when Roosevelt suggested a visit or a statement on a national issue, or even when Roosevelt
arranged for the governor of Virginia, Harry Byrd, to invite Smith to speak
before a prestigious audience at a one-day institute on public affairs at the
University of Virginia. "I honestly think that in view of the distinguished
membership, it would be a splendid thing if you could run down to it

even for a day," Roosevelt told Smith. "[This] is the kind of an event which is non-political and distinctly along the line of your governmental endeavors. Try to do it."

Smith declined, politely and with a good excuse—his daughter, Emily, was about to give birth to her first child.[10]

An opportunity lost, in Roosevelt's view. "He is not known enough for his real accomplishments as Governor," Roosevelt lamented to a friend about Smith. But he also concluded that for all his brilliance, Al Smith was flawed, perhaps fatally, as a national candidate, for he saw the great mass of land west of the Hudson River as alien territory about which he preferred to know as little as possible. Roosevelt certainly would have agreed with the great newspaperman Mencken, who had a soft spot for Smith but recognized his limitations. "The plain fact is that Al, as a good New Yorker, is as provincial as a Kansas farmer," Mencken wrote. "He is not only not interested in the great problems that heave and lather the country: he has never heard of them." In the company of trusted friends, Roosevelt had been telling a story from the 1924 convention, when Smith actually crossed paths with Mencken's proverbial Kansas farmer. In Roosevelt's telling, Smith, with a big cigar stuck between his teeth, chatted up the Kansans with a story about Wisconsin, which made perfect sense to a provincial New Yorker but perhaps not to anybody more familiar with the heartland's geography. "Y'know, the other day some boys were in from Wisconsin, and I learned something," Smith said, according to Roosevelt's story. "I always thought Wisconsin was on this side of the lake. It's on the other side. Glad to know it. Glad to know more about the place where good beer comes from." Roosevelt told the story and rolled his eyes, for the delegates lived nowhere near Wisconsin and, worse, they were as dry as the prairie in August. Then, perhaps with the shake of his head, Franklin Roosevelt got on with the business of attaching himself to Al Smith's cause.[11]

A letter arrived in Warm Springs in early March 1927 from an old Roosevelt acquaintance, Ellery Sedgwick, Groton 1890, Harvard 1894.

Sedgwick was the editor of the prestigious journal *Atlantic Monthly*, and he was about to publish an essay that figured to have an enormous impact on the presidential campaign of 1928; more specifically, on the all-but-announced campaign to nominate Al Smith for president. The essay was in the form of an open letter to Smith from a prominent lawyer named Charles Marshall. Stripped of its lawyerly language, the essay reprised the argument of the Ku Klux Klan in 1924: Al Smith could not serve as president of the United States because his first and true loyalty was to a foreign power in Rome whose edicts through the centuries were at odds with Anglo-Protestant ideas of liberty and democracy. Sedgwick sent Roosevelt an early version of Marshall's essay, asking him if he would forward it to Smith and perhaps persuade the Happy Warrior to respond in a subsequent issue.

Roosevelt knew that thousands of elite opinion makers would read Marshall's attack on Smith and his religion. He sent a copy of the essay to Albany along with a long letter emphasizing the importance of the moment and outlining Smith's options as Roosevelt saw them. Smith could ignore it, Roosevelt said, but silence might only empower bigots. Perhaps a Protestant ought to reply? If so, Roosevelt volunteered for the task. But he had a better idea: Smith himself should respond to it. "You can do it in such a way that people all over the United States will respect you even more than they do now," he wrote.[12]

Smith would have none of it.

He read the essay and recognized in Marshall's writing nothing of the Catholicism he practiced. "I don't know what the words mean," he told Joseph Proskauer, the Alabama-born Jewish lawyer and judge who was a constant presence in his office. "I've been a Catholic all my life—a devout Catholic, I believe—and I never heard of these encyclicals and bulls and books that he writes about."[13]

Proskauer and Belle Moskowitz agreed with Franklin Roosevelt. They, too, believed Smith ought to respond—that he had no choice. His fitness for office had been challenged in a highly influential periodical, and silence would be taken to mean that he quite literally had no response.

Smith waved them away, and when Roosevelt wrote Smith again to ask when he would reply, the governor said he was "holding off."[14]

While they argued in Albany, Roosevelt was trying to persuade Sedgwick to spike the Marshall essay. "It will stir up discussion on religious issues which is not for the good of the country," Roosevelt told him. If he were asked to respond to Marshall, he told Sedgwick, "I should do so in a humorous vein by quoting certain Unitarian ecclesiastical dignitaries to prove that Unitarianism is not Christianity and that, therefore, President Taft was not even a Christian. Further, I could easily quote from the sayings of individual Episcopal or Baptist or Presbyterian luminaries to prove that Wilson, Roosevelt, McKinley and Cleveland were, as members of various churches, secretly obligated to put the church ahead of their oath of office." The whole thing was ridiculous, Roosevelt said. Al Smith had never taken orders from priests and bishops about public policy and never would.[15]

Smith finally decided he had to respond, and certainly not in a "humorous vein." He asked Proskauer to draft a reply. Perfect, the judge said: "A Protestant lawyer challenges a Catholic candidate on his religion, and the challenge is answered by a Jewish judge." Perfect indeed, although Smith and Proskauer thought it wise to consult with one of the most famous Catholic priests in America, Father Francis P. Duffy, chaplain of the Fighting 69th during its deployment in France. The composing and editing in the governor's office went on for days, and when parks commissioner Robert Moses interrupted a session with a matter of state, he quickly concluded that he was out of his element—no small concession for a man with a towering opinion of his own intellect.[16]

The result of that erudite conversation was a masterly exposition of the role of faith in a secular republic, of the ways in which a civic leader can balance religious conviction with his or her obligations to the law and to the people. It refuted Marshall's contention that Catholicism and Americanism were in conflict, and it invited readers to look at the record, to see that the governor of New York called on the best men and women to serve the state regardless of their religious faith. Smith's reply to Marshall was one of the most anticipated literary events of the year, and it was a success, then and in years to come, when other candidates would find themselves under attack because they worshipped in ways the majority found strange and offensive. His final line was filled with hope: "I join with fellow Americans of all creeds in a fervent prayer that never again in this land will any public servant be challenged because of the faith in which he has tried to walk humbly with his God."[17]

Roosevelt was preparing to leave Warm Springs in early May when Smith's reply was published. He seemed to be delighted with the piece. More to the point, he noticed that the reply to Marshall had the intended effect on wavering Democrats, especially in the South. Roosevelt returned north convinced that the tide was turning in Smith's favor. Besides, who else did the party have?

The problem for Smith now, at least in Roosevelt's view, was overconfidence. "I want to urge you to impress on your friends the danger of getting over enthusiastic and making all kinds of rash claims that the fight is over and you are certain to be nominated," he told Smith. The goal was to prevent the emergence of a single alternative to Smith and to win the nomination without a repeat of 1924. Otherwise, Roosevelt said, the nomination "would be of little value as the chances of your election afterwards would be destroyed."[18]

Message received, Smith said. "I have been talking to everybody and advising silence," he told Roosevelt. The momentum in his favor, he agreed, was coming too early. Al Smith thought of himself as Irish, and there was nothing so Irish as to consider the appearance of good fortune as a sure sign that something very bad was about to happen.[19]

History certainly seemed to be breaking in Al Smith's way, for in the summer of 1927 the most popular politician in America, President Calvin Coolidge, announced in famously cryptic language that he did not choose to run for reelection. Not long thereafter, the man who might have fought a rematch for the nomination, William Gibbs McAdoo, said rather more emphatically that he, too, would not be a candidate in 1928. Roosevelt wrote to his hundreds of contacts around the country, telling them that the party no longer had a choice. "The simple fact is that whatever the convention does we Democrats have no chance of electing a president unless the nominee [is] Smith," he told a friend. The cities would support him, which would give him many of the eastern states, and he was convinced that "the South will hold its nose and vote for him."[20]

As the calendar turned and the press installed Smith as the favorite in the coming presidential primaries, it was becoming clear that 1928 would present a test for the American people: Did they agree with Charles Marshall and the Klan that no Catholic could lead a nation founded on liberty, which was a Protestant idea? Or would they evaluate Smith on his merits and record, regardless of how he chose to worship and where his grandparents were born? Or would it all simply come down to drink? The nation's most prominent clerical voice of Prohibition, Methodist bishop James J. Cannon, put the question more bluntly in an essay in the liberal journal *The Nation*. "Shall Dry America . . . elect a 'cocktail President'?"[21]

The political commentator and essayist Walter Lippmann was fairly certain how the American people would answer. They would choose fear over hope; they would choose to stay on their side of the divide. They believed that "the clamorous life of the city should not be acknowledged as the American ideal," he wrote. An acquaintance of William Gibbs McAdoo complained bitterly that Smith represented "aliens . . . Catholics . . . northern negroes [and] Jews" who were seeking to overturn "the America of Anglo-Saxon stock." They would not and could not win, McAdoo's friend predicted. "Old America, the America of Jackson, and of Lincoln and Wilson'" would rise to the defense of their values and their culture if Smith and his people sought to claim the White House.[22]

Smith's people—Moskowitz and Moses; Proskauer and Rosenman; Farley and Flynn—were intelligent enough and well-traveled enough to know that their candidate inspired the lesser angels of the American character. They certainly had not forgotten what happened in Madison Square Garden in 1924. They had watched with horror when the Ku Klux

Klan marched along Pennsylvania Avenue in 1925, columns of men in white robes showing off their hatred of those who threatened their version of America. The nation's cultural divide made it all the more important that somebody from Old America speak up for the New America that Al Smith represented. So Franklin Roosevelt became Al Smith's answer to the fears of Old America, and it was through Al Smith's New America that Franklin Roosevelt continued to make himself relevant, even as he spent nearly half the year in a rundown spa in rural Georgia in search of a miracle. He had contacts in places that Smith's brain trust had never heard of and preferred to keep it that way. An Old America judge from rural Nebraska told Roosevelt, "I am drier than a bone that has lain in the middle of the desert of the Sahara one thousand years, but it [seems] to me that Alfred E. Smith is the one man in our party that can be elected." It was just what Roosevelt had been telling other friends, other Old Americans—"Governor Smith's support is by no means confined to the Wets," he wrote. "There are thousands of Up-State New York Dry Democrats and Republicans who keep on voting for him for the very good reason that they believe him to be the best Governor and most progressive Governor this state has ever had."[23]

Roosevelt performed his duties as Old America's voice for New America with sincerity and enthusiasm, a task that required no small amount of humility given how little Smith's advisers appreciated the effort. Robert Moses expressed his opinion of Roosevelt in the most ruthless way he could—with drastic budget cuts to the Taconic Park Commission that Roosevelt ran. Roosevelt generally tried to ignore Moses's condescension, at least publicly, but this time he exploded, and if there was any doubt whether he noticed the years of slights and smirks from Smith's top aides, the mystery was over. He most certainly had. He fired off an extraordinary letter to Smith, raging about Moses, calling him a liar. "I wasn't born yesterday!" he told Smith. "You know, just as well as I do, that Bob has skinned us alive this year. . . . I am sorry to say it is a fact that Bob Moses has played fast and loose with the Taconic State Park Commission since the beginning." He told Smith he would resign as the commission's chairman.

Smith chose not to accept Roosevelt's resignation, saving him from what might have been an impulsive bit of theater designed mainly to get the governor's attention. "I know of no man I have met in my whole public career who I have any stronger affection for than yourself," he wrote in fatherly fashion. "Therefore, you can find as much fault with me as you like. I will not get into a fight with you for anything or for anybody." But the older man couldn't resist the opportunity to offer the onetime young whippersnapper a lecture: don't act like you know everything if you're just guessing. "I have lived, ate, and slept with this park question for three and one half years," he told Roosevelt. He certainly didn't need the head of the Taconic Park Commission to tell him what was going on in his own administration.[24]

Roosevelt did not resign.

It was extraordinary: the party that tore itself to pieces in 1924, the party that could not find the courage or moral authority to condemn the Ku Klux Klan, the party that seemed to equate Protestantism with Americanism and the consumption of alcohol with Satan himself came together in the early months of 1928 behind the candidacy of an Irish Catholic from New York City who refused to allow his police officers to enforce the Eighteenth Amendment. Al Smith swept the primaries in the North, in New England, in the Midwest, and even in California.

As Smith's campaign team began to look ahead to the coming convention in Houston, the press speculated that the governor would ask his increasingly famous protégé, Mayor Jimmy Walker, to place his name in nomination. Quick-witted, dashing, handsome, and eloquent, Walker seemed like a good choice, but word leaked out in late April that the Smith team had changed its mind. Rather than Walker, Franklin Roosevelt would get the assignment, and there was no mystery about the reason. Walker was, like Smith, a Catholic. The press noted that Smith and his advisers decided they needed their favorite Protestant to perform the chore. Roosevelt's reaction to this blunt assessment of his utility was not recorded, but from his perspective, it didn't matter very much because once again he would be at the very center of American politics. He was relevant. His voice would be heard by millions over the radio. Roosevelt told journalist Walter Lippmann that he would design his speech "wholly for the benefit of the radio audience."[25]

Assured of victory, the New Yorkers packed their bags and headed to Houston in late June, just a few days after the Republican Party nominated Herbert Hoover as its nominee. Smith himself remained in Albany, playing the role of disinterested candidate. A friend sent him a gift to bring him good luck: thirteen freshly caught trout. The old Fulton Fish Market man promised to have the fish for breakfast the following morning.[26]

Smith and his allies had agreed to hold the convention in Houston as a sop to the dry, rural, Jim Crow South that would have a hard time backing an Irish Catholic from New York for president. Smith, like every other Democratic presidential candidate in the first half of the twentieth century, had no hope of winning without the Solid South—and part of what made the South so solid was the Democrats' explicit support for brutally enforced segregation and oppression. Just days before the convention opened, a young black man named Robert Powell was accused of killing a Houston detective in an exchange of gunfire that left him seriously wounded. A group of locals marched into the hospital, named for Jefferson Davis, president of the Confederacy, removed Powell from his bed, stuffed him into a car, and hanged him under a bridge a few miles outside the city limits. There was no protest from the Smith campaign. The convention opened as scheduled about a week later, and when it did, black spectators were escorted to a segregated pen on the convention floor, separated from the delegates and guests by chicken wire.[27]

Conspicuous by their absence in Houston were Smith's most-prominent women supporters. Belle Moskowitz stayed in Albany to be with the governor when the great moment arrived. Eleanor Roosevelt, who worked closely with Moskowitz during the brief primary season, decided she had no interest in what she called the "hurly-burly" of convention politics, not after the ugliness of 1924. Frances Perkins, the highest-ranking woman in state government, remained home to tend to her ailing husband. They would all follow the convention by radio.[28]

All the others who made the trip to Houston were on their best behavior, for Franklin Roosevelt, serving as Smith's convention floor manager, had told them to accept their man's victory with grace and humility. No sirens, no displays of triumphalism. It was not only unseemly, it simply wasn't smart, for there still were voices from within the party itself warning that Smith's nomination was part of a crafty plot by the pope and his minions to take over the United States and—who knows?—perhaps declare Protestant marriages illegal, or impose a new inquisition. The reliable bigot and future Klansman, Senator Cotton Tom Heflin of Alabama, warned that Smith and his fellow Catholics were determined to "crush the life out of Protestantism in America." He suggested that the time was coming to deport Catholics because their allegiance was to Rome first, and he warned that Smith's views on African Americans, Prohibition, and immigrants were "directly opposed to the things that are near and dear to the Democratic South." Faced with such rabid opposition from within his own party, Smith wanted no demonstrations that would feed the paranoia of awful men like Heflin.[29]

Roosevelt delivered his nominating speech for Smith on the night of June 27 to an audience of twenty thousand in the hall and fifteen million listening by radio—among them, Al Smith, gathered with his family and longtime aides around an enormous wooden box with a pair of dials. Those in the hall who had watched Franklin Roosevelt propel himself on crutches at the 1924 convention saw firsthand what he had been writing in so many letters. He really seemed to be getting better (even though he wasn't, not anymore). His upper body, his chest and shoulders, were bigger and muscular. And the crutches were gone. He "walked" with a cane in one hand and his hand on the arm of his son Elliot. The crowd cheered as he reached the podium and he waved with one hand while holding the podium with the other, an extraordinary display of grit that the millions listening on the radio could only imagine. And then he began: the governor of New York, he said, was not only immensely popular but was enormously qualified. He understood what people needed from government because he knew what it was like to struggle. He had a heart, and he had a brain, and that made him a leader. "Between him and the people is that subtle bond which makes him their champion," he said, his voice clear and resonant. "America needs not only an administrator but a leader—a pathfinder, a blazer of the trail to the high road that will avoid the bottomless morass of crass materialism that has engulfed so many civilizations of the past. . . . To stand upon the ramparts and die for our principles is heroic. To sally forth to battle and win for our principles is something more than heroic. We offer one who has the will to win—who not only deserves success but commands it." He paused, and then delivered his punch line:

"Victory is his habit—the happy warrior, Alfred E. Smith."[30]

Back in Albany, Al Smith wiped his eyes. Franklin Roosevelt had done it again. Will Durant, historian and a commentator for the Smith-friendly *New York World*, wrote, "Nothing better could be said for the Governor of New York than that Franklin Roosevelt loves him."[31]

Franklin Roosevelt once again rose to the occasion on behalf of Al Smith. And Smith knew it: he put pen to paper and dropped Roosevelt a note, saying that the speech brought tears to his eyes.[32]

Balloting began the following night. Roosevelt was with the New York delegation on the convention floor; Smith and his family, joined by Belle Moskowitz, Robert Moses, and other aides who stayed home rather than travel to Houston, set up chairs around the executive mansion's enormous radio to listen to the roll call. They took notes, counted the votes, exchanged looks as each state's chairman announced the tallies. The roll call ended with 724⅔ votes for Al Smith, far, far ahead of his competitors but nine votes shy of the two-thirds necessary. The head of Ohio's delegation suddenly raised his voice and got the attention of the convention chairman and said that the Buckeye State wished to change its vote, which had been split. Ohio now wished to cast all forty-five of its votes for the governor of New York. Smith had all the votes he needed.

Alfred Emanuel Smith was standing by the radio, his Great Dane, Jeff, lying at his feet, when Ohio made its announcement. He took off the glasses he was careful to not wear in public very often, and people in the room noticed his hand was trembling. Then he looked at the small gathering around him: his daughter, Emily, and her husband, Moskowitz, Moses, and several other friends. Emily practically leaped into his arms. Moskowitz turned to Moses, "It's over, Bob." It is hard to imagine either one of them considering this moment with dry eyes. Thousands were gathered outside the executive mansion on Eagle Street, cheering for their hero although it was past midnight.[33]

All the while, Franklin Roosevelt was in his seat on the convention floor, watching the children and grandchildren of immigrants marching through the aisles on behalf of Al Smith. They passed men who did not share their joy, who remained in their seats because they hated what they saw. A delegate from Texas watched the Smith people pass by his seat near the center aisle. "I wondered, 'where were all the Americans?'" he later said. The Smith people, the non-Americans, the New Americans, were so overjoyed that they did not notice that die-hard Smith foes in the South declined the usual custom of making the convention's choice unanimous.[34]

The convention quickly agreed on Smith's choice for vice president, Senator Joseph Robinson of Arkansas, who had risen to Smith's defense in Washington when Cotton Tom Heflin insisted that the governor of New York was nothing more than a stooge of the pope. Robinson was from the South, he was dry, and he was Protestant. The ticket was balanced.

And so was the party's platform, designed to offend the fewest number of voters on the most important cultural issue of the day, Prohibition. A compromise plank pledged that the party and its nominees would make an "honest effort" to enforce the Eighteenth Amendment. It was an artful evasion, for who could say what was an "honest effort" and what was not, and by making such a declaration the party simply said that it would respect the law of the land. Nobody would like it but nobody would hate it.

Nobody except the party's nominee. "This isn't on the level," Al Smith grumbled after the plank's language was read to him on the phone. "It doesn't say anything." That, of course, was the idea. The day after his nomination was made official, Smith dashed off a telegram to the convention saying that he was honored to be the party's nominee, that he would support the party's platform. Sort of. Because he could not help himself, he added this: "It is well known that I believe there should be fundamental changes in the present provisions for national prohibition." The fervent drys in the convention hall and around the country were aghast. And so was Franklin Roosevelt, who later called it "that fool telegram." But Smith was tired of the lies and the hypocrisy, tired of the liquor straddle. Other politicians could choose to say nothing; he would not. He'd enforce the law but he would not hide his contempt for it.[35]

Roosevelt's despair only worsened when Smith announced his choice as chairman of the party's national committee, the prerogative of all presidential nominees. Smith chose John Raskob, a fabulously wealthy businessman, a Catholic, a wet. Like Smith, he was self-made—he had seen his opportunities, and he took them. In 1901 he was hired to be a secretary to Pierre DuPont, a member of one of the nation's wealthiest families. Less than two decades later he was helping to run the DuPont enterprises and their new venture, General Motors. Smith saw in Raskob what he might have been had he chosen business rather than politics.

Everyone, including Belle Moskowitz, told Smith that Raskob was a bad choice. But Smith decided he was smarter than they were. Raskob would show the nation's business community that they could trust a man often criticized for his expansion of government, his expensive social programs, his populist persona. But there was more to Raskob's appointment than political pragmatism: Smith told Moskowitz that Raskob was a friend who had never asked for anything in return—until he asked to head the Democratic National Committee. Smith came of age in a political clubhouse, and the clubhouse had certain rules, one of which was you did right by your friends.

Roosevelt believed Smith should have chosen somebody who could speak to both sides of the liquor issue and somebody who could bridge the religious divide. He told his mother that he had been offered the chairmanship before Smith turned to Raskob, but he declined. The offer seems to have been made to Roosevelt in his sleep, while he was dreaming.

He retreated to Warm Springs after the convention, and he made a promise to his mother. Just as he had declined the national chairmanship, he wrote, he would "decline the nomination for Governor" if it was offered. For the first time since 1916, the Democratic Party of New York would have to find somebody other than Al Smith to run for governor. And that somebody would have to be well-known and popular, somebody who could help Smith win his home state, for without New York, Smith's presidential campaign was doomed.[36]

Smith's aides were beginning to talk about finding this somebody, and the more they thought about it, the more they realized that they once again needed Franklin Roosevelt. But then again, if Roosevelt ran for governor and won, reporters would descend on Albany just as they did in 1911 when the young Roosevelt made such a show of thumbing his nose at Al Smith's mentor, Charlie Murphy. They would make him into a hero, perhaps even a threat to Al Smith at some point. An empowered Franklin Roosevelt could be a dangerous Franklin Roosevelt.

When Smith's aides raised these concerns, he dismissed them with a wave of the hand.

"He won't live a year," Al Smith said of Franklin Roosevelt.[37]

fifteen

CONFRONTING OLD AMERICA

AL SMITH ACCEPTED HIS PARTY'S nomination for president more than four weeks after his first-ballot victory, in a ceremony of manners and protocol that remained stuck in the nineteenth century, as stilted and formal as a Victorian courtship. The event was carefully programmed: a glee club would begin performing on the massive capitol steps fronting State Street at six o'clock. The governor would show himself at the top of the steps at seven, buglers would sound flourishes, and then the governor would walk down the capitol's long staircase while a band played "The Sidewalks of New York." He would then take a seat on a platform while prayers were offered and speeches recited, and then the party's elders would inform him that he had won the nomination. Humble and proud, he would then accept the party's call to service at precisely 7:30—precise because the speech would be broadcast by radio around the nation.

The morning brought rain to Albany. Still, they gathered by the thousands in a grassy area at the foot of the capitol's staircase, waiting for the moment when Al Smith would stand at the top and wave. Franklin and Eleanor Roosevelt found their seats and tried to ignore the rain that turned the lawn into a sponge and the gutters into small streams. Finally word was passed that the ceremony would take place in the assembly chamber, where Smith started his public career a quarter century earlier. Franklin Roosevelt took one look at the throng heading inside, hundreds of men and women brushing up against each other, jostling with each other, and decided that he was not about to chance an accident—the press reported that "Mr. Roosevelt, who walks with the aid of a crutch and a cane, did not venture into the crowd." He stayed in his seat despite the rain and would listen to the ceremony on loudspeakers. Eleanor remained seated with him.[1]

Wearing a light-colored bow tie and a darker, double-breasted suit, Smith spoke not only to the hundreds jammed inside the assembly chamber but to millions listening on radio, most of whom were hearing his voice, and such a voice, for the first time. No presidential nominee in the history of the republic spoke as Al Smith did with his peculiar pronunciations, straightforward style, and gravelly voice. The language was more formal than he generally preferred but the message was almost radical in its embrace of an activist government after eight years of Harding-Coolidge passivism. He condemned reactionaries who put government on the side of "material things" rather than people, but he also said it was possible to protect "the rights of the people, including the poor and the weak," while also looking after "the rights of legitimate business." In his administration, government would intervene on behalf of farmers and workers who were at the mercy of economic forces beyond their control. He would "advance the safeguards of public health," expand the national park system, and build a social safety net to protect families from falling into the abyss. Included in the list of ambitious though somewhat vague promises was one very specific vow: Smith said he wanted the federal government to play a leading role in preventing and controlling floods in the Mississippi Valley. Franklin Roosevelt, sitting in the misty rain outside and staring at the loudspeaker carrying Smith's words, would have been forgiven if he smiled at the mention of the Mississippi Valley—he had urged Smith to pay attention to the issue more than a year earlier.[2]

Smith made another promise, one that seemed certain to alienate many in his own party and surely many more listening on the radio, but one he believed he could not avoid. If people in the heartland knew anything about the governor of New York, they knew that he was a wet—not moist, but as drenched symbolically as Franklin and Eleanor Roosevelt were in reality as they listened to his words. Smith saw no reason to pretend otherwise, so he proposed a new constitutional amendment to supersede the hated Eighteenth. Leave it to the states, he said. And in the meantime, rewrite federal law to allow for the sale and consumption of low-alcohol beer. His voters cheered. His enemies, and they included many Democrats beyond the Hudson River, shook their heads in disgust and saw why the noted newspaper editor William Allen White had lashed out at their candidate. "The whole Puritan civilization which has built a sturdy, orderly nation is threatened by Smith," wrote White, editor of the *Emporia Gazette* in Kansas.[3]

Smith spoke for a portion of the nation that had no time for Puritans, then and now, a portion that lived in places that were proud to be not quite as orderly as the town of Emporia. His voice, his delivery, and the very words he spoke were quite literally foreign to many of those who heard them through their magical talking boxes. He sounded like nobody's neighbor save for those listening in the tenements of the Lower East Side. He said things that sounded dangerous, things that challenged the great American myth of rugged individualism. But in the assembly chamber and in the rain outside the capitol, everything Al Smith said sounded familiar. They cheered him on, no louder than when he pledged that in making appointments he would not be influenced by a candidate's religion, "by what church he attends in the worship of God." It was a subtle nod, and the only one, to the unspoken issue of Al Smith's campaign of 1928.[4]

This was the moment Al Smith's enemies had been preparing for since 1924, when for the first time in American history a non-Protestant was seriously considered as a nominee for the nation's highest office. It wasn't just the Klan; it wasn't just the dry fanatics; it wasn't just the latter-day Bryans of the vast American heartland. Mainstream preachers and pamphleteers across the country mobilized on behalf of a great crusade to prevent the White House from falling into hands that clutched rosary beads, to challenge the loyalty of a man who answered not to the Founding Fathers but to the Holy Father in Rome. They printed handbills and leaflets filled with claims that the pope and his cardinals were packing their bags and preparing to cross the Atlantic to declare the United States one nation under a Catholic God. There were pictures of Al Smith standing in front of a tunnel—and that tunnel led directly to the Vatican! (It was actually the Holland Tunnel, a marvelous piece of engineering connecting the island of Manhattan with the mainland of the United States, via New Jersey.) A publication called the *New Menace*, filled with diatribes against Smith and Catholics, found its way into the mailboxes of homes in Missouri. In Virginia, thousands of copies of a vicious anti-Smith, anti-Catholic broadside titled *Romanism, Rum, and Rebellion* were distributed throughout the state as an alternative to the state's newspapers, which were said to be controlled by Catholics. Other leaflets asserted that Catholics would use a Smith presidency to murder Protestants, to void Protestant marriages, abolish public schools, and generally destroy all American institutions. The Klan's propaganda sheet, *Fellowship Forum*, had no shortage of "news" about the pope's plans for a Smith administration, the most noteworthy being that the Vatican intended to take over management of the Post Office. Perhaps the pope, like Franklin Roosevelt, was a stamp collector.[5]

The Klan also encouraged like-minded racists to consider the possibility that Al Smith's break with tradition was not simply confined to his faith. The *Fellowship Forum* screamed that Smith and his friends in Tammany Hall "approved of race equality" in the parceling out of municipal jobs and that Smith regularly spent time "among the Negroes of Harlem." The paper ran a picture of a prominent black supporter of Tammany and Smith, Ferdinand Morton, standing near his secretary, a white woman, in his "private office." It was an image that ought to "nauseate any Anglo-Saxon," the paper said. Morton was one of New York City's three civil service commissioners, along with a Catholic and a Jew, leading the *Forum* to conclude that Protestants had no chance of being hired under the likes of Smith. And even worse, black people could be in charge of hiring.[6]

Smith himself was careful not to further antagonize the white South. He allowed racists and their foes to read what they would from his record and his silence. Some of his supporters assured voters in the Deep South that Smith could be counted on to enforce white supremacy, while some black newspapers in the North saw Smith as a voice for racial progress. "What the Democratic party stood for 40 years ago the Republican party stands for today," said the *Chicago Defender*, a prominent black voice in the Midwest that vigorously supported Smith.[7]

Still, it was religion, not race, that added heat to the fire and brimstone of Protestant clerics throughout the country. The Rev. Billy Sunday, soon to gain fame as a radio preacher, told a gathering in the Methodist summer colony of Ocean Grove, New Jersey, that Al Smith's election would be "the greatest calamity that can befall America," for Smith represented "the forces of hell." The Rev. John Ham, a Georgia cleric, said he had heard it on good authority—from Catholics he knew personally—that the pope had a plan to "make America Catholic."[8]

Smith's Catholicism made him unacceptable or worse to fellow Democrats who trafficked in the same conspiracy theories that were brought to vivid life in hundreds of pulpits across the heartland. Old reliable Cotton Tom Heflin, U.S. senator from Alabama, told a Klan rally in Pittsburgh that he was prepared to be a martyr, to die by an assassin's bullet like Abraham Lincoln, James Garfield, and William McKinley (all of whom, one California preacher said, had been killed by Catholics), in order to save the country from Al Smith and the pope.[9]

The New York press called it a "whispering campaign" against Smith but it was much louder than a whisper. It was a full-throated shout by mid-September, when his eleven-car campaign train made its way to the Midwest, where he hoped to win the support of farmers who might disregard his city-slicker pose and see him as a champion of ordinary people. The results were mixed. Frances Perkins, whose bond with Smith now stretched nearly twenty years, didn't think the governor of New York was fooling anybody. "He did not sound like a man who knew pigs and chickens," she said. The whole effect—the cigar, the voice, and his headgear, a jaunty brown derby that practically screamed urban, ethnic, sidewalks of New York—was something the sons and daughters of the soil had never seen or heard before.[10]

After a speech in Omaha, the train headed south, through the endless prairie of Nebraska and Kansas into Oklahoma. It was dark by the time the train approached Oklahoma City, dark save for the glow on the hilltops, where local Klansmen greeted the Catholic candidate with a display of burning crosses.

He spoke that night in Oklahoma City about religion, about tolerance, about the diverse nature of the country he loved and cherished. He had not intended to make such a speech, at least not in Oklahoma, where a former U.S. senator, Robert Owen, had announced with great fanfare that he would desert the Democratic Party of Al Smith and his ilk and instead vote for Herbert Hoover. But some of his aides, including his campaign finance chairman Herbert Lehman, believed the time was right to call out bigotry and prejudice for what it was.

Thousands gathered in an auditorium in Oklahoma City. Joseph Proskauer, Smith's longtime aide, saw "groups of thin-lipped, evil-looking, sneering men." Smith spoke without a text, glancing occasionally at a piece of paper in his hands, as he said what others were thinking and whispering. He named former senator Owen and the Ku Klux Klan, saying they were responsible for the spread of "bigotry, intolerance and un-American sectarian division."

"I here and now drag them into the open and I denounce them as a treasonable attack upon the very foundations of American liberty," he said. No good citizen, no true American, would vote against him based on his religion, he said, and the same could be said of those of his own faith who might vote for him for no reason other than his religion. "Let the people of this country decide this election upon the real issues of the campaign and nothing else," he said.[11]

The thin-lipped men learned, perhaps to their surprise, that they were outnumbered by those who heard in Smith's speech a call to their better angels. They cheered him and his message, and Smith left the hall and the city in triumph. He saw no reason to take back what he told reporters before setting out on this journey into the heartland. "I'm going to beat the pants off Hoover," he promised.[12]

Franklin Roosevelt was no more than an observer as the Smith presidential campaign got underway. That wasn't his intention, but when he began showing up at Smith headquarters in New York, he could not help but notice that Smith's top aides, particularly Belle Moskowitz, had little use for him. In their eyes, he had done his duty—he gave a nice speech at the convention—and now the professionals would take care of the rest. He stopped going to headquarters and left town altogether, first to Hyde Park, then to Warm Springs. But he seized on whatever opportunities were offered him to promote Smith and keep active in the campaign. He accepted a job as a columnist for a Dutchess County weekly newspaper based in the small city of Beacon, where he penned pro-Smith pieces. ("I'll do anything to help Al," he told the newspaper's publisher.) He journeyed from Hyde Park to the Connecticut city of Bridgeport to give a speech on Smith's behalf just as anti-Catholic propaganda began circulating in early September. "We know [Smith] over in the state of New York. That is why we have elected and re-elected and re-elected him," he said. "Over in New York the question of his religion has never entered into politics and it never will."[13]

When he went south to Warm Springs in late September, he made a special trip to Atlanta to address a gathering of Georgia Democrats and assail Smith's anti-Catholic critics. He had known many presidents, Roosevelt told the crowd. "I can tell you that Alfred E. Smith will be in dignity and ability a fit successor to the most illustrious of them," he said.[14]

The single phone at the Warm Springs spa rang one day in late summer. On the other end was the unmistakable bellow of Al Smith, calling from the campaign trail to see if Frank would consider running for governor in November. Smith and his friends had been thinking it over and they thought he was the natural choice. The enthusiasm in Smith's voice showed that he hadn't lost his touch as an actor, because the truth was that Smith did not think Roosevelt was the natural choice, at least not at first. Smith preferred Herbert Lehman, who had served on his campaign finance committee and who entered public life because he believed in the work Al Smith was doing in Albany. But when others pressed the case for Roosevelt, Smith gave in. Lehman, it was decided, would make a great lieutenant governor.

Roosevelt told Smith that as much as he'd love the chance to be his successor, he simply couldn't do it—he needed more time to rebuild his legs. Someday he would throw away the crutches, he was sure of that, but he needed another year or so of exercise and therapy in Warm Springs. It was an argument Smith had to accept. "Well," he said, "you're the doctor." But it wasn't just about his legs—it was about his political future. Louis Howe believed the country was in no mood for a change, for the twenties still were roaring and the Republican administration was not shy about taking credit. Democrats were doomed in 1928, Howe believed, and there was no reason for Franklin Roosevelt to take one for the team.[15]

New York Democrats gathered in convention in Rochester in early October to nominate a candidate for governor to succeed Al Smith. The problem was, they had no candidate. Roosevelt was in Warm Springs, hiding, determined to be out of touch.

A telegram was awaiting Smith as he arrived at the Hotel Seneca in downtown Rochester. Franklin Roosevelt wished to remind him that he would not be a candidate for governor. "[My] nomination would make no difference to your success on the New York ticket," Roosevelt wrote.[16]

Smith put aside the telegram and made his way to a smoky conference room in the hotel, where it took only a moment to realize that others were not quite so ready to give up on Franklin Roosevelt. In the room were Jim Farley, the political genius Smith had made secretary of the state party; Ed Flynn, the boss of the Bronx; and an assortment of grim-faced upstate leaders. They all wanted Roosevelt. They all knew that Al Smith needed to win New York, and so Al Smith needed the best possible candidate for governor—that candidate's name was Franklin Delano Roosevelt.

Smith retreated to another room where the air surely was fresher. Eleanor Roosevelt, in town as a delegate to the convention, was awaiting him. John Raskob, chairman of the Democratic National Committee, joined Smith for a heart-to-heart talk with Eleanor while reporters waited in anticipation of some dramatic development. The convention already had been called to order and the Democrats still had no candidate for governor. But Eleanor emerged to say that she would not try to influence her husband.

Hours later the phone rang at Warm Springs and a loud man with a strange accent once again asked to speak with Mr. Roosevelt. An attendant asked the loud man to hold on while he tracked down Mr. Roosevelt. He was by the pool, and he told the attendant to tell the loud man that he was away on a picnic. And then after the picnic he had an important meeting, and that also was far away. Mr. Roosevelt would be completely out of touch for hours. Such bad luck!

Later that night, Smith begged Eleanor to intervene. The party needed Frank, he explained. He would have a capable lieutenant governor—Herbert Lehman. It was all arranged. But she wouldn't do it. "I feel this is Mr. Roosevelt's problem," she told Smith, who simply would not accept such an answer. Finally she gave ground on one point: she told Smith she would try to reach him by telephone—not at Warm Springs, but at a school nearby, where he was giving a speech on Smith's behalf. The call came in on a public phone, Roosevelt was summoned to a phone booth, and more than a thousand miles away in a hotel suite in Rochester, Eleanor Roosevelt surrendered the phone to the governor of New York. "Hello, Frank!" Al Smith said.

Roosevelt claimed that he couldn't hear Al. There was something wrong with the line, he said, so he was going to hang up. But an operator called back with a message: Al Smith would call him shortly at an inn near Warm Springs.

He could have ignored the message. He did not. He made his way to the inn and, seated in his wheelchair, phone pressed to his ear, he heard the pleas of desperate men: Raskob, the wealthy chairman of the party, said he would cover Roosevelt's personal investment in Warm Springs. Lehman, Roosevelt's would-be running mate, said he would fill in for him whenever he felt the need for treatments at Warm Springs. Then Smith got on the line and made it personal: he asked Franklin Roosevelt to run for governor of New York as a favor, because without him, he would lose the race for president.

It was a humbling admission from Smith, but Roosevelt remained noncommittal. Still, he hadn't said no. Smith sensed an opening.

"I just want to ask you one more question," he said. "If those fellows nominate you tomorrow and adjourn, would you refuse to run?"[17]

He hesitated. He told Smith he wasn't sure what he would do. That was good enough for Al Smith, who put down the phone and told those fellows to go ahead and nominate Franklin Roosevelt.

Jimmy Walker, mayor of New York, did the honors the following morning, linking the names of the candidate for governor with the party's candidate for president, reminding delegates of Roosevelt's brilliant speech on Smith's behalf in Madison Square Garden four years earlier. "There never was any fear in the mind of Franklin D. Roosevelt about the Americanism of Alfred E. Smith," Walker said. The delegates burst into cheers.[18]

Eleanor Roosevelt dispatched a telegram to Warm Springs: "Regret that you had to accept but know that you felt it obligatory." Louis Howe's telegram was more succinct: "Mess has no name for it."[19]

Al Smith was overjoyed. He had what he wanted, what he needed, to make sure that New York turned out for the Democratic ticket in November. And such a ticket! Smith, an Irish Catholic from the sidewalks of New York; Roosevelt, a Protestant patrician from upstate; Herbert Lehman, a Jewish banker and philanthropist; and, running for U.S. Senate, Royal

Copeland, a friend of William Randolph Hearst—from a New Yorker's point of view, the Democrats had their ethnic, cultural, and political bases covered. Such a combination would have been unthinkable a generation earlier, even in New York, but times were changing: not only was a Catholic running for president, but New York's Republicans chose a Jew, Albert Ottinger, to run for governor against Roosevelt.

Upon his return to Albany after the convention, Smith told reporters and a crowd of several hundred gathered at Albany's Union Station that he had no doubts about Roosevelt's ability to lead the largest and greatest and most powerful state in the union. "Frank Roosevelt today is mentally as good as he ever was in his life," he declared. "Physically he is as good as he ever was in his life. His whole trouble is in his lack of muscular control of his lower limbs. But the answer to that is that the governor does not have to be an acrobat. We do not elect him for his ability to do a double back flip or a handspring. The work of the governorship is brain work."[20]

The newspapers, however, declared that Smith and his top aides were asking too much of his friend and ally. "They demanded of Roosevelt a cruel physical sacrifice for the sake of helping Smith carry New York," the New York Post wrote. Smith "has asked and accepted a greater sacrifice than a friend should ask from a friend. And it is more than ever evident that Mr. Roosevelt is a sport of the first order."[21]

Roosevelt was indeed a sport. He announced from Warm Springs that he was "amazed" that anyone would think Al Smith had "dragooned" him into running for governor. Why, it was nothing of the sort! "[Smith] fully appreciated the reasons for my reluctance and was willing to give up any such advantage as he felt my candidacy might bring in deference to my wishes," he said. The governor made no personal appeals—reports to the contrary were simply nonsense—but when the party drafted him as its nominee, well, he had no choice. He was determined to carry forward Al Smith's policies, he said, and if that meant running for governor, he would do it. He left Warm Springs and traveled to Cleveland, where he denounced the anti-Catholic "whispering campaign" against Smith and charged that opponents were using the issue of Prohibition as a "cloak for something else."[22]

He met with Smith in New York City on October 8. Election Day was only a month away and yet the campaign was just getting started—a team had to be assembled, appearances needed to be booked, speeches had to be written. Roosevelt's team consisted of Louis Howe. But Al Smith had a generation of young Democrats at his command and he was willing to share, although there was one prominent supporter of his who declined the opportunity to campaign for Franklin Roosevelt: Eleanor Roosevelt. She had no interest in her husband's campaign, but she threw herself into the effort for Smith, often in close collaboration with Belle Moskowitz and Frances Perkins. "Comparatively speaking, I knew very little about the 1928 campaign for the governorship," she wrote, dryly, years later.[23]

Others, however, were dispatched from Smith's circle to help the new candidate for governor: James Farley, the back-slapping Irishman who was with Smith as early as 1922, was assigned to organize upstate for Roosevelt. Ed Flynn, the Bronx boss, was conscripted to work with Louis Howe on strategy and tactics. Smith's onetime speechwriter, Samuel Rosenman, was told that he would be writing Roosevelt's speeches, not Smith's, an assignment he dreaded, for he had heard the talk in the Smith campaign. Roosevelt, they were saying, was a lightweight, nothing like their hero Al, who climbed to the top on his own accord, on his own merits. Rosenman was told to pack his bags and keep Roosevelt company as he toured the cities and villages of upstate New York. Frances Perkins, too, found herself working as much for Roosevelt as she did for Smith, serving as the candidate's liaison to organized labor, a group with which he was only vaguely familiar.

As Perkins and Rosenman watched Roosevelt work the crowds in places like Oriskany Falls and Skaneateles, Oswego and Salamanca, they realized that Franklin Roosevelt was not the man he once was, not the man so easily dismissed in Al Smith's inner councils. Perkins saw it in the way Roosevelt was able to adjust to the unpredictability of a campaign, the canceled stops, the unplanned remarks, all without complaint. "If you can't use your legs and they bring milk when you wanted orange juice," he said, "you learn to say, 'That's all right,' and drink it."[24]

Rosenman saw a profoundly more serious man than he expected. He took speechmaking seriously, often dictating revisions on his own, at the last minute, breaking down complex issues into simple sentences. He stood up to give his speeches and never let on that he could achieve this amazing feat only because he wore heavy braces and had a steely determination that nobody back at Smith headquarters seemed to understand or appreciate. And yet so many of the words he spoke were devoted not to his campaign but to that of Al Smith. Rosenman might well have wondered if Belle Moskowitz and Robert Moses and others had any idea what Franklin Roosevelt was saying about their boss, and, if they did, why they seemed so unwilling to acknowledge it.

He told an audience that the great question of the campaign was simple: "Shall the State of New York carry through, consolidate, and make permanent the great reforms which for all time attach to the name of Alfred E. Smith? My answer is, 'yes.'" He adopted Smith's controversial view that the state, not private industry, should develop New York's fledgling hydropower capacity—because the people, not corporations, owned the rivers. And in a speech in upstate Binghamton, a small city that was said to be the headquarters of the KKK in New York State, he went out of his way to assail the bigotry and hatred aimed at Smith, his wife, and the nation's Catholics. "Circulars are being distributed in the South that you persons would be ashamed of to have in your homes," he said. "I have seen circulars that were so unfit for publication that the people who wrote them ought not to be put in jail, but ought to be put on the first ship and sent away from the United States." In Buffalo, Roosevelt said that he hoped God would show mercy toward any "miserable soul . . . who [would] cast a ballot for intolerance."[25]

Smith's old enemy William Randolph Hearst, following the race from the ostentatious comfort of his California mansion, fired off a telegram declaring that Franklin Roosevelt was "trying to drag the religious question into politics." Roosevelt, the publisher said, "comes dangerously near to being a traitor to the country."[26]

"There can be no question as to the plain duty of all Presbyterian church members," announced a high-ranking clergyman as Election Day approached. "The plain duty of every churchman is to work and pray and vote for the election of Herbert Hoover." The first American woman to bear the title of bishop, Alma White, a Methodist evangelist, referred to Smith as "the papal governor of New York."[27]

They were talking about religion, all right. Talking about it in every corner of the country. In Tennessee, part of the old Democratic Party's heartland and a state that even John Davis carried after the debacle of 1924, officials told the press that Al Smith's Catholicism was splitting the party and leading to mass defections to Herbert Hoover. In Alabama, a noted evangelist named Bob Jones, a friend of the late William Jennings Bryan and founder of a university that bore his name in South Carolina, made a hundred appearances on behalf of Herbert Hoover, telling his listeners, "I'd rather see a saloon on every corner than a Catholic in the White House." He offered a variation on that theme in some places, saying that he'd rather "see a nigger" in the White House than Al Smith. In Oklahoma, a Baptist minister told congregants, "If you vote for Al Smith, you're voting against Christ and you'll all be damned." One young woman rose in her pew and said she had heard enough: she was leaving the church and might even consider becoming Catholic. "All right, goodbye lady," the preacher replied.[28]

When Frances Perkins visited Independence, Missouri, for a campaign rally, U.S. senator Harry Hawes warned her to expect something other than a warm reception when she spoke on Smith's behalf. Still relatively innocent, she asked why. "Smith's religion," Hawes said. "They don't like it." He was right—they booed Perkins and Hawes as they made their case for Smith, and when the meeting was over Perkins had to be whisked to a car that sped out of town as quickly as possible. This was hardly the outcome envisioned by one of the rally's organizers, a local Jackson County official named Harry Truman.[29]

Perkins returned to New York having seen and heard things she had not imagined and could not have imagined. Other Americans were speaking about a man she did not recognize as the Al Smith she knew. Nothing she could say about his record and his character mattered. She told Belle Moskowitz at headquarters about her misgivings.

"You're quite mistaken, Frances," Moskowitz replied. The country was eager to hear Al Smith's message of social and economic justice, she said. "This is what the country is longing for."[30]

It was not an implausible argument as Al Smith toured the country for a second time in mid-October. Armed with his brown derby and brimming with confidence, he drew adoring crowds in Nashville, St. Louis, St. Paul, and Omaha. When the campaign swung back east, there was even more reason to believe that Belle Moskowitz had it right and Frances Perkins had it wrong. Fourteen thousand people in Baltimore hardly allowed him to speak, so fervent were their cheers. And when he named the Ku Klux Klan and said that it would be hard to imagine an organization that was less Christian and less American, they stood and cheered for nearly twenty minutes.

It was the same in Boston, Philadelphia, Wilmington, Newark, Brooklyn. Immigrants and outsiders, Catholics and Jews, city dwellers and wets—Smith saw hope in their faces, and he believed hope would get him to the promised land. "I know politics and I know political crowds," he told Perkins. "I've run for election before and this is not just an ordinary election. This is something."[31]

Al Smith and Franklin Roosevelt joined forces for one last massive rally before voters went to the polls on November 6. Twenty five thousand people jammed Madison Square Garden, singing "The Sidewalks of New York" over and over again as they awaited Smith's appearance on a platform covered in red, white, and blue bunting. Outside the Garden, fifteen hundred police officers tried to keep order among those who arrived too late to get inside but who had no intention of leaving, for they wished to be a witness to history.

While they waited for Smith, they heard from Roosevelt, who knew his audience. He launched a stinging attack on his opponent, Albert Ottinger, for his silence on Prohibition. Roosevelt then gave way to the city's most prominent rabbi, Stephen Wise, who said he was a Republican and a dry and a Jew but said he would vote as an American "for a Democrat, a Catholic, and an American—Alfred Emanuel Smith." The place went wild. But that was nothing compared to the cheers that greeted the governor himself when he appeared on the platform at about ten o'clock. He wore a dark suit, a bow tie, a bright handkerchief in his left breast pocket. He raised his right arm to acknowledge the roars as Jimmy Walker, the master of ceremonies, moved in close and spoke directly into Smith's right ear. Roosevelt joined the party on stage and somehow the cheering grew even louder. Confetti fell from the cheap seats and the band played "The Sidewalks of New York" because it could not have done otherwise.

His voice was hoarse and raspy after weeks on the campaign trail but it remained filled with conviction. He spoke of those who launched "an attack upon me because of my religious faith and an attack on nearly twenty million people in the United States who share that faith with me."[32]

There was little doubt that those in the Garden agreed with him. But there was more to America than twenty-five thousand adoring people in the heart of New York City.

On their way from Springwood to the town hall in Hyde Park on Election Day, Franklin Roosevelt and his mother, Sara, passed a huge "Roosevelt for Governor" banner stretched across the Albany Post Road. Local Republicans and Democrats alike had paid for the advertisement to salute the village's favorite son. Roosevelt said he was touched: if he lived to be a hundred years old—and he fully expected to do so, he said—he would never forget the kindness of his friends and neighbors.[33]

Mother and son pulled up at town hall at about eleven o'clock to find a battery of newspaper photographers and newsreel cameramen awaiting them. The candidate flashed his famous smile but then reminded the photographers of the rules of engagement: no pictures as his chauffeur helped him out of the car. They obliged, and did likewise when Roosevelt reemerged from town hall and returned to the car.

He spent the rest of the day on the banks of the Hudson River, where the trees he studied and loved had shed their leaves, offering a clearer view of the river and the Shawangunk Ridge in the distance. He was prepared for the worst, as he had been since he started this adventure only five weeks earlier.

His friends and neighbors didn't think much of his candidacy, even if they didn't say so to his face. They spoke with their ballots: Franklin Roosevelt lost his own election district in Hyde Park in a relative landslide. Of his friends and neighbors, 168 voted for him; 240 voted for his opponent, Ottinger.

Later in the afternoon he and Sara got back into the car for the two-hour ride to Manhattan to monitor the results over a buffet dinner at the Biltmore Hotel. Howe would be there, of course. And so would Ed Flynn, James Farley, Sam Rosenman, and Frances Perkins, all of whom had one thing in common: they had all worked for Al Smith in some capacity but were gathered together on behalf of Franklin Roosevelt. He was their candidate now.

The Biltmore, on Madison Avenue in midtown, happened to be the residence of Al and Katie Smith since they moved uptown from Oliver Street several years earlier. Smith left the hotel that morning and walked across the street to cast his ballot in one of the city's new-fangled mechanical voting machines. He emerged from behind the curtain not with a smile but with the look of somebody deep in thought. He asked to be left alone. He told his police escort they wouldn't be needed for a few hours and told reporters that he needed some privacy. He disappeared into the streets of New York, of the city he loved, and made the short but ever so distant journey from midtown's skyscrapers to the walk-up tenements of the old neighborhood.

He showed up in Tom Foley's old clubhouse, the Downtown Tammany Club, just a few steps away from his old flat on Oliver Street. He sat under a painting of the burly boss, which was hanging near a picture of his protégé, the young assemblyman, Alfred E. Smith. He chatted with some old friends, and when word made its way into the streets that once were his playground, people began gathering outside, calling his name, cheering, laughing. A couple of priests from St. James Church, where he served as an altar boy and where he received his only formal education, rushed over to greet him. Somebody asked him about the inevitable brown derby he was wearing: it was, he said, one of about forty given to him as presents since he made the derby his signature. Everybody laughed.

After a while it was time to return to the Biltmore to prepare for whatever the night might bring. He stepped back into the street and saw the bootblack, Steve Roberto, who used to shine his shoes at the corner of Madison and Oliver. And then he saw Mrs. Morris Sunshine waving from her laundry at 30 Oliver. She and her husband laundered Al Smith's shirts for twenty years. The local block captain reported that all eligible voters on Oliver Street had already cast their votes, some of them, workmen mostly, after waiting in line at the crack of dawn that morning. The men who lived in boardinghouses on the Bowery were accounted for as well. "You would think you were in a little country town instead of the Lower East Side of New York," the captain said.

And then Al Smith looked across to the old place, the three-story walkup where he used to greet his friends and neighbors on the stoop on election night, where he and Robert Moses used to finish their talks when he was out of office but still filled with ideas. There were pictures in every one of the apartment's eight windows, pictures of the most famous tenant who ever lived or who would ever live at 25 Oliver Street, pictures of the Democratic Party's candidate for president of the United States, Alfred E. Smith.[34]

The police closed off Times Square to accommodate the tens of thousands of New Yorkers who gathered in the streets to watch election returns as they were projected on large screens near the *New York Times* building. The square was packed shoulder to shoulder by the time night fell as New Yorkers waited to see if the rest of the country shared their love for Al Smith.

They didn't have to wait long.

Smith and his wife arrived at the Democratic Party's election headquarters in the 71st Regiment Armory on Park Avenue at about nine o'clock. He stuck a cigar in his mouth and never bothered to light it as he joined two men who were waiting for his arrival, Franklin Roosevelt and U.S. senator Robert Wagner.[35]

The returns came in early and often and they had nothing but bad news for Al Smith and alarming news for Franklin Roosevelt, who soon retreated to his campaign headquarters in the Biltmore. The Democrats were losing in the North. They were losing in the border states. They were losing the upper South. They were losing in the Midwest and the far West. They were losing in places where Smith had drawn huge crowds, and they were losing in places where the crowds wore hoods and robes. Most disheartening of all, Smith was behind in New York, and not by a small amount. By tens of thousands, then more than a hundred thousand. If Al Smith could not carry New York, he could not win. And if Al Smith could not carry New York, it seemed highly unlikely that Franklin Roosevelt could survive.

By ten o'clock, men and women began to leave the armory. "Well, the time hasn't come yet when a man can say his beads in the White House," Smith said as it became clear that he was on the wrong end of a landslide. Al and Katie Smith left the armory, quietly, and returned to the Biltmore, where the Roosevelt team was monitoring results from upstate. Roosevelt was ahead, but not by much. Frances Perkins sat with Sara Roosevelt while the Smith men on loan to Roosevelt—Farley and Flynn and Rosenman—joined Louis Howe in poring over the numbers, looking for messages of hope in the figures from Erie County and Syracuse and Albany. They noticed an unexpected bump developing in Republican counties upstate, places that were supporting Hoover but seemed to be supporting Roosevelt as well. Perhaps it was the magic of that Roosevelt name. Or perhaps it was because Franklin Roosevelt's opponent was a Jew.[36]

Perkins watched as Smith tried his best to play the role of gracious loser, mixing with so many of his old friends and allies who were now working and sweating to ensure the election of Franklin Roosevelt. He wasn't fooling anyone—his eyes were glassy and Perkins saw in his expression something she had never seen before. He was no longer the Happy Warrior. "So unlike himself," she later recalled. Eventually, at about midnight, the Smiths retreated to their apartment, where the defeated candidate for president celebrated his wife's birthday.[37]

Franklin Roosevelt left the Biltmore shortly thereafter, convinced that he, too, had lost. The professionals remained in place, still hoping, squinting at pieces of paper and reciting the names of far-off towns and cities and checking columns of figures. Soon, well after midnight, Ed Flynn began calling clerks in upstate counties where votes were being counted very slowly, telling them that if they were up to any funny business, lawyers from New York City would be on their way to help speed up the counting.

Franklin Roosevelt woke up a winner.

He won by twenty-five thousand votes out of more than four million cast. There was some uncertainty for a day or two, talk that Albert Ottinger might contest the result but he eventually conceded. Herbert Lehman, running separately from Roosevelt as the Democratic candidate for lieutenant governor, also won a narrow victory. The Roosevelt team was exhausted but ecstatic, save for one. Asked what she thought of her husband's victory, Eleanor Roosevelt said it meant nothing to her because Al Smith had lost. "If the rest of the ticket didn't get in, what does it matter?" she said.[38]

Al Smith suffered a loss of historic proportions. Herbert Hoover took more than 58 percent of the popular vote and 444 votes in the Electoral

College. Smith won a mere 41 percent of the popular vote and a humble 87 electoral votes. He won eight states, six of them in the South, plus Massachusetts and Rhode Island. And while the numbers stung, nothing hurt more than the rejection of his fellow New Yorkers. He lost his home state by more than a hundred thousand votes after having piled up historic wins in his campaigns for governor.

Historians and political scientists would analyze his defeat in the decades to come, searching for clues about the statement the nation made about itself on November 6, 1928. Was it simply a wish to keep the prosperous status quo? On election eve, the *New York Post* had summed up its support for Herbert Hoover with a single phrase: "Why change?" Hoover was very different from Calvin Coolidge and Warren Harding, but still, he was a Republican and he represented continuity. Why change? Many observers in later years would make the argument that a nervous Louis Howe made at the time: 1928 was no year to be a Democrat.[39]

But 1928 was unlike any other presidential campaign, because one party had chosen a candidate from a religious minority thought to be something other than truly American. Religion may not have been the decisive factor, but it surely brought out hatred and ugliness the likes of which the nation had not seen in some time.

Al Smith never got over it, they said. Frances Perkins, who so many years ago saw him as the eager champion of causes she and other reformers believed in, now saw in his eyes not the mirth of the Happy Warrior but the sadness of a broken man, a lost soul. It was not so much that he lost but how he lost. It was not so much that he lost Virginia or Montana or California. It was that he lost New York. And he was not alone: Around the country, Catholics, especially the Irish, concluded that they had been wrong about their fellow Americans. In the Irish neighborhoods of the northeast, stories were passed down from parent to child, stories of defeat that sounded so much like the sad stories that were told in the old country as the turf smoldered and the sky wept gently, stories of men and women who took down their American flags on November 6, 1928, the day of Al Smith's sacrifice, and never raised them again.[40]

A day after the election, Joseph Tumulty, an Irish Catholic product of Jersey City machine politics who rose to become personal secretary for President Woodrow Wilson, saw a young boy, the son of a friend, carrying in his hands two pictures of Al Smith. The boy told Tumulty that he intended to save the pictures, to keep them in his room. "For memory's sake," he said. Tumulty, a battle-hardened veteran of New Jersey and Washington politics, nearly burst into tears. He channeled his sadness and bitterness in a letter to Smith written that very day: "It seems from what happened yesterday that, as of old, the mob loves to crucify its Redeemer, but those engaged in that unwholesome task failed to realize that there inevitably comes the Day of Resurrection."[41]

Even some Hoover supporters felt that Smith had been treated unjustly, for it was one thing to fail—somebody always did, every four years—but it was another thing to be rebuked so harshly and for reasons that did not reflect well on the character of the electorate. "From the standpoint of courage and character, he did not deserve so humiliating an outcome," wrote the *New York Post* of Smith. "He did not pretend to be anything other than his natural self. . . . [Whatever] the years may bring forth, Alfred E. Smith may always walk amongst us unafraid and unashamed."[42]

It wasn't particularly noted at the time, but Al Smith's fifteen million votes were the most any Democrat had ever won, and nearly as much as Calvin Coolidge collected in winning the 1924 election. The nation's largest cities saw an upsurge of support for the Democrat, signaling the beginning of a new power center for the party in the years to come and a movement away from the South and border states. New America, the America of the twentieth century, turned out for the man who seemed so much like them. There weren't enough of them, not yet anyway, but their day would come.

Somewhere in Al Smith's apartment in the Biltmore on election night was a lovely leather-bound book presented to him from his old friends and neighbors on the Lower East Side. Inside were the names of first-time voters in Smith's old election district who had pledged to support the one-time tenant of 25 Oliver Street. There were hundreds of names: Isador

Goldstein, George Trattollone, Benjamin Weinstock, John Marchese, Carmela Ambrosio, Madeline Perrone, Isadore Schneider, Giuseppe Picciotto, Hans Neilson, Carl van Soosten, Marie G. Hayes, Pasquale Lo Presti, Ida Levine, Evelyn Ricci. On it went, fifty names on a page, thirteen pages, men and women with names that spoke of crossings across the Atlantic in steerage, of neighborhoods where old men and women spoke languages other than English but who would tell you that they were American and proud of it.[43]

For many decades the Democratic Party had been the party of rural America, a party of populists and preachers who saw in the cities a danger to the country they imagined and the culture they cherished. In the South, the party was the means by which Klansmen sought power and influence as they kept African Americans oppressed while countering the growing presence of Catholics and Jews in government. The great cities with their mongrel populations had turned out in large numbers for Al Smith and the Democrats, and it was not just New York and Boston and Chicago but Pittsburgh and Detroit and Cleveland and Milwaukee. Never before had a Democrat captured the combined votes of the nation's twelve largest cities.

One political scientist would later declare that Al Smith's campaign of 1928 may have been a failure but it foreshadowed his party's historic successes from 1932 through the 1960s. But those successes, the coalition that delivered those victories, would be associated with the skills and charisma of the man who succeeded Al Smith as governor of New York: Franklin Delano Roosevelt.[44]

The governor-elect paid a visit to the outgoing governor at the Biltmore two days after the election, as Smith was preparing to head back to Albany for a few days before going on a desperately needed vacation. Roosevelt's visit was more of a courtesy call than anything else, a show of support for the valiant loser from an unexpected winner. "Get a rest now," Roosevelt told Smith as photographers recorded the beginning of the transition from one governor to another. "Well," Smith said, "I may see you in Georgia." Both men would soon be on their way south to recover from their ordeals, but Smith did not, in fact, stop by Warm Springs on his way to or from Florida.[45]

Roosevelt spent late autumn in Warm Springs preparing to be governor. Smith spent his time in Florida preparing to be the invisible governor, anticipating that he would be a power behind the scenes while his successor focused on his health and rehabilitation. He and his friend Herbert Lehman, the lieutenant governor–elect, would run the state during Roosevelt's inevitable absences. Smith asked Belle Moskowitz to work up drafts of an inaugural address and a message to the legislature for Roosevelt to deliver when he returned from Georgia. Frank, he figured, would surely be grateful for the assistance. Smith told his old friend Frances Perkins, who not only stayed on under Roosevelt but was promoted to the post of industrial commissioner, that he would be happy to be on call as a shadow governor. "I could see people for him," he said, referring to Roosevelt. "I could keep track of things and be around all the time."[46]

Smith and his allies soon learned that Franklin Roosevelt considered himself to be more than capable of running Albany by himself. He had campaigned, in essence, as a Smith surrogate, as an extension of the Smith administration, and he quickly signaled that he intended to keep to that vision. Smith appointees like Frances Perkins were welcome in Franklin Roosevelt's Albany. He asked Smith for permission to retain a longtime aide named Robert Fitzmaurice as the top person in the state's executive department, which delighted the outgoing governor to no end. "He has been identified with the government since 1911," Smith told Roosevelt. "He hears more gossip, gets more dope, gets more inside information than any two men around the Capitol." Nearly all of Smith's top aides, in fact, were kept on—nearly all. But Robert Moses was dismissed as secretary of state, a job he had turned into something akin to assistant governor, and Roosevelt could find no good use for the services of Belle Moskowitz. When Smith and Roosevelt returned from their southern jaunts, the outgoing governor pleaded with his successor on behalf of Moses and

Moskowitz, but Smith was blind to the plain political truth that was evident to everyone else. Eleanor Roosevelt told her husband that Moskowitz was very capable, but, she added, "you have to decide, and decide now, whether you or Mrs. Moskowitz is going to be governor of this state." He made the decision, but he simply could not look Al Smith in the eye and tell him that Belle Moskowitz was not wanted in Albany anymore.[47]

As for Moses, Roosevelt had suffered his slights for years, and now was his chance to exact a measure of revenge. He didn't want Moses strutting the corridors of the capitol's second floor as though he were the second-most powerful man in Albany, as he was under Smith, but Roosevelt did allow him to remain as state parks commissioner. When Roosevelt finally summoned the courage to tell Smith that Moses would no longer be secretary of state, he explained, simply, "He rubs me the wrong way." In place of Moses, Roosevelt chose Ed Flynn, who got his start in politics under Tammany boss Charles Francis Murphy. If there is indeed a heavenly afterlife and if Murphy managed to gain entrance—he was a man with connections, after all—he surely found the whole business amusing. Franklin Roosevelt turning to the protégé of a man he once called a "noxious weed"—how in the world did that happen?[48]

Roosevelt was sworn into office on January 1, 1929, in a ceremony arranged by the man he had fired, Robert Moses. The *New York Times* noted that special accommodations had to be made in the assembly chamber because the "crippled condition of the new governor made it impossible for him to proceed to his place." He was wheeled up a ramp to the rostrum and then he performed his well-rehearsed walk, with the support of a cane and his son James, to his place at the podium.[49]

Roosevelt graciously turned his inauguration into a salute to the passing of an era, to the end of Al Smith's long tenure as governor. Smith stood to Roosevelt's left and delivered an impromptu farewell address. "I am turning the government over to you, not perfect—no human instrumentality achieves perfection—but as good as it can be made," Smith told Roosevelt and their audience. "Frank, I congratulate you. I hope you will be able to devote that intelligent mind of yours to the problems of this state." He then acknowledged Roosevelt's mother, seated in the front row. "It is a great day for her," he said. "I remember my mother. My mother was on the platform with me for two inaugurations." Sara Roosevelt, no softie, teared up as Smith spoke of his mother, who died a few weeks before the 1924 Democratic convention in New York. Sara Roosevelt was not particularly fond of the company her son kept now that he was a professional politician, but Al Smith, coarse though he was, at least had charm.

And with that, Smith turned over the ceremony to Franklin Roosevelt, who acknowledged him as "Governor Smith," and then, with a smile, said, "I mean, Al."

"This day," Roosevelt said, "is notable not so much for the inauguration of a new governor as that it marks the close of the term of a governor who has been our chief executive for eight long years." No governor in New York's history, he said, had achieved more and was more "attuned to the needs and hopes of the men, the women and the children" of New York.[50]

While Roosevelt presided over an inaugural parade, Smith quietly disappeared and made his way over to Eagle Street for a final farewell to the staff at the executive mansion, and then, escorted by the new governor's son, James, Al and Katie Smith were driven to a waiting train at Albany's Union Station. They arrived in Grand Central Terminal in Manhattan a few hours later to find members of the 69th Regiment's band on hand to welcome them. They struck up "The Sidewalks of New York," because it was, after all, mandatory. Then they played "Auld Lang Syne," and people noticed that the former governor's eyes were moist and red.

He waited for the inevitable call from his successor asking for advice and guidance. As he told the story, those calls and letters never came, but in fact they did. Roosevelt dropped him a note several weeks after the inauguration, asking him to stop by to see him in Albany. "There are many things I would like to talk to you about," the new governor told the old governor. He asked for Smith's advice on appointments to a transit commission not long after the election, and in the months that followed he sent Smith several notes seeking his guidance and sharing some political intelligence with him. He kept Smith posted about political maneuvering at the Port Authority, the transportation agency that was a special cause of the former governor. When Smith asked him to hold off on making an appointment to the state Bridge and Tunnel Commission, Roosevelt wrote that he wouldn't "do a thing" until they discussed it. "I do wish that we could have a good long talk and perhaps around October 20th you and your Missus would come up here and spend a Sunday at Hyde Park," he wrote Smith in September. He couldn't resist teasing his predecessor after having seen a picture of the Smiths' new, temporary home on lower Fifth Avenue near Washington Square Park. It looked as though it had no roof, Roosevelt wrote. "Is this the idea of getting closer contact with heaven or are you trying to get back to nature?" It seems as though Smith did not avail himself of Roosevelt's invitations, or if he did, they led to little more than small talk.[51]

Roosevelt's gestures seemed warm and deferential, but Smith was not only dissatisfied, he managed to convince himself that they were a mere courtesy from a man who hid his ruthlessness behind a façade of private-school manners. "Do you know, by God, that he has never consulted me about a damn thing since he has been governor," Smith blurted out to a friend. "He has ignored me."[52]

Roosevelt was aware of how Smith felt but decided there was only so much he could do. He had promised to honor Smith's legacy and build on Smith's achievements with some of Smith's own people. But the squire of Hyde Park understood what the Fulton Fish Market man seemed incapable of acknowledging: he was in power now and Al Smith was not, and that, as any protégé of Charlie Murphy ought to know, changed everything.

"I've got to be governor of the state of New York and I have got to be it myself," Roosevelt told Frances Perkins. "I'm awfully sorry if it hurts anybody, particularly Al."[53]

It did. Oh, how it did.

sixteen

FRANK OR AL

THEY ROSE TOGETHER, the two of them, to see the city as few had ever seen it before. Al Smith and Franklin Roosevelt were side by side on the observation deck of the tallest building in the world, posing for photographs and marveling at the views, on the afternoon of May 1, 1931, the day the Empire State Building opened for business with Al Smith as its president, public face, and resident cheerleader.

Smith, dressed in a dark suit and dark bow tie, raised his right hand and pointed out distant landmarks as Roosevelt, his leg braces snapped tight and his double-breasted jacket buttoned up against the wind, stood erect while holding onto a waist-high wall with his left hand. He said that from eighty-six stories in the air, the Hudson River looked like a simple creek in Dutchess County and Central Park seemed no more impressive than a simple cow pasture in Hyde Park.[1]

But there were people living in the park, living in shacks and tents because they had been forced from their homes when jobs disappeared and there was no help to be had. Not even Al Smith's New York, with the safety net he built during his years in Albany, could keep people in their homes and off breadlines in the spring of 1931, eighteen months after the stock market crash that led to a catastrophic economic depression.

Smith and Roosevelt lingered on the deck for several minutes, smiling for newsreel cameras and dashing off lighthearted commentary. "When I came up in the elevator, I went so high that I expected to be above snow level," Roosevelt said. When a reporter prefaced a question with the word, "Governor," Smith quickly interjected: "Which one?"[2]

Roosevelt, speaking to a crowd of about 350 gathered in a lounge area on the eighty-sixth floor, was careful to credit Smith for the building's speedy construction and for making good on a vow to open the building as scheduled. Work on the massive building had begun on Saint Patrick's Day, March 17, 1930, in honor of Al Smith's heritage. It was now complete, all 102 stories, on May 1, 1931.

"All I am going to ask him to do is to reserve for me an office in this building so that when I leave Albany I will have some place to go," Roosevelt said in that avuncular tone of his. Smith was quick on the uptake, a salesman now. "About that office," he said, "the next day you are in town, I will have you down in the rental department."[3]

They were in good form and they seemed for all the world to be enjoying each other's company. One measure of the genuine bond that had formed between them was evident in a letter Roosevelt sent to Smith in early 1930, when Al Smith's granddaughter, Mary Warner, the child of Smith's daughter Emily and her husband John Warner, spent the afternoon at the executive mansion with one of Roosevelt's granddaughters. John Warner was the superintendent of the state police, which likely explained his little daughter's friendship with the governor's granddaughter. "A few weeks ago," Roosevelt wrote Smith, "when my granddaughter was here, your granddaughter came to the house to spend the afternoon and five minutes after I had joined the party, Mary was calling me 'Ganpa.' I felt highly honored and have certainly cut you out." Smith replied by saying that as soon as he returned to Albany, he'd be sure to take the child away from Roosevelt so that she could be with her rightful grandfather.[4]

These were the words and sentiments of men who surely were more than allies of convenience, for there were too many connections, too many shared friendships and enemies, too many important partnerships to dismiss their relationship as merely a function of power and ambition. Smith volunteered to deliver Roosevelt's renomination speech in 1930 and did so in a manner that suited the nickname Roosevelt so reluctantly gave him in 1924. He was a happy warrior indeed, and with good reason: the state Democratic convention that year not only renominated Roosevelt but, to Smith's delight, adopted a plank in its platform calling for an immediate end to the noxious experiment known as Prohibition. That was an Al Smith plank—his people had demanded it, twisted arms for it, and no doubt made a threat or two in order to get it passed. Roosevelt reluctantly agreed.

In his nomination speech for Roosevelt, Smith reveled in the party's unequivocal position on drink, mocking Republicans for trying to have it both ways on Prohibition. "Wet when you are among the wets," he said of the GOP's position, "and when among the drys . . ." He didn't finish the sentence, but assumed the pose of a man at prayer, his head down, his hands joined together with fingers pointed skyward. The audience loved it and loved him. That made his testimonial to Roosevelt all the more powerful. "In all my experience no man has accomplished more in the office he occupied than has Franklin Roosevelt. He has a clear brain and a big heart."[5]

A month later, Roosevelt won reelection by the largest margin in state history, some seven hundred thousand votes, far larger than Smith's own landslide victory in 1922. A day later, Roosevelt's campaign manager, James Farley, told the press, "I do not see how Mr. Roosevelt can escape becoming the next presidential nominee of this party, even if no one should raise a finger to bring it about."[6]

Roosevelt's rise to national prominence, his success as governor, and the talk of Roosevelt campaigning for president in 1932 aroused no small amount of resentment among Smith's old friends. The two spurned staffers, Belle Moskowitz and Robert Moses, continued to make their low opinion of Roosevelt known—Moskowitz referred to Roosevelt as *"your governor"* in conversations with her friend Frances Perkins, while Moses, who also was friendly with Perkins, did little to hide his contempt for the lightweight usurper installed on the capitol's second floor. But none of this should have mattered to Al Smith, for he had announced on that shattering night in 1928 that he was through with politics, although he later amended his remarks to say that he would never be through with politics, just political office. His new job as head of the Empire State Building's management company paid $50,000 a year, and by 1931 he needed every penny of it. True, his family was in no danger of becoming squatters in Central Park—as a matter of fact, Al and Katie had moved to a swanky apartment on 820 Fifth Avenue directly across from the park. But he had lost tens of thousands of dollars, perhaps much more, when the stock market crashed. His sons had borrowed money from a bank owned by his old and dear friend, James Riordan, and they used the funds to play the stock market. When the market collapsed, Smith's sons lost nearly everything they had. The bank was ruined, and so was Riordan, the trucking executive who had found a job for Smith when he lost his reelection bid as governor in 1920. One afternoon in early November, James Riordan sat down in a chair in his apartment and blew out his brains with a .38-caliber revolver. Smith was in tears at the funeral of his friend.

Another friend, John Raskob, the DuPont executive whom Smith chose to head the Democratic National Committee, was the man and the money behind the Empire State Building, the man who hired him to be the building's president. He came up with the plan to redefine New York's skyline when the twenties still were roaring and saw no reason to change his plans or temper his ambitions when Wall Street collapsed. Hard times didn't slow construction, but they brought the need for new office space to a grinding halt. The Empire State Building was little more than an empty shell. On the day Smith and Roosevelt enjoyed the view from the eighty-sixth floor, there was nothing below them—nothing, that is, in terms of tenants. Seventy-five percent of the space was vacant and there was no sign, not in May 1931, that prosperity was right around the corner. Much of Smith's time at the building was spent showing celebrities the view from the observation deck in hopes of drawing attention to the enterprise and perhaps enticing tenants. Winston Churchill paid a visit and received the full treatment from Smith, who pointed out that they could see Sandy Hook if they looked south. Churchill was content to admit that he had never stood so high above the earth. "Highest for me, too," Smith said. It was all good publicity for what seemed like a very bad investment.[7]

For Franklin Roosevelt, the Depression posed a very different kind of challenge. He had campaigned and won in 1928 on the promise that he would continue Al Smith's work on expanding and modernizing government's role as a mediator and regulator. Early in his first term, he directly challenged private utilities, as Smith had done, on the development of hydropower. But the general plan for a fifth Al Smith term, this one presided over by Franklin Roosevelt, was tossed aside in the aftermath of the stock market crash. The state's jobless demanded action, and action now.

It began with Roosevelt's industrial commissioner, Frances Perkins, in early 1930. Without consulting her boss, Perkins publicly challenged President Herbert Hoover over national employment figures. The White House said employment was gaining after weeks of losses following October's stock market crash. Perkins and her staff produced figures that showed that the very opposite was true: things were getting worse. Her challenge to the president of the United States became national news, not least of all because she was a woman. Roosevelt learned of his commissioner's temerity in the newspapers. He called Perkins and said he was glad she spoke up.

That conversation with Perkins seemed to awaken Roosevelt to the extent of a catastrophe he had originally dismissed as "a little flurry down town." In March 1930 he appointed a commission to devise a solution to the state's growing unemployment crisis, the first governor in the nation to sound the alarm over the frightening disappearance of jobs as the unemployment rate rose from about 3 percent in 1929 to about 15 percent in 1931. In Washington, the Senate's commerce committee was beginning to hold hearings on a controversial bill to provide some measure of relief for the unemployed. Its sponsor was Al Smith's old roommate in Albany, Senator Robert Wagner of New York.[8]

Roosevelt journeyed to a conference of governors in Salt Lake City in late June to deliver a speech Perkins had prepared for him, suggesting that the time had come for the nation to offer insurance against unemployment just as so many states now offered insurance against injuries in the workplace. "Careful planning, shorter hours, more complete facts, public works and a dozen other palliatives will in the future reduce unemployment, but all of these will not eliminate unemployment," he said. "Some form of insurance seems to be the only answer." His fellow governors, Democrats and Republicans alike, gave him a rousing, loud ovation. He insisted that the display embarrassed him. "I felt like crawling under my desk," he said afterward.[9]

The Salt Lake City speech established him as the voice of the nation's governors as they all sought to find some local solution to the national problem of mass unemployment. The press reported that he was beginning to receive "more than casual mention as a Presidential possibility," and his smashing reelection a few months later added a level of seriousness to those more than casual mentions. Roosevelt summoned his new political adviser, Ed Flynn, to an intimate dinner at the executive mansion in Albany in late 1930 with longtime loyalist Louis Howe. The three men chatted amiably through the meal and then afterward retired to the library for the inevitable post-dinner cigarettes, when Roosevelt revealed why he wished to speak with Flynn that night. "Eddie," he said, "I believe I can be nominated for the Presidency in 1932 on the Democratic ticket."[10]

Preparations were set in motion. Roosevelt soon dispatched his campaign manager, the gregarious James Farley, around the country to speak with other Democrats under the pretext of carrying out his role as an exalted ruler of the Elks Club. Flynn and Howe, comfortable with each other but few others, began the chore of quietly contacting wealthy donors, including a Boston businessman named Joseph P. Kennedy.

The first test of Roosevelt's organizing strength came in early 1931, weeks before the Empire State Building's opening, when the building's owner, Raskob, chairman of the Democratic National Committee, abruptly announced a special meeting of the committee to consider the party's strategy in the run-up to the presidential election of 1932. More specifically,

Raskob wanted the committee to commit to repealing Prohibition, the very commitment New York Democrats made in 1930.

Roosevelt and his advisers were beside themselves. Raskob, they thought, was out of his mind. Why return to the debacles of the past when the country was sliding ever deeper into the Depression and Herbert Hoover was becoming one of the most unpopular presidents in American history?

The press saw the coming battle over liquor as a test between two old friends who had dominated the nation's most important state for more than a decade, one of whom was the nation's most prominent wet, the other of whom was, like a damp towel left on a sunny beach, dry enough. Roosevelt tried reaching Smith by telephone to talk about Raskob's proposal but never made the connection. Clearly frustrated, he wrote a note to Smith to say that he was "very disturbed" about the plan and that it would be contrary to party policy for the national committee to adopt policies between conventions. Roosevelt had a well-deserved reputation for evasion in dealing with unpleasant topics among friends and allies, but he could not have been clearer in his letter to Smith: this Raskob proposal, he said, was a bad idea.[11]

For Smith's supporters, however, the hypocrisy of Prohibition was simply intolerable, for it was not just about drink. It was about culture. It was about religion. It was about cities. It was about New America. And, to be sure, it was about Al Smith and all that he represented. For his allies and friends, Al Smith was more than simply another in the long list of failed Democratic presidential candidates since the Civil War. Al Smith was a symbol of the ambitions and hopes of those who saw something of themselves in him. John Raskob was among them, and he still had hopes that Smith might yet try again the prize so cruelly denied him in 1928. As chairman of the Democratic National Committee, Raskob was not without resources if his friend chose to make a go of it in 1932. Belle Moskowitz, one of several Smith allies (Roosevelt among them) appointed to the party's executive committee in 1928, seemed certain that her hero would run again. The party, she told Frances Perkins, owed Smith another try after he was treated so poorly in '28. Raskob's summons to the Democratic National Committee was an early test to see how many Democrats felt as Belle Moskowitz did.[12]

The battle between the two New York governors took the form of phone calls and letters and personal appeals, and there was nobody in the country better at these tactics than James Farley. He built alliances with southern Democrats who shared Roosevelt's horror that any Democrat, never mind the chairman of the Democratic National Committee, would be so foolish to start talking about booze when people were living in shacks. Raskob met privately with a Roosevelt ally, Virginia governor Harry Byrd, the night before the highly anticipated committee meeting and was presented with the result of Farley's politicking: Raskob's wet resolution, Byrd told him, was doomed to failure on the floor. It was an astonishing defeat for the party's chairman and for Smith, the party's most prominent wet. And it was a masterful victory for Roosevelt and his growing number of allies.

Raskob chose discretion over valor, announcing that he would not put his repeal proposal to a vote that he was destined to lose. But he did insist on a full, public discussion of the party's position on drink. Raskob gave a fiery speech about the evils of Prohibition, which led Al Smith's running mate in 1928, Senator Joseph Robinson of Arkansas, to argue with equal passion on behalf of the dry and the moist. Liquor would kill the party's chances in 1932. Leave it alone, he said.

Smith himself then addressed the group on behalf of Raskob. He was received respectfully, but in the end, it didn't matter. The party was in no mood to take on the darned old liquor question, not when victory in 1932 seemed within its grasp. Al Smith was out of step with the party's consensus.[13]

But after the committee officially adjourned and delegates began milling about, hundreds formed a line to shake hands with Al Smith. He kept smiling, saying nothing, when some of the delegates said they hoped he would run again for president. Roosevelt's people were careful to take note of this spontaneous display of affection for the Happy Warrior and soon began telling reporters that they believed Al Smith would run for president in 1932.

Not long thereafter, Frances Perkins noticed that whenever Roosevelt's speechwriter Sam Rosenman submitted drafts containing a favorable reference to Smith, the references were edited out of the final copy. She suspected the heavy hand of Louis Howe.[14]

And if Frances Perkins noticed Al Smith's absence from Franklin Roosevelt's speeches, surely Smith did as well.

In the eight years that Al Smith served as governor of New York, he compiled a long list of achievements, from social welfare legislation to administrative reform to the construction of great public parks. Reforestation, that is, the replanting of trees throughout the state, was not on the list. Reforestation sounded like one of those boring upstate issues people like Franklin Roosevelt were always trying to bring to his attention.

But in the fall of 1931, Al Smith suddenly became intensely interested in reforestation, and that was because Franklin Roosevelt had proposed and supported an amendment to the state constitution committing $19 million in state funds over eleven years to replant trees in rural areas outside of the state's two great mountain preserves, the Catskills and the Adirondacks. The proposal, which required approval from voters, was near and dear to the governor's heart, for he had learned from his father the story of seemingly every tree that canopied the fields of Springwood, and in later life he delighted in describing his occupation as "tree farmer" on official documents. He likely could not imagine how or why anybody would oppose the use of state funding to grow more trees—even the state's Republican Party supported his idea. But in mid-October, an angry and offended Al Smith announced that while he had nothing against trees, he didn't care for the way Franklin Roosevelt proposed to go about paying for their replenishment. Policy had no place in the state's constitution, its basic set of laws, he said. If the governor decided that replanting trees was a priority, he ought to ask the legislature for an appropriation to pay for the cost.

Smith delivered a fiery denunciation of Roosevelt's proposal in a radio address from the stage of Carnegie Hall. His opposition—the vehemence of it, and the obscurity of the argument—caught Roosevelt by surprise, suggesting that Smith, who placed such a priority on communication from his successor, never gave the governor advance warning of his position. Several days later, the mayor of Chicago, Anton Cermak, an immigrant from Central Europe and onetime coal miner, paid a visit to New York and declared that the Democratic Party's next presidential nominee ought to be "a man of the 'Al Smith' type." He was quick to add that he did not necessarily mean Smith himself. No, not at all, he said. What he meant is that he wanted somebody who would promise to get rid of Prohibition once and for all. Which meant that by an "Al Smith type" he was definitely not referring to Franklin Delano Roosevelt.[15]

Smith's speech and the mounting speculation about presidential politics put Roosevelt on the defensive. The *New York Times* reported that Smith's opposition to the reforestation measure "has been resented by Governor Roosevelt's friends who believe that it has shown definitely that Mr. Smith intends to do everything he can to prevent Governor Roosevelt from obtaining the Presidential nomination." The governor delivered a radio address of his own in Poughkeepsie just before voters went to the polls to decide on the amendment. He made no mention of Smith's criticisms but it was evident that they had gotten under his skin. Anyone, he said, "who knows anything about the growing of trees . . . understands why continuing appropriations are necessary." His argument carried the day: voters approved the reforestation amendment with ease and the press recorded another victory for Franklin Roosevelt over Al Smith, although nobody was quite sure precisely what the conflict was all about.[16]

He was a gracious winner.

A few days after the reforestation vote, Roosevelt dropped a note to Smith asking him to come to lunch at the townhouse on East 65th Street to talk over the state budget. Smith agreed, although the invitation seemed to do little to change his view that Roosevelt was ignoring him. And while there were few people in the state who knew more about the budget than Smith, he and Roosevelt had a good deal more to discuss beyond figures and estimates.[17]

Reporters were on hand when Smith showed up at lunchtime on November 18 wearing his trademark brown derby. "I'm here to eat," Smith told them as he crossed the threshold. Smith greeted Roosevelt as "governor." Roosevelt greeted him as "Al." And then the doors were shut.[18]

They spoke for two hours, after which they separately told reporters that they had discussed state finances. Roosevelt said this with a slight smile. Smith said it through clenched teeth. Nobody particularly believed it. But some days later Smith told one of Roosevelt's friends what had not been discussed: the governor's presidential ambitions, about which there was no mystery.

"By God," Smith said, "he invited me to his house . . . and did not mention to me the subject of his candidacy."[19]

Soon the emissaries began to arrive at the Empire State Building. Ed Flynn had already cast his lot with Roosevelt, but like so many New York Democrats, particularly the Irish, he still loved Al Smith for all that he was and all that he stood for. When Flynn told Roosevelt that somebody ought to sit down with Smith and speak candidly about the coming presidential race, Roosevelt said he had just the man for the assignment: Flynn himself.

And so he made his way to Smith's office to ask if Smith planned to challenge Roosevelt. They were speaking as friends, personal friends, he said.

Smith opened a desk drawer. He took out stacks of documents, spreading them across his desk. They were official documents, financial documents. "Ed," Smith said, "these are all the debts I must clear up. Financially, I am in an extremely bad position." The debts were not just his, but those of his sons as well.[20]

Flynn took that as a no. Not long thereafter, Roosevelt's lieutenant governor, Herbert Lehman, made the same call with the same purpose.

Lehman owed as much to Smith as Flynn did, for he had entered politics in the mid-1920s because of Smith, and it was Smith who, at the height of his power in 1928, insisted that the party nominate Lehman for lieutenant governor. But now Lehman had little choice but to support his boss. He, too, left his meeting with Smith convinced that the former governor was done with running for office.

Those reassurances did nothing to tamp down speculation in the press that he might be up to something. Democrats in the Dakotas and in the territory of Alaska were beginning to sort out their presidential endorsements in mid-January. Roosevelt was the clear preference, but Smith's absence, his silence, won almost as many headlines as Roosevelt did with these early signs of support far from his presumed base in the northeast. As the press watched and waited, an anonymous political writer at *Collier's* magazine, an influential weekly, reported that Roosevelt had said some rather unkind things about his predecessor. "Smith was a rotten governor," Roosevelt supposedly said, according to the report. Roosevelt issued a furious denial, saying that "any man who circulates a story of that kind is not only a liar, but is a contemptible liar."[21]

The governor announced shortly thereafter that he had invited Smith to Albany and was expecting him in a week or so.

Smith's office released a statement saying that the former governor had no plans to visit Albany any time soon. The *New York Times* reported that "most of the political prophets" in New York "did not know what to make of the situation."[22]

Roosevelt made the inevitable reality in late January 1932 when he sent a letter to the Democratic state committee in North Dakota accepting the committee's endorsement for president and giving his permission for his name to appear on the state's primary ballot. It was Roosevelt's first formal acknowledgment that he was a candidate for president, but the press considered it to be no more newsworthy than an announcement that the sun was due to rise in the east the following morning. Roosevelt's announcement, wrote the *New York Times*, "long ceased to be an unknown quantity in our political algebra."[23]

Several weeks later, something unexpected and jarring took place: Al Smith summoned reporters to his office in the Empire State Building on a Saturday afternoon, February 7, took his place in a green leather armchair, and grabbed a pile of papers. There was mischief in his voice when he reminded his guests that he had been saying for some time that if he had anything to say about the presidential campaign, well, he would say it to them first. "Well, here it is, boys," he said, gesturing to the papers in his hand. They were mimeographed copies of a short statement in his words: "If the Democratic National Convention, after careful consideration, should decide it wants me to lead I will make the fight."[24]

He would not campaign for the nomination, he said. But if the convention wanted him, well, he was available.

His announcement was a stunning development, treated as front-page news across the nation, never mind that the Roosevelt people had been whispering about Al Smith's ambitions for months now. Editorial comment from Boston to Los Angeles framed the coming battle as a contest between friends, between mentor and protégé, between, in the *Baltimore Sun's* words, "hero and eulogist." One thing seemed certain, at least in the view of editorial writers: the Democratic Party was about to be split open, again.[25]

The following day, Roosevelt and Smith were together in lower Manhattan at the funeral of the ceremonial head of Tammany Hall, John Voorhis, who had been taken abruptly from his earthly existence at the tender age of 102. The governors shook hands after the service.

"Come on up to the house with me," Roosevelt said. Smith agreed, and the two men rode together to the Roosevelt townhouse on East 65th Street. Smith watched as Roosevelt was carried out of the car and wheeled into his home, and then the two of them spoke for nearly an hour.

Smith returned to the Empire State Building later in the afternoon, still dressed in black mourning clothes and a black top hat, a cigar tucked into the side of his mouth. Reporters who saw him leave the funeral with Roosevelt were waiting. He showed them telegrams of congratulations he received after his dramatic announcement a day earlier. Was there one from Governor Roosevelt, a reporter asked.

Not yet, Smith said, but there were so many more to read.

What did he and Roosevelt talk about?

It was all social, Smith said. Reporters noted that Smith seemed to be enjoying this.

Another reporter called Roosevelt's people to ask for the governor's version of the meeting with Smith. The reporter noted that Smith said that no politics had been discussed, that the visit was simply social.

"Then it was social," Roosevelt's man said. "Whatever Smith says on the subject goes."[26]

It was time to choose sides—Frank or Al—and while for most the decision was obvious, it did not make it any less painful, for everybody loved Al, even those who had thrown in their lot with Roosevelt and those who concluded that the country was not ready for a Catholic president, an overly urban president, a wet president. They felt badly for Al, but 1932 was not a time for sentiment: the Democratic Party had produced two winning candidates since the Civil War—*two, in seventy years!*—but the Depression and Herbert Hoover's ineffective response to it meant that the party had a chance not simply to win but to win without sweating over late returns. The party, so many believed, could not take another chance on Al Smith.

They had all been on the same team once, but now people like Ed Flynn and James Farley and Frances Perkins and Sam Rosenman were with Roosevelt while Smith held onto his nearest and dearest, Belle Moskowitz, Robert Moses, Joseph Proskauer, Jimmy Walker. Others sought to negotiate a middle ground where they could somehow please both governors. Senator Robert Wagner tried mightily to stay above the battle, a job made easier when he chose not to be a delegate to the national convention. James Hoey, an insurance executive and member of the Democratic National Committee, was a Smith man, always had been, but through Smith and politics he had become friendly with Roosevelt as well. Hoey was publicly pledged to Smith, but by early 1932 he found himself in touch with another old friend, Roosevelt's campaign manager, Farley. "I am doing everything I can in my own way to help the cause in which you are interested," Hoey told Farley after explaining that he would continue to publicly support Smith. Soon he was passing along intelligence about delegate counts to the Roosevelt campaign.[27]

With Al Smith in the race, the seemingly inevitable Roosevelt campaign would now have to compete for the love and affection of fellow New Yorkers, particularly those in the powerful Tammany Hall machine. Tammany had reverted to its bad old days of conspicuous corruption under its favorite son, Mayor Jimmy Walker, but Roosevelt had chosen not to notice, at least not until he was shamed into opening an investigation of city government at the insistence of the high-minded reformers who used to think of the governor as one of their own. As his presidential campaign was beginning in earnest, Roosevelt was feeling the heat from the stalwart prosecutor of all that was evil and bad about politics, the indefatigable Samuel Seabury, the only man to cast a vote against Al Smith's gubernatorial nomination at the Democratic state convention in 1918. Seabury, acting as counsel to a legislative commission investigating corruption in Jimmy Walker's New York, delivered a fiery speech broadcast around the country in early 1932 all but calling Roosevelt a political coward for trying to appease Tammany rather than joining him to eradicate it from the face of the earth. "Tammany's power," Seabury pronounced, "drives public men, whose instincts would lead them to speak out in protest against corruption that has been revealed, to a sullen silence. They know the conditions are evil, but they fear to antagonize the power of Tammany Hall." The press saw Seabury's speech as an attack on Roosevelt and as the opening statement in an unannounced Seabury presidential campaign.[28]

Roosevelt kept his counsel. If he went after Walker, he went after the heart of Tammany, and if he lost Tammany, he could lose New York to Smith. The pressure of it all got to him, and he lashed out not at Walker and not at Tammany but at two of the city's most distinguished citizens, Rabbi Stephen Wise and the Rev. John Haynes Holmes, who visited his home on Saint Patrick's Day, 1932, to demand further action against an array of corrupt officials. Roosevelt released a statement assailing them for "rushing into print early and often with extravagant and ill-considered language." The two of them, Roosevelt wrote, should spend less time telling the governor what to do and more time educating their flock so they might choose better public officials. The tirade shocked Roosevelt's supporters.[29]

Several days later, Roosevelt delivered a national radio address from Albany in which he condemned the Hoover administration for neglecting what he called "the forgotten man at the bottom of the economic pyramid." It was just a single line, a clause, in a longer speech about tariff policy, farm prices, and relief for homeowners. But to some listeners, Roosevelt's invocation of the "forgotten man" had about it more than just a whiff of Bolshevism. The *New York Times* complained that the speech, "coming as it did from a man of intellect and experience in large affairs, was of a sort to make his friends sorry and the judicious grieve."[30]

And it was enough to make Al Smith, who gleefully identified himself as a child of the city's streets, incandescent with rage. Once upon a time, when a wealthy landowner from Long Island complained that Robert Moses's parks would attract the rabble from the city, Smith interrupted the man and said, "Rabble? That's *me* you're talking about." But now it was Franklin Roosevelt of the Hudson Valley Roosevelts who was talking about the plight of the forgotten man. As if he knew.[31]

Smith held his tongue for a day while he and Roosevelt were together again, this time at the Hotel Astor to raise funds for Catholic Charities. They were seated in places of honor, separated only by their host, Cardinal Patrick Hayes, and in a moment captured in a news photograph, Roosevelt chatted amiably with the cardinal, seated to his left, while Smith looked out into the distance. When it was time to speak, Roosevelt heaped praise on "my old friend Al" and Smith tried his level best to respond in kind, recalling how confident he had been four years earlier that Roosevelt would continue the good work he had started. He then went on to talk about the awful plight of so many New Yorkers who were out of work, out of their homes, and perhaps out of hope. But unlike Franklin Roosevelt, Smith did not describe them as forgotten.[32]

Less than a week later, Smith and many other leading Democrats—but not Franklin Roosevelt—gathered in Washington to celebrate the birth of Thomas Jefferson, an annual event in honor of the party's founder. Smith was one of the event's featured speakers, and the press and other Democrats piled into the Willard Hotel ballroom to hear what Franklin Roosevelt's old friend Al would have to say.

He gave them more, far more, than they expected. Yes, he talked about the hypocrisies and evasions of Prohibition, and that surprised nobody. He said the country might have to cancel the debts it accumulated during the world war, and that was mildly radical. But then he turned his attention to people, or a person, he did not name. "I will take off my coat and fight to the end against any candidate who persists in any demagogic appeal to the masses of the working people of this country to destroy themselves by setting class against class and rich against poor," he said, spitting out the words as the eyes of two thousand Democrats widened.[33]

The speech was a sensation in every possible sense of the word because everyone knew he was talking about Franklin Roosevelt. "There is no question that the two are now fighting in the middle of the ring," wrote the *Boston Globe*. The *Milwaukee Journal* said that Smith had put himself at the head of "big business opposition" to Roosevelt, which was certainly the first time that Al Smith had ever been accused of serving as the voice of big business. The *Kansas City Star* decided that Smith was a man of "courage and sincerity," while Roosevelt's speech was "unworthy" of him.[34]

A man named James Francis Burke announced that he was simply delighted with Smith. "It was a fine speech," Burke said. "It will have a fine effect." Burke was the counsel to the Republican National Committee.[35]

Smith's words and his tone and most of all his anger meant that

Franklin Roosevelt would certainly not have an easy path toward the nomination so many considered inevitable. Roosevelt's old friend and Woodrow Wilson's onetime adviser, Edward House, now a grand old man of the Democratic Party, offered Roosevelt some unrequested advice: "[You] should take no notice of Smith's statement."[36]

Roosevelt took House's advice. Not that it mattered—Al Smith believed Franklin Roosevelt hadn't taken notice of him for years.

Whether Smith liked it or not, Roosevelt's invocation of the forgotten man resonated with the party's rank and file. Victories in state conventions and the all-important New Hampshire primary allowed Roosevelt to pile up the delegate count while Smith found himself dispatching letters to supporters assuring them that he was indeed a serious candidate even though he had pledged that he would not campaign for the nomination. Some of Roosevelt's supporters wondered what kind of game Smith was playing, indeed, why he was playing it at all. Felix Frankfurter, a future Supreme Court justice, put the question to Smith's most ardent supporter, Belle Moskowitz, and in her reply she refused to even speak the name of Frankfurter's preferred candidate. "Many of us feel that the party needs a well-equipped candidate, able to lead, courageous and willing to take responsibility," she said, adding that "the candidate . . . who is leading the field" didn't fit the job description.[37]

Democrats in Massachusetts concurred with Moskowitz's assessment. Smith won the commonwealth's primary with a stunning 75 percent of the vote, a shocking outcome that added to growing restlessness within the party. When FDR barely won Pennsylvania and suffered another humiliation in Rhode Island's state convention—all of this without Smith publicly soliciting votes—the old Smith people in Roosevelt's campaign may have begun to wonder about the choice they had made.

A bold James Farley had predicted months earlier that Roosevelt would win a first-ballot victory. Nobody believed that, not anymore. Talk began to focus on the non–New Yorkers in the field, particularly on John

Garner of Texas, winner of the California primary, the chosen candidate of William Randolph Hearst and of the man Smith thwarted in 1924, William Gibbs McAdoo, who saw the battle between his onetime colleague Roosevelt and his onetime rival Smith as benefitting only Herbert Hoover. "The Smith and Roosevelt contest is bound to have the most-hurtful reactions," McAdoo wrote.[38]

In early June, with the convention just three weeks away, a time bomb landed in Roosevelt's lap in the form of a letter from prosecutor Samuel Seabury, summarizing the case for removing New York mayor Jimmy Walker from office on grounds of corruption. Seabury said he was acting simply as a private citizen whose only interest was in achieving better government for the city of New York. Roosevelt and others, including his adviser Ed Flynn, suspected Seabury was intent on winning the Democratic Party's presidential nomination himself as a compromise candidate, and when delegates began receiving a worshipful biography of Seabury in their mailboxes, this suspicion seemed to be confirmed.

Charming Jimmy Walker, the life of a party that had become a distant memory, quickly became a test of a would-be president's principles, a symbol of the discredited excesses of the Roaring Twenties. One prominent Manhattan attorney had a particular interest in this business—Walker's personal lawyer, Basil O'Connor, former law partner and current close friend of Franklin D. Roosevelt.

Reformers, influential journalists like Walter Lippmann, and even members of Roosevelt's unofficial family, especially Eleanor's friend Marion Dickerman, believed FDR had no choice: he had to remove Walker. But Roosevelt vacillated. He told journalist and historian Claude Bowers, "Never has a governor been asked to remove an elective officer on such evidence." Publicly, he announced that he was carefully studying the issue. He continued to carefully study it for two weeks before forwarding Seabury's letter and list of charges to Walker himself, telling the mayor that he would await his reply.[39]

By then, Democrats were boarding trains bound for Chicago to choose a candidate for president. Would it be Frank or Al? Or perhaps neither?

Al and Katie Smith took the Twentieth Century Limited from Grand Central Terminal in Manhattan to Chicago's LaSalle Street Station, with a stop in Albany to rally his troops almost within earshot of the executive mansion on Eagle Street, where Roosevelt would monitor the convention by radio and phone, playing the traditional role of the frontrunner. The captain of the railroad's police force introduced Smith to about eight hundred supporters, presenting the candidate with a clock symbolizing Smith's role as "the man of the hour." Smith promised the crowd that win or lose, he would return to Manhattan via Albany and have another chat with them.[40]

Chicago was baking in an early summer heat wave when Smith arrived, so he ditched the brown derby for a straw hat as he addressed reporters gathered to record the coming spectacle of New Yorker vs. New Yorker, Frank against Al, Protestant patrician vs. Catholic plebian. They were not the only candidates—House Speaker John Garner; Newton Baker, who had been Woodrow Wilson's secretary of war; and Governor Albert Ritchie of Maryland were considered serious contenders. But Roosevelt and Smith had the most pledged delegates—Roosevelt had between five and six hundred, short of the 769⅓ required for victory, and Smith had a little less than a hundred. (Some delegates still cast only a fraction of a vote under party rules.)

James Farley and Ed Flynn were already in Chicago, plotting behind the scenes to ensure that the Al Smith comeback story ended in defeat at the hands of his chosen successor. They shook their heads when Smith's floor manager, Jersey City mayor Frank Hague, told reporters that Roosevelt was the weakest Democrat in the field, never mind that he had more pledged delegates than all other candidates combined. He had no chance of winning, Hague insisted in what was considered a shocking breach of decorum. Farley replied regally that the Roosevelt team had no interest in criticizing or defaming other Democrats.

Even deeper behind the scenes, Al Smith was doing all he could to make sure that Roosevelt was stopped, even if it meant sacrificing his own candidacy. Smith even sat down for a closed-door meeting with his bitter rival from 1924, William Gibbs McAdoo, emerging afterward all smiles and hearty handshakes and held tongues. The press speculated that something was up and noted that Roosevelt's enemies were whispering that he would never carry New York in the general election because Samuel Seabury had planted the Walker stink bomb, and when it went off and Roosevelt was forced to remove Walker, the city's Democrats would stay home on Election Day and Herbert Hoover would take the nation's biggest electoral prize. Seabury showed up in Chicago for no apparent reason save to draw attention to himself and to his crusade to force Franklin Roosevelt's hand in the matter of James J. Walker.

Smith, Roosevelt, Walker, Seabury: the Chicago convention was filled with intrigue involving New Yorkers, all of whom had known each other for years. The intensity of the personal drama, the pathos of old friends divided, led Ed Flynn to seek an audience with Smith on the eve of the convention's first gavel. He arrived at Smith's room in the Congress Hotel to find the candidate surrounded by friends who took one look at the Roosevelt man in the doorway and quickly left the room. It was just the two of them, Smith the wounded warrior seeking some form of redemption; Flynn, the pragmatist who decided that his old boss and friend simply could not win and his new friend and boss could. Many years later, Flynn would say the meeting was one of the "saddest experiences I have ever had."

"Ed," Smith said, "you are not representing the people of Bronx County in your support of Roosevelt. You know the people of Bronx County want you to support me."

Flynn conceded the point. The people of the Bronx were no different than the people in Manhattan or Brooklyn or Boston or Chicago or any other city where immigrants and their children and grandchildren saw this man Smith as their champion and their voice. But, Flynn said, he had pledged to support Roosevelt after Smith said he was through with politics, and he could hardly turn his back on Roosevelt now. He had given his word, and Ed Flynn and Al Smith learned from Charlie Murphy that when you gave your word in politics, there was no going back.

Smith offered his hand, and Flynn took it. He would recall years later that the handshake was weak and perfunctory.[41]

He had lost a friend.

The convention's first skirmish was over the liquor question. Roosevelt's supporters backed a plank calling for the issue to be settled by individual states; Smith delivered a speech demanding full repeal, and Roosevelt's people cleverly let it be known that either plank was acceptable—they refused to be drawn into a battle over liquor when so many went to bed at night without bread. The repeal plank passed overwhelmingly, and so, with little more than a whimper from the dogmatic drys, the darned old liquor question that had so fiercely divided the party for years was removed from further discussion, forever.

The delegates shuffled into the cavernous Chicago Stadium on the morning of June 30 to hear the names of nine candidates placed in nomination, a process that continued until it was past three o'clock in the morning. It was evident that Roosevelt had the most delegates, but Smith had all the energy. His supporters jeered every positive mention of Roosevelt, their voices amplified because Chicago's mayor, Anton Cermak, was a fervent Smith supporter and he was careful to pack the galleries with his friends and allies. Roosevelt's old friend from Dutchess County, John Mack, delivered a tepid, uninspired nominating speech, one that Roosevelt had hoped Senator Robert Wagner would give, but Wagner declined to be drawn into the bitter battle between two friends and allies. Massachusetts governor Joseph Ely placed Smith's name in nomination with an inspired oration that did justice to Roosevelt's own Happy Warrior speeches of the last two conventions. Delegates in the hot, steamy Chicago Stadium erupted in an hour-long demonstration that did nothing to deflate the dreams of Smith's true believers. But amid the din on the convention floor, James Farley knew that cheering and stomping meant nothing. "We have the votes and that's what counts," he told Maryland's governor Ritchie.[42]

The first ballot began at the ungodly and inhumane hour of 4:28 a.m., after all of the candidates were nominated and seconded and seconded again for good measure. Roosevelt's managers insisted on going through to the first ballot without an adjournment, for they wished to show their man's overwhelming strength without giving Smith's allies an opportunity to conspire and whisper in hotel lobbies and speakeasies. The leather-lunged conscripts of Mayor Cermak's army retreated in exhaustion. Convention chairman Frank Walsh's voice bounced from wall to wall in the mostly empty hall as he ordered the states to announce their votes.

The Smith forces wanted to stall, to prolong the ballot, to find the backers of favorite sons and dark horses and beckon them into quiet corners where they would speak of the need to unite behind a single candidate who could stop Franklin Roosevelt, a certain loser in the fall. As the balloting proceeded, Smith-controlled delegations requested that Walsh call on each delegate to announce his or her vote individually rather than have the state chairman simply announce the collective total. It not only prolonged the ballot, which was the idea, it also forced public figures to announce their positions in full view of other delegates, assuming they were awake. Frank or Al? Or somebody else? There would be no ducking the choice.

Rote exercise became high drama, however, when the New York delegation also requested that its members be polled publicly. There were ninety members of the convention's largest and most important delegation, and Walsh began calling their names, one by one. Time to choose sides, publicly—James Farley: Roosevelt. John Curry, boss of Tammany Hall: Smith. Herbert Lehman: Roosevelt. Edward Flynn: Roosevelt. Daniel O'Connell, legendary boss of Albany: Smith. Henry Morgenthau: Roosevelt. Joseph McCooey, boss of Brooklyn: Smith. On it went. When the name of delegate Jimmy Walker was called there was no response. He had left the hall, whereabouts unknown.

But just as the delegation's chairman, Tammany boss Curry, prepared to announce New York's tally—sixty-five votes for one son of the Empire State, Smith, and twenty-five for the other, Roosevelt—men and women in the aisles began to murmur and point their fingers as a tall, slender figure made his way past slumping, sleepy delegates. Jimmy Walker, the mayor of New York, whose fate was in Franklin Roosevelt's hands, demanded to be recognized by the chairman.

"Who is the gentleman who addresses the chair?" asked Walsh from the podium.

"Walker, a delegate from New York," came the reply.

"For what purpose does he address the chair?" Walsh asked.

"The delegate was not here when his name was called and his alternate voted in his stead. The delegate is now here and requests permission to cast his own vote," Walker said.

"The request is granted."

Walker looked triumphant and defiant, all at once. "One half vote for Alfred E. Smith," he bellowed. And the place exploded, glassy-eyed delegates in rumpled suits and dresses, hair askew, reeking of smoke and sweat. Even the Roosevelt forces had to admire the mayor's guts.[43]

When it was over at nearly seven in the morning, Franklin Roosevelt had 666¼ votes, well more than a majority but short of the 769⅓ he needed. Smith had 201¾, Garner had 90¼, Ritchie of Maryland had 21, and the other candidates divided up the rest. Roosevelt's supporters expected those backing dark horses and favorite sons to jump aboard the frontrunner's bandwagon at once so that they might be able to say that they helped tilt the convention in favor of Franklin Roosevelt. But no announcement came. There would be a second contested ballot, beginning immediately. It ended with little change. The Roosevelt forces were stalled. A third ballot was ordered, beginning immediately. Outside the hall, the people of Chicago went about their business on a bright early summer morning. Inside the hall, a haze of blue smoke clung to the ceiling as men

and women, their clothes stained with sweat, their breath fouled by tobacco, went through the motions again, with the Smith people hoping
that the cranky delegates would somehow blame Roosevelt for this mar-
athon. Roosevelt, after all, had resisted adjournment hours earlier, at 4:30,
when the nominations were done.

The third ballot ended in stalemate, again, with Roosevelt gaining just
a few delegates. The session adjourned at 9:15 in the morning. Delegates
were told to return in twelve hours.

There was no time for sleep. There was hardly time for a bath. Al Smith
and his supporters believed they had stopped Roosevelt, and Roosevelt's
forces feared the Smith people were right. Meetings were called, phone
calls placed, telegrams dispatched. Roosevelt needed a deal. Smith needed
an alliance. And it all needed to be in place by the time delegates took
their seats at nine o'clock on Friday night, July 1, 1932.

Glassy-eyed, hoarse, and aching, they whispered behind closed doors.
They all knew that Texas held the card they wanted, held it in the form
of House Speaker John Garner, who had the support of his own state and
of California, under the control of William Randolph Hearst and William Gibbs McAdoo, men who shared a history of losing to Al Smith and
who were not particularly happy about it.

In the inner sanctum at Smith headquarters, Belle Moskowitz, the
most powerful woman at the convention and perhaps in all of national
politics at this moment, knew the history, the politics, and the danger.
An old ally, journalist Herbert Bayard Swope, was deputized to contact
McAdoo to feel him out. The call was not returned. Another Smith stalwart, Joseph Proskauer, tried and tried and tried and failed to reach Garner
by telephone. Hours were passing and, at least in Smith's headquarters,
nothing had changed since the morning and that was not good. Moskowitz
herself called the manager of the hotel in Washington where Garner was
staying and demanded to know the whereabouts of the Speaker. She
was calling on behalf of Governor Smith, she said.

"You may tell Governor Smith from me that Speaker Garner is here," the manager said. "The reason you can't get him is that he refuses to answer the phone."[44]

Roosevelt's men were having much better luck, for they were working an angle that was unavailable to Al Smith because it involved a man who had been waiting for such a moment for a long time: William Randolph Hearst.

Pausing for neither bath nor shave, Jim Farley called meetings and whispered into phones all morning. He had one more ballot left: if Roosevelt didn't clinch the nomination later that evening, he was finished. So he and Ed Flynn and Louis Howe—seemingly near death from an asthma attack, lying on the floor of his room in the Congress Hotel—sought to shore up wavering delegates and cut a deal with somebody who could put them over the top. During one of those meetings, with Mississippi senator Pat Harrison, Farley drifted off into a deep and exhausted sleep while he was trying to reach Texas congressman Sam Rayburn, a man Farley had cultivated for months and who now would be his point of contact to reach the unreachable John Garner.

He was awakened, gently, when Rayburn arrived and immediately went back to business. He had an offer for Garner and asked Rayburn to communicate it: the vice presidency, in return for Garner releasing his delegates to Roosevelt.

As Farley made his pitch, William Randolph Hearst decided the time was right to strike. He had no great love for Franklin Roosevelt, whom he considered an internationalist like Woodrow Wilson. But he was not Al Smith, and that meant something. Hearst's friend Joseph Kennedy, a Roosevelt man, called from Boston to warn him that the convention could easily devolve into a slog like 1924 and if it did, there was no telling how it might end. It could end with Al Smith accepting the nomination.

Hearst supported Garner. Not coincidentally, the California delegation, led by William Gibbs McAdoo, supported Garner. But the time had come for a deal: Hearst, through an intermediary, told Garner it was time to withdraw. Garner called Rayburn at three o'clock that afternoon to say he was withdrawing from the race. Roosevelt, Garner said, should be nominated later that night, with the support of Texas and California.

John Garner never returned Belle Moskowitz's call.

The convention was called to order at nine o'clock, and for a short time it all looked familiar, just like the first three ballots. Chairman Walsh then called on California, and the delegation's chairman, McAdoo, asked for time to explain the state's vote. In the New York delegation and in other Smith strongholds, there were nervous glances and furrowed brows. California, as far as most of them knew, was for Garner. Why would McAdoo need to explain its vote? Others on the floor knew, or suspected, what was about to happen. They, too, grew quiet as the tall, slender McAdoo made his way to the podium.

"California came here to nominate a president of the United States," he said. "She did not come here to deadlock this convention or to engage in another desolating contest like that in 1924." That should have been his year, McAdoo's year, but Al Smith had blocked him. McAdoo could not help but conjure that bitter memory as he prepared to plant a knife in the back of Alfred E. Smith.

He continued to explain, going on about unity and harmony, and then said that "when any man comes into this convention with the popular will behind him to the extent of almost seven hundred votes . . ." Now it was clear: he was switching to Roosevelt. The galleries, packed again with Smith supporters thanks to the careful organizing of Chicago's pro-Smith mayor, exploded: boos, jeers, screams, the sounds of people who were facing not simply defeat but betrayal. McAdoo said he would continue to speak no matter what the galleries thought, and then he displayed his weapon: California and Texas, he said, had decided in tandem to do what was best for the party and the country. "And so, my friends, California casts forty-four votes for Franklin Roosevelt!"[45]

It was over, save for the actual counting. After the cheering and the shrieks and even tears, the balloting continued. Al Smith's agony and Franklin Roosevelt's ecstasy, played out in alphabetical order: Maryland, Massachusetts, Michigan . . . Vermont, Virginia, Washington. Roosevelt finished with 945 votes—well more than the 769⅓ he needed—but when the counting was done there was no move from the second-place finisher, Al Smith, to make the choice unanimous. It was not mandatory, but it was expected of a gracious loser in the interests of party unity.

"I won't do it," Smith said. "I won't do it. I won't do it." Soon after he packed his bags and left Chicago as delegates cheered for the new ticket of Franklin Delano Roosevelt and John Nance Garner. He returned to New York and told reporters that he had nothing more to say. "I am tired," he muttered, "and I just want to get a rest."[46]

In a break with precedent, Franklin Roosevelt flew from Albany to Chicago to accept the nomination in person, the nomination delivered to him by two of Al Smith's enemies in a deal sealed in part through the help of two old Smith men, Farley and Flynn. He made a memorable speech promising Americans a new deal, a speech that was partly the work of another old Smith man, Sam Rosenman.

The band in Chicago Stadium played Roosevelt's new campaign song, "Happy Days Are Here Again."

seventeen

FRANK VS. AL

HE WAS NOT INCLINED to help Franklin Roosevelt, not yet any-way, not while the wound was still fresh and seemed to bleed anew every morning. An old acquaintance from Buffalo named Norman Mack, an-other onetime Smith man who was now with Roosevelt, decided he had the credentials and the manner to talk sense to his friend Al. So he set out for the Empire State Building from Roosevelt headquarters in Man-hattan, determined in manner and elegant in bearing. Roosevelt's cam-paign manager, James Farley, noticed too late, as Mack disappeared into the street, that the old man was wearing slippers rather than shoes. He returned from Smith's office some time later with a dour expression and sore feet. Farley asked him how it went.

"No one can talk to that man in the frame of mind he's in now," Mack replied.[1]

But Smith couldn't help himself, no matter how grouchy and bitter he seemed to Mack and others, and so he did a favor for Franklin Roose-velt just as the general election campaign was beginning in earnest.

Al Smith got rid of the Jimmy Walker problem.

And a problem it was, worse after the convention than before, because the pressure was that much more intense now that Roosevelt was the nom-inee and the favorite to defeat the wildly unpopular Hoover. People like Harvard law professor Felix Frankfurter and an irascible liberal Republi-can from Chicago named Harold Ickes told him he needed to get rid of

Walker to win over independent-minded voters and Republicans who had soured on Hoover.

Roosevelt summoned Walker to the state capitol in mid-August for a hearing to answer the charges raised in the Seabury investigation. He did so with only limited enthusiasm, for he surely would have preferred to be on a boat in the Florida Keys or in a pool in Warm Springs, resting for the coming campaign. Instead, public pressure demanded action on Walker, and so Franklin Roosevelt took on the role of judge and jury as the charming rogue Walker and the stern moralizer Seabury spent the last two weeks of August locked in verbal combat in the state capitol's Red Room, and the exchanges were sometimes so sharp that the governor had to ask both men to mind their manners. As August neared an end, the mayor's brother died at age forty-eight, leading Roosevelt to order the proceedings halted while Walker mourned. The irrepressible mayor had been transformed over the two weeks into a physical wreck, so frail and ill that doctors ordered him to bed after he buried his brother. Press coverage of Seabury's pointed questions and the mayor's evasive answers indicated that Jimmy Walker's troubles were only just beginning.

And so Al Smith intervened during the interregnum in late August, perhaps out of guilt, for Smith had talked Walker into running for mayor in 1925 at a time when the man they called "Beau James" might have been content to remain in Albany. Did Smith understand that Walker posed a serious threat to Franklin Roosevelt's chances in November? Did he wish to spare the city the spectacle of a mayor removed on corruption charges? He never said.

He met with Walker at the Plaza Hotel and pronounced his judgment. "Jim," he said, "you're through." The words surely stung, for not only was Al Smith the revered elder statesman of New York politics, but many years earlier the two had been roommates in Albany when Walker was a young assemblyman. Smith took Walker under his wing, but the young man never developed Smith's work ethic and discipline—amazingly, though, he had been an effective lawmaker in Albany despite his preference for carousing late into the night. Such a waste, and now it had come to this: scandal and disgrace. Smith had no doubts: his friend and protégé had to go.[2]

The phone in the governor's mansion rang on the evening of September 1, 1932, as Roosevelt was weighing his options—the Walker hearings would resume soon, but the outcome already was clear. Seabury was demolishing the mayor. Among those gathered around Roosevelt was Basil O'Connor, the governor's former law partner, trusted friend . . . and Walker's personal lawyer, although he had been careful to recuse himself for the Seabury hearing. It wasn't much of a recusal—O'Connor may not have represented Walker during his interrogation, but now, behind closed doors, he served as his advocate, telling Roosevelt that he ought to go easy on his client. Otherwise, he said, the mayor's friends in Tammany Hall will sit on their hands in November, which could lead to disaster. Roosevelt said he no longer had a choice. Walker had to go. "So you'd rather be right than president!" O'Connor shouted.[3]

Then the phone call: there was news from New York City. Jimmy Walker had submitted his resignation effective immediately.

He soon set sail for Europe to meet his lady friend, leaving behind a relieved governor and a long-suffering wife.

Al Smith was quiet all summer, and that gave Republicans some hope that the voice of the party's urban machines and immigrant-stock voters would sit out the campaign, signaling to supporters that they should do likewise. He was quiet, but he hadn't disappeared from public life—he simply made himself unavailable for comment about Franklin Roosevelt, preferring to talk about his new job as editor of an influential magazine about politics and culture called the *Outlook*, which Theodore Roosevelt had helped to edit many years earlier. (The magazine was rebranded as the *New Outlook* when Smith took over.) He agreed to be interviewed in mid-September for a new but obscure medium called television, speaking for fifteen minutes on the Columbia Broadcasting System about the life of an editor—among other things, he said he was amazed at how many poems were submitted to the magazine every month. Sweat was streaming down his face by the time his fifteen minutes were up, and afterward he told the production people that unless they could do something about the heat, politicians would stay away from television and stick to radio. He did not volunteer a single thought about the presidential campaign.[4]

Roosevelt's supporters soon were spreading word that they needed Al Smith and were counting on him to be the Happy Warrior of old. The New York press reported that Roosevelt's managers were worried about their man's prospects in New England, especially after a campaign stop in Bridgeport, Connecticut, attracted a less-than-enthusiastic crowd. New England, or more particularly Massachusetts and Rhode Island, was considered Smith country. With more than a hint of desperation—or manipulation disguised as desperation—unnamed sources from within the Roosevelt camp told the *New York Times* that they considered Smith to be the key to their hopes in New England.[5]

Still, he remained aloof. And so it was with some trepidation that New York's Democrats came together for a state convention in Albany in October, for both Smith and Roosevelt would be in attendance and nobody quite knew what would happen or, more to the point, what Al Smith would say when he was summoned to the podium to nominate his friend Herbert Lehman to be the next governor of New York, since Roosevelt could not run for both governor and president in 1932.

Roosevelt was seated in a place of honor at the front of the convention hall when the time came for Smith to deliver his speech for Lehman. As he made his way to the podium from the convention floor the cheers began, and reporters turned away from their notebooks and typewriters to watch for any sign of hostility between the two recent rivals. Smith moved not toward the podium but toward Roosevelt. He shook hands with James Farley, who was now chairman of the Democratic National Committee, replacing Smith's friend John Raskob. He moved down the line of dignitaries and then came to Franklin Roosevelt. Smith put out his hand. "Hello, Frank, I'm glad to see you."

The governor flashed his famous smile. "Hello, Al," he said, taking Smith's hand, "I'm glad to see you, too, and that's from the heart."[6]

All was well again in New York.

Smith did his duty over the next six weeks, accepting Roosevelt's challenge to persuade the city dwellers and mill workers of New England that the Protestant patrician from Hyde Park understood them, respected them, and was ready to help them without passing judgment about their religion or their drinking habits or the ways in which they organized their lives. And Smith did so with gusto, although it could hardly escape anybody's attention that he often spoke not so much about Roosevelt and 1932 but about Smith and 1928 and the ways in which America had let him down and did him wrong. He assailed Republicans for their supposed hypocrisy on drink and attacked "the spirit of bigotry" that doomed his chances for president. Thousands of New Jerseyans turned out to hear Smith at a Roosevelt rally in Newark in late October, but the hall was decorated with posters displaying Al Smith's mug, not the candidate's. A reporter noted dryly that Franklin Roosevelt was the "forgotten man" of Al Smith's campaign speeches.[7]

Roosevelt didn't mind: Smith was drawing tens of thousands to his speeches—two hundred thousand during a series of rallies in New Jersey alone. The cities were mobilized and ready to heed Smith's plea on behalf of the Democratic ticket, even if he didn't really have much to say about the ticket save to assure the crowds that Franklin Roosevelt was okay with him and ought to be okay with them.

Smith stopped off to visit with Roosevelt at the executive mansion in Albany just before midnight on October 28 after the governor called to congratulate him for a speech in Boston the previous night. They talked over the changed situation in New England for an hour in a room that quickly filled with smoke, cigars for Smith, cigarettes for Roosevelt. Fifteen reporters eventually were allowed into the room, billowing smoke of their own, to ask what they discussed. Not surprisingly, neither man had much to say. One reporter asked if the meeting could be described as "an old-fashioned Frank and Al get-together."

"If we were a couple of Frenchmen," Smith said, "we'd kiss each other. As it is, we have to rely on a handshake."

So they were friends again?

"Well," Smith said, "you don't see any blood, do you?"

They all laughed, including Roosevelt, who was letting Al Smith do all the talking. He was enjoying himself and there was no reason to interrupt him.[8]

They were together again, for one last time before Election Day, on the night of November 4 in the Brooklyn Academy of Music, where four thousand people rose to their feet when Franklin Roosevelt shuffled out on stage with Al Smith discreetly but firmly grabbing hold of his right arm at the crook of the elbow while thrusting his own right arm into the air to salute the crowd. The crowd stood and cheered for nearly ten minutes, applauding the past, saluting the present, anticipating the future. "Flags waved and yells of approval arose as Frank and Al each acknowledged the greeting," wrote the *New York Times*. Roosevelt was introduced, inevitably, as the "next president of the United States." Perhaps just as inevitably, Smith was introduced as "the best-known and best-loved man in America."[9]

They shared the stage with the man they agreed should be the next governor of New York, Herbert Lehman, and with U.S. senator Robert Wagner, who was running for reelection. The tableau offered a glimpse of the Empire State at the height of its power: Smith, Roosevelt, Lehman, Wagner. Three of them, Roosevelt, Lehman, and Wagner, were about to lead a revolution in the relationship between government and the governed, Roosevelt as the implementer of the New Deal, Lehman as the author of New York's so-called Little New Deal, which expanded on federal relief programs and public works projects, and Wagner as the prime sponsor and mover of the Social Security Act and the National Labor Relations Act, both among the greatest legislative achievements of the era.

All three men took inspiration from the policies and vision of the best-loved man in America, Alfred E. Smith.

Franklin Roosevelt voted for himself in the town hall in Hyde Park, and then he and Eleanor and their friends formed a motorcade that took them through flag-lined streets in the river towns and villages of Dutchess, Putnam, and Westchester counties before heading into the city, to the Biltmore Hotel, where the professionals—James Farley, Ed Flynn, Sam Rosenman, Louis Howe, and all the others—were watching over twenty young women working the phones, writing figures on paper, and passing them on to those who knew the code. It was clear very early that Franklin Roosevelt would be the next president, that he would have a Democratic Congress on his side, and that his friends in New York, Lehman and Wagner, would win as well. Not all elections make history, but the returns of 1932 surely did, for they would be a starting point for a new era in American politics, a new political coalition that would last for nearly forty years. Steelworkers and grocery store clerks, those who sewed and those who sowed, children of immigrants and the descendants of founding fathers—they were divided before 1932 but found common ground in the candidacy of Franklin Delano Roosevelt, the patrician who mixed with the machines.

Al Smith, looking overjoyed, burst into Roosevelt headquarters at 9:30. They all stopped what they were doing and what they were saying to applaud the Happy Warrior as he and Roosevelt clasped hands and smiled. Smith stayed in the room for about ten minutes but then cleared out to leave the stage to his successor. By night's end, Roosevelt had one of the great landslides in American history, winning all but six of the forty-eight states. Smith's hard campaigning helped to deliver Massachusetts and Rhode Island to Roosevelt. Until 1932, both had been Republican states; they would become predictably Democratic for generations.

Franklin Roosevelt turned to the task of preparing to be president during the greatest crisis the country had faced since the Civil War. Smith returned to his job at the virtually vacant Empire State Building while playing the role of New York City's cheerleader in chief. He intervened with bankers when they were reluctant to do business with the cash-strapped city. He led charity drives to help the 30 percent of New Yorkers who were jobless. As Christmas neared, a telegram arrived from the president-elect wishing him and his family season's greetings. "I desire to extend the same to you and all your family," Smith wrote back. "Any time I can be of service, I hope you will feel free to give me a ring."[10]

Smith had the pleasure of traveling to Albany to witness the inauguration of another protégé, Herbert Lehman, as governor on January 2. Roosevelt, as the outgoing governor, and Smith, as New York's elder statesman, both were honored guests at the ceremony and delivered remarks broadcast around the country on two radio networks. Lehman linked the two of them together in his inaugural address, saying to Roosevelt, "The policies and principles of sound and liberal government, which were enunciated more than a decade ago by our great predecessor Alfred E. Smith, have been safe in your hands."[11]

If Smith yearned for respect and deference, he received both on this typically cold inauguration day in Albany. He basked in his role as founder of the feast and then returned to the Albany home of his daughter and son-in-law to relax before a round of inaugural social events. But then the phone rang, an urgent call from Manhattan: the woman who was at Al Smith's side through every triumph and every defeat since 1918, Belle Moskowitz, was dead of a heart attack at the age of fifty-six. Smith wept as he put down the phone. Plans were canceled and Smith boarded the next train to Manhattan, arriving in Grand Central Terminal with his head bowed, barely able to speak to waiting reporters. The *New York Times* noted that Belle Moskowitz "came nearer than any other woman had come before to being the maker of a President." She had never reconciled herself to Franklin Roosevelt, never saw him as much more than a pretender. He had a prize that ought to have been Al Smith's, and at her death she was grieving for Smith and the opportunity denied him. And now he grieved for her, his friend who had the greatest brain he ever knew.[12]

The mayor of Chicago, Anton Cermak, had backed the wrong man in 1932 and, as a veteran of his city's rough and rumble politics, he knew that some politicians never forgot who supported them and who opposed them when it mattered. Franklin Roosevelt, for all of his bonhomie, was one of them. He and his loyalists had a designation for those who were with him from the start. They were known by a set of initials: FRBC— For Roosevelt Before Chicago. Anton Cermak was an Al Smith man before there was even a Smith candidacy. So now fences required mending for many reasons, not least of which was the dire financial plight of Cermak's city. The Depression left many a municipal treasury bare but Chicago was a special case: the city's real estate owners had stopped paying property taxes in 1931 to protest what they regarded as unfair treatment in tax policy. The tax strike was nearing an end, but the damage to the city's finances was done. Cermak hoped Washington would lend a hand.

And so when the president-elect went south to Miami from Warm Springs in February, Cermak found an excuse to journey to Florida in hopes of delivering a message of peace and goodwill. The mayor was among several dignitaries gathered in Miami's Bay Front Park on the evening of February 15 to greet the president-elect when he arrived to give a short talk to members of the American Legion. Roosevelt delivered his speech from the backseat of a convertible, telling the legionnaires a few fish stories about his cruises off the Florida coast, and when it was over Cermak hurried over to the president-elect and put out his hand. Roosevelt accepted it with warmth and the two of them began a friendly conversation. They agreed to meet later to talk business. Cermak stepped away, and as he did so a thirty-two-year-old bricklayer from Italy, Giuseppe Zangara, leaped up on a park bench and opened fire with a revolver about forty feet away from Roosevelt's car. A woman standing near Zangara had the presence of mind and the courage to strike Zangara's arm as he got off five shots in the president-elect's direction.

Miraculously, the bullets missed Franklin Roosevelt. But others were hit, including Cermak, who was struck in the torso. Roosevelt's driver instinctively tried to get his passenger out of harm's way but the president-elect ordered him to back up the car so they could retrieve the crumpled mayor, his shirt stained red with blood. Roosevelt used his muscular upper body to lift the stricken mayor into the back seat, held him with his left arm as they sped to hospital, and talked to him even though the mayor seemed to be dead. "Tony," he called him, "keep quiet. . . . It won't hurt you if you keep quiet." Raymond Moley, a member of Roosevelt's brain trust, later said that he had never seen anything more magnificent than Roosevelt's absolute calm during the crisis.[13]

They got Cermak to a hospital in a few minutes. The bullet he took, the bullets that hit three other people, were meant for the president-elect. The would-be assassin explained that he had nothing against Roosevelt personally, but he hated all presidents and hated the rich.

Anton Cermak died on March 6, his condition made worse by an assortment of other ailments. Zangara was arrested, tried, convicted, and executed by March 20, 1933. The process took just over a month.

Inauguration Day, March 4, 1933, brought them all together: Al Smith and Robert Wagner; Frances Perkins and Sam Rosenman; James Farley and Ed Flynn, all of whom were present at the creation of a new kind of politics in their state and now were gathered in the nation's capital to hear the wonderful voice of Franklin Roosevelt reassuring Americans that they need fear only fear itself. These were the words of a man who strapped on steel braces so he could stand up and wave and smile to the crowds, the words of a man who had no time for discouraging words and dire prognoses. The sentiments he expressed were fresh and new for a nation accustomed to the glum assessments from the Hoover White House, but they were familiar enough to the New Yorkers on hand, for they had heard his unfailing optimism before.

After taking the oath of office and delivering his inaugural address, Roosevelt stood and watched a parade in his honor, one hand gripping a rail in front of him while he waved with the other. There was, suddenly, a commotion, a stirring in the crowd, shouts audible over the sounds of band music. Some, with fresh memories of the assassination attempt in Florida, looked up and down Pennsylvania Avenue anticipating danger—a riot, perhaps. It was nothing of the sort. It was just the crowd acknowledging Al Smith as he marched at the head of the Tammany Hall delegation, inspiring cheers on either side of the avenue as he passed. The press reported the next day that Smith received the loudest and most prolonged cheers of anybody in the parade, except for the new president himself.

Smith turned to his right when he reached the reviewing stand, took off his hat, and saluted the man who had what was denied him. And then he moved on, cheers ringing in his ears.[14]

Some of Smith's old friends and allies remained in Washington once the ceremonies were over and the bunting put away for another day. Frances Perkins, brought into government during the Smith administration, would be the nation's first woman cabinet officer, accepting Roosevelt's offer of secretary of labor. Robert Wagner, freshly reelected to a second term in the U.S. Senate, would go on to become the greatest legislator of the coming New Deal. Jim Farley, who first got a glimpse of power and politics in the Smith campaign of 1922, would be Roosevelt's postmaster general, a position that would allow him to spend most of his time tending to his other job, that of chairman of the Democratic National Committee. Sam Rosenman, trained to be a speechwriter for a man, Smith, who hated giving formal speeches, would go to work crafting words the nation would hear by its firesides. Ed Flynn, whose first government job was with Al Smith, had no formal position but was on call as a political wise man, a job that became more important when sickly Louis Howe died in 1936. Flynn would eventually succeed Farley as chairman of the Democratic National Committee in 1940.

The White House bore more than a little of Al Smith's influence, but it did not have the man himself, despite press speculation that he might be in line for a job in the new Roosevelt administration that looked, from some angles, like an old Smith administration. So he stayed in New York where there were many opportunities to remain in public life—some he took, and others he put aside. New York would choose a new mayor in 1933 in the aftermath of the Walker scandals, and even Walker's vanquished foe from 1929, Fiorello La Guardia, a Republican, urged Smith to enter the race and said he would pass up the chance to run again if Smith wanted the job. He declined, leading to La Guardia's victory over two Democratic opponents. But Smith was happy to accept the post of chairman of a state convention called to ratify the Twenty-First Amendment to the U.S. Constitution, which repealed the despised and now doomed Eighteenth Amendment. On the afternoon of April 7, 1933, a team of six Clydesdales pulled an Anheuser-Busch wagon across 34th Street in midtown until it reached the Empire State Building. There, Al Smith was waiting, cigar stuck in his mouth, to accept the delivery of a case of Budweiser, or at least the watered-down version—3.2 percent alcohol— that was allowed under a relaxation of Prohibition prior to its outright repeal. The beer had been flown in from St. Louis the night before, a gift from the brewers to the nation's most stalwart wet.

"This is surely a happy day for all," Smith said, echoing Roosevelt's campaign song, "because it will on some measure deplete the ranks of the unemployed and promote happiness and good cheer."[15]

Less happy and far more important was his leadership of a small but prescient group of New Yorkers who saw the rise of Adolf Hitler in Germany as a threat not only to German Jews but to the world in general. Smith was the featured speaker at an extraordinary anti-Hitler rally in Madison Square Garden in late March 1933, less than three months after Hitler's appointment as Germany's chancellor. Smith addressed an audience of twenty thousand inside the building and another thirty-five thousand listening on loudspeakers outside the Garden, comparing Hitler and the Nazis to the Ku Klux Klan and the forces of bigotry whose power he saw firsthand in 1928 and had never forgotten. "It don't make any difference to me whether it is a brown shirt or a night shirt," Smith said. He would speak up "against intolerance, against bigotry, against the suppression of freedom of speech" whether the offenses took place in Germany, Russia, or the United States. It was the finest hour of his life as an elder statesman and conscience of the Democratic Party.[16]

He had much to say about Franklin Roosevelt's aggressive attempts to revive the nation's economy and most of it was good. But, through his bully pulpit as editor of the *New Outlook*, he expressed little but disdain for the academics who were lured from the classroom to advise Roosevelt and who were engaging in what he saw as dangerous experimentation based on theory rather than practical experience in actual governance. "I am for experience as against experiment," he wrote. He assailed one of the most prominent members of Roosevelt's brain trust, Columbia University economics professor Rexford Tugwell, because Tugwell believed in what he called "the magnificence of planning." It sounded to Smith's ears like so much socialistic and even communistic balderdash. "Let Tugwell get one of those raccoon coats that the college boys wear at a football game and let him go to Russia, sit on a cake of ice and plan all he wants," Smith wrote. In another piece in the *New Outlook*, he took note of the extraordinary growth of new agencies with, in his view, unclear or uncertain missions, many identified, as the president himself was, by their initials: the NRA, AAA, CWA, and PWA, and many more to come. Smith, who prided himself on streamlining New York's government during his eight years as the state's chief executive, referred to the collection as an "alphabet soup" cooked up by the New Deal's professors. The colorful criticism stuck.[17]

He was careful not to criticize Professor Tugwell's boss, Roosevelt, and when Smith and Roosevelt were together in early October, again at a dinner for Catholic Charities, the two men were all smiles as the president made his awkward way to his seat in the grand ballroom of the Waldorf Astoria. It was Roosevelt's first appearance in New York City as president, and that he chose a Catholic event for the occasion and would be seated next to the pope's apostolic delegate in the United States was a tribute to all that Al Smith meant in American culture and a sign of how much had changed since 1928, when bigots and demagogues were warning of the imminent Catholic takeover of American life. Roosevelt stopped to greet Smith, already seated on the dais, and as the crowd cheered Roosevelt bent to whisper something in Smith's ear. He burst into laughter and, as Roosevelt turned, he slapped him on the back. A news account described it as a "resounding whack."[18]

There were more whacks, just as resounding and not nearly as friendly, in the weeks to come. Smith delivered a national radio address three weeks after the Catholic Charities event that sounded as though it might have been given by Herbert Hoover or Calvin Coolidge. He railed against the "heavy, cold, clammy hand of bureaucracy," saying that private enterprise "still is vastly superior to government planning and government control of business and all of human effort." Progress, he said, was the work of "private individuals, working without compulsion, control, of even suggestion, from the government itself." His remarks were front-page news, a seeming rebuke of the unfolding New Deal. An invitation to the White House was quick in coming, and Smith and his close friend John Raskob enjoyed a spot of tea with the president on the evening of November 14, 1933, leading the New York press to speculate that Smith and Roosevelt were about to revive their alliance.[19]

It was a nice thought, but it was put to rest a week later when Smith assailed Roosevelt over monetary policy, particularly his abandonment of the gold standard, in an open letter addressed to the New York Chamber of Commerce and printed in his magazine. The letter was filled with a special kind of bitterness and invective—"I am for gold dollars as opposed to baloney dollars," he said, arguing against Roosevelt's efforts to make the dollar cheaper and perhaps stimulate demand for American goods overseas. Farmers, as William Jennings Bryan knew so well, preferred cheap money and inflation, but high prices inevitably hurt wage-earners in the cities. Smith and his new friends in the business community, especially Raskob, saw Roosevelt's policy as a sop to the old party of Bryan, the rural, dry farmers of the West and South. And Smith was an eastern businessman now, not only in charge of the nation's largest office building but also a bank, County Trust Company, that his friend James Riordan founded and led until he killed himself when the market crashed in 1929.[20]

Smith never cared for economic demagogues, whether they were named Hearst or Bryan, but he, too, had played the class card in his younger days. Now that he was keeping company with business leaders, Smith's rhetoric lost some of the grit from the sidewalks of his youth. He wore silk hats now, not brown derbies, and it showed.

"If I must choose between the leaders of the past, with all the errors they have made and with all the selfishness they have been guilty of, and the inexperienced young college professors who hold no responsible office but are perfectly ready to turn 130 million Americans into guinea pigs for experimentation, I am going to be for the people who have made the country what it is," Smith wrote. The tirade prompted no comment from the Roosevelt White House, but a singular figure rose to the president's defense with an equally blistering message: "Are we to forget that Mr. Smith is a wealthy banker?" asked Father Charles Coughlin in one of his famous radio addresses from the Shrine of the Little Flower in Detroit. He called Smith's attack "a poisoned dart aimed at a leader who is endeavoring to save capitalism itself." Al Smith, proclaimed the nation's best-known Roman Catholic priest, had written his political obituary.[21]

The press announced that the relationship between Smith and Roosevelt had turned from friendship to a feud of historic proportions. Writing in the *New York Times*, journalist Arthur Krock noted that, until recently, "most people would have said that 'Frank' Roosevelt and 'Al' Smith might differ, but they would differ with affectionate reluctance. Destiny had not permitted this to be true."[22]

He was wrong, though: behind the scenes, out of the public eye, the two men still were on good terms thanks in large measure to Roosevelt's admirable graciousness. Three weeks after Smith's stinging attack on his monetary policy, the president dispatched a bouquet of flowers to Al Smith's home on Fifth Avenue to wish him a merry Christmas. Smith responded with a "Dear Frank" note, telling him that the display "added much to the cheer of Christmas." And as the press continued to speculate about their feud, Smith sent Roosevelt a friendly personal letter in March 1934 asking for the president's permission to use a photograph of the two of them together on opening day of the Empire State Building in promotional material for the still-struggling skyscraper. "Love to all the family," Smith wrote. The president gave his blessing: "It certainly will be all right for you to use this picture."[23]

They were trying to remain civil. But as the months passed, Al Smith became angrier, raging against the professors of the New Deal in conversations with his daughter, Emily, and just about anyone else who would listen. "Franklin Roosevelt and these 'brain trusters' of his are giving people the idea that the government owes them something," he said.[24]

He was surrounded by people who nodded in agreement. Nobody pointed out that there was a time in Albany when people said the same thing about Al Smith.

The break with Roosevelt came in late summer 1934, when Smith joined forces with some of the nation's wealthiest business leaders to create a new organization called the American Liberty League. Many of the founders were Republican businessmen who had come to loathe Franklin Roosevelt and the broad powers his administration sought to exert over private enterprise through the National Recovery Administration, the Agricultural Adjustment Act, and other foundational New Deal creations. But its leaders were delighted to point to high-profile Democrats who joined. They included John Davis, the party's nominee at the infamous convention in 1924; John Raskob, former chairman of the Democratic National Committee; and Jouette Shouse, former chairman of the committee's executive board under Raskob.

Smith was the league's biggest catch, becoming a founding member and member of its executive committee at the suggestion of his friend Raskob, even though he didn't share the blind hatred of Roosevelt that motivated so many of the league's funders. He dutifully attended league meetings in the struggling property he managed and Raskob owned, the Empire State Building, and kept company with some of the most conservative business leaders in the country. And even as he did so, even as he heard the sputtering invective of his fellow Liberty Leaguers for "that man" (they couldn't even bear to say the president's name), Franklin Roosevelt was putting into place measures that sounded a good deal like the laws Al Smith supported when he was in Albany. Roosevelt signed the Social Security Act in 1935, a landmark piece of legislation cosponsored by Smith's old friend Robert Wagner, and what was Social Security but a logical extension of the pensions for widows and children that Smith won for New Yorkers when he was in the New York Assembly? It was Al Smith who stood against the forces of reaction in 1915 at a state constitutional convention to defend laws intended to benefit the poor and the vulnerable, asking if it were right and proper for modern government to be reduced to what he called the "caveman's law." That same year, 1935, Robert Wagner and Frances Perkins persuaded Roosevelt to go along with a new bill, the National Labor Relations Act, enshrining the right to organize labor unions. Labor had been on Smith's side in every race he ran in New York, and in return for union support, Smith presented working people with the invaluable gift of Frances Perkins. The Liberty Leaguers saw these measures as the beginning of the end, and Al Smith would have heard their bitter condemnations in the lonely corridors of the Empire State Building.

The league announced with great fanfare in late 1935 that Al Smith would be the featured speaker at an event in the Mayflower Hotel in Washington in January, just as a new election year got underway. There was no mystery about Smith's intentions, for the league was delighted to advertise his speech as an all-out assault on Roosevelt and the New Deal.

Eleanor Roosevelt, like everybody else in Washington, knew what was coming. And she did something extraordinary for this man she admired and for whom she campaigned against her own cousin in 1924. She invited him to stay in the White House while he was in Washington to deliver a speech that would attack her husband.

"Franklin and I hope very much that you and any of your family will stay with us at least for the night," she wrote.

It is hard to know what Smith made of this extraordinary gesture, save that he knew he could not accept, and did not. The correspondence somehow became public and it made Smith look bad, turning down an invitation from the president and first lady. That led to a more private correspondence between the two, and in it Smith revealed himself as he almost never did in written word. Eleanor told him she thought it a "great pity" that people "who have had respect and admiration for each other" were being dragged into "antagonistic personal feelings."

Smith's discomfort was evident in his reply. He, too, thought it a pity that political differences might lead to "personal animosities," and because he knew what was coming he felt the need to point out that he had been by her husband's side in the past. "I earnestly supported Frank in 1928, 1930 and 1932," he wrote, "and if I take any issue now with some of the policies of the administration it is not with any personal animosity towards him or you."[25]

And so on the night of January 25, 1936, in a ballroom filled with two thousand men and women in fine evening clothes, Alfred E. Smith, himself dressed in white tie and tails, delivered what would become one of the bitterest, fiercest, and, for those reasons, best-remembered attacks on Franklin Roosevelt and the New Deal.

It was hard, he said, to attack his own party—he said nothing about any pain he felt about assailing a man who had placed his name in nomination for the presidency twice and who ran for governor of New York as a personal favor. He said he feared the power of demagogues he did not name who would "incite one class of our people against the other." He railed against the "vast building up of new bureaus of government" that would "redistribute" the nation's resources. He complained about the "young brain trusters who caught the socialists in swimming and ran away with their clothes."

All the resentment, all the anger, all the grievances—real or imagined— were laid bare not only in front of two thousand Roosevelt haters in the ballroom but hundreds of thousands listening on their radios. "There can be only one atmosphere of government, the clear, pure fresh air of free America or the foul breath of communistic Russia," he said in a shout that might well have been heard up and down Pennsylvania Avenue without benefit of microphones or a radio. "There can be only one flag, the Stars and Stripes or the red flag of the godless Union of the Soviet."[26]

They cheered him, men and women of means gathered in a glittering ballroom at a time when nearly 17 percent of Americans were out of work, Americans who looked to the president's alphabet soup and concluded that no matter how the letters were arranged they spelled hope. Republicans quickly announced that Al Smith had said what many Democrats were thinking and that this was the beginning of a split in Franklin Roosevelt's party. But Alabama senator Joseph Robinson, who ran for vice president with Smith in 1928 and stood by him when he was assailed in the South for his religion and his wetness, summed up the views of most Democrats. Al Smith, Robinson said, had gotten rich. He "has turned away from the East Side with those little shops and fish markets, and now his gaze rests fondly upon the gilded towers and palaces of Park Avenue."[27]

As for Roosevelt himself, he shook his head and wondered what might have prompted Al to say these things.

He took aside his labor secretary, Frances Perkins, who remained friendly with her old boss Smith, and asked her what had gone wrong. "I just can't understand it," he said. "All the things we have done in the federal government are like the things Al Smith did as governor of New York. They're the things he would have done as president. What in the world is the matter?"[28]

She didn't know. When reporters caught up with her and asked what she thought of her former boss's speech, she said, sadly and simply, that Al Smith was her friend. "I believe he'll come back," she said.[29]

Al Smith would never reveal why he broke so bitterly with Franklin Roosevelt. His old roommate from Albany days, Robert Wagner, would blame it on the company Smith kept after 1932, the DuPonts and Raskob and all the other high hats who flattered him and paid attention to him in ways Franklin Roosevelt did not, at least as Smith saw it. Others would say that he never got over the wounds of 1928, and still others would say no, it was 1932 that put him over the edge. Robert Moses, who loved Al Smith and hated FDR, would write that Smith was a "congenital conservative" in matters of economics while Roosevelt was a "country squire liberal." Joseph Proskauer, who shared Moses's opinions of Smith and Roosevelt, argued that Smith found Roosevelt's centralization of power alarming—state and local governments were closer to the people and better placed to serve their constituents, as the machine that raised Smith to power, Tammany Hall, demonstrated in the wards and clubhouses of old New York. Others who knew and worked with both men, people like Frances Perkins, would point out other differences. Al Smith was direct and Franklin Roosevelt was not. Al Smith, Perkins would say, always told her the truth, and as for Franklin Roosevelt, well, her silence on the topic was persuasive. She nevertheless worked for Roosevelt for his entire presidency.[30]

And then there were the slights, real or imagined. Smith did not suffer in silence when he believed Franklin Roosevelt was neglecting him and all the wisdom he had to offer. Roosevelt was more reticent about conjuring memories of the way the Smith camp used to talk to and about him, what it was like to be treated simply as Al Smith's designated Protestant, a mere decoration. He said nothing, but he remembered.

And so they were both ready to take offense, and they did so early and often, even before Smith joined the Liberty League. Smith was enraged when Roosevelt's head of the Democratic National Committee, James Farley, began replacing local party leaders in New York who were judged to be insufficiently supportive of Roosevelt before his nomination. Smith saw it as a power play directed at him and pleaded with his friend, Governor Herbert Lehman, to take a stand against Farley and, by extension, Roosevelt. "I cannot be expected to sit by and remain quiet if the men who voted for me in Chicago are to be driven out of the party," he told Lehman, who wisely chose not to intervene.[31]

And when Roosevelt cooked up a scheme to get rid of New York's se-nior U.S. senator, Royal Copeland, by naming him to be ambassador to Germany and replacing him with reliable ally Ed Flynn, Smith crossed his arms and stood in the way. The plan depended on Lehman's cooperation, for the governor was empowered to fill vacancies in the Senate. Lehman told Flynn he'd be happy to accommodate the president's wishes, but Flynn needed to talk to Al Smith—the press and the people surely would expect the beloved former governor to have the right of first refusal if a Senate seat were to open. So Flynn found himself having yet another unpleasant conversation with Al Smith on behalf of Franklin Roose-velt. Over a scratchy phone connection, Flynn heard the sound of bitter indifference as he told Smith of Roosevelt's plan. The president wanted him, Ed Flynn, in the Senate, Smith was told. Did he have any objec-tion? Smith said in so many words that he'd have to think it over. Years later Flynn would remember the tone and tenor of Al Smith's voice on the telephone line. It was obvious, he said, that "the sores and hurts" of the recent past remained fresh in his memory. He continued to think about it, for days, for so long that Flynn gave up and told Roosevelt that without Smith's approval, the scheme was doomed. Royal Copeland re-mained in the Senate and soon became a vociferous critic of the New Deal.[32]

In late 1934 and early 1935, Roosevelt sought to exact revenge on the man Al Smith had plucked from academic obscurity so many years ear-lier, Robert Moses, who had consolidated his power as state parks czar and extended his reach into New York City after the election of Fiorello La Guardia as mayor in 1933. Together, they were planning new highways and tunnels and bridges to be paid for with money from Franklin Roo-sevelt's Public Works Administration, led by interior secretary Harold Ickes. But in late 1934, Ickes told La Guardia that the city would not be getting the money for a centerpiece of the master plan for New York, the Triborough Bridge, unless and until Robert Moses quit the city agency that was building the span. With Roosevelt's knowledge and agreement, the PWA issued a piece of legalese known as Administrative Order No. 129, which in essence said that no agency funds, not a penny, would go to any entity that saw fit to employ Robert Moses. Ickes had a simple explanation for the federal government's wrath: "Moses is a bitter personal enemy of the President's," he wrote. "He is a very close friend of Al Smith."[33]

By early 1935, the Triborough Bridge Authority was nearly down to its last dollar, and without funds from the PWA it would have to halt work on one of the city's most important public works projects, throwing thousands of workers into the street.

The feud between Roosevelt and Moses became national news, with Roosevelt cast in the role of the villain, no easy assignment given that his antagonist was the imperious and unlikable Robert Moses. It was a terrific drama featuring four headstrong characters—Roosevelt, Ickes, La Guardia, and Moses—and nobody was quite sure how it would end until Al Smith summoned reporters to his office on the thirty-second floor of the Empire State Building on February 27, 1935. He handed out copies of a written statement calling the administration's move against his friend Moses as "vindictive" and "ridiculous." In more diplomatic language, he said it was hard to believe that Roosevelt was behind it, although he knew the president was out to get Moses and certainly was aware of what Ickes was trying to do.[34]

Roosevelt backed down the next day, wondering aloud why he wasn't entitled to satisfy a personal grudge. But even in retreating from a grudge there was begrudgery. Ickes, with Roosevelt's approval, sent a letter to La Guardia informing the mayor that Moses could continue to serve on the Triborough Bridge Authority, but it was backdated to February 26 even though it was written after Al Smith's statement of February 27. Ickes admitted it was all about grudges: he and Roosevelt didn't want to give Smith the satisfaction of knowing that he had outmaneuvered them.

City and country, north and south, east and west—they came together for a Democratic president in 1936 as they had never done before, at least not since the reelection of Andrew Jackson a hundred years earlier. Only a dozen years had passed since the long convention of 1924, when it seemed as though the cultural and geographic and demographic gulf between the Democratic Party's factions could never be bridged. But Franklin Roosevelt and his New Deal and winning smile and unshakeable optimism changed everything. He campaigned for reelection speaking words written by Sam Rosenman, following a strategy laid out by Jim Farley and Ed Flynn, touting achievements that bore the imprint of Frances Perkins and Robert Wagner, friends, protégés, and onetime allies of Al Smith.

Smith himself campaigned not for Franklin Roosevelt but for Alf Landon, the governor of Kansas and the Republican Party's designated sacrificial lamb in the 1936 presidential campaign. His announcement for Landon was intended to be a moment of high drama, and one of the two NBC radio networks, NBC Blue, agreed to broadcast Smith's speech from Carnegie Hall between nine and ten o'clock eastern time on the night of October 1, 1936. But when Jim Farley's Democratic National Committee caught wind of Smith's plan, it arranged with two competing networks, CBS and the other NBC network, NBC Red, for Roosevelt himself to address the nation for half an hour beginning at the same time. It was a ruthless, even pitiless, tactic, and it was brilliant: Smith was a performer made for vaudeville and the Bowery, but this was the age of radio, and Roosevelt was a master of a medium Smith still mispronounced as "rad-dio."

Outmaneuvered by his old friends, Smith backed down and dispatched a telegram to Roosevelt informing him of his surrender. Its very salutation spoke of the breach between the two old allies, for it began not with "Dear Frank" but with a cold "The President." Smith went on to tell Roosevelt that he had rearranged the timing of his speech in "deference to the high office of the President" so he would start speaking at 9:30, after Roosevelt was finished. He signed it not as "Al" but as "Alfred E. Smith," a formality he generally avoided.[35]

The show went on as planned on October 1. Smith spent a good portion of his speech talking about himself, saying that he had heard what people were saying about him and that it wasn't true. Yes, he had a high hat now, but he still had the brown derby. He hadn't forgotten his roots, but, he said, Franklin Roosevelt was pitting class against class, and that was wrong and dangerous. He mentioned that he had spoken with the president only once since his inauguration even though he had made it plain that he was available for consultation—he couldn't help but lay bare his sores and wounds. He said Roosevelt had commandeered the Democratic Party and made it into something else, a New Deal Party, he said. Finally, at the end of his hour, he announced his support for Landon.[36]

Republicans were ecstatic—one top party official predicted that Smith's speech would be good for three million votes in the places where Al Smith still was considered a political martyr to the forces of hatred and bigotry.

The Roosevelt White House said nothing, and on Election Day, Franklin Roosevelt defeated Alf Landon by more than ten million votes. Roosevelt received 523 Electoral College votes. Landon received eight—five from Maine and three from New Hampshire.

Smith showed up at his local polling place on Madison Avenue on Election Day wearing not a high hat but his brown derby, ready to cast his vote against Franklin Roosevelt. A Republican poll watcher greeted Smith and his wife and escorted them to the front of the line.

He and Katie strolled the sidewalks of New York back to his apartment on Fifth Avenue. His fellow New Yorkers—city people, ethnic people, Al Smith people—spotted him on his way home. And some of them booed.[37]

And so it ended, an unlikely, convenient, and historic relationship that spanned a quarter century and helped change the very nature of politics and government in ways that few would have predicted in the Gilded Age into which Al Smith and Franklin Roosevelt were born. Two New Yorkers reared on a riverside ninety miles and nine years apart somehow had found each other useful and helpful, two very different things, and by force of will and personality together they dragged their party into the twentieth century, into the America of cities and immigrants and men and women who toiled with their hands in factories and sweatshops. One was born into that America, the other had to learn about it, and perhaps it helped that he came to know what it was like to be vulnerable, and that vulnerability was not a sign of weak character or bad genes. That man would be credited with creating a new and inclusive brand of politics— the New Deal coalition—that made him a secular messiah, savior of the Democratic Party. The other was forced to the sidelines, wondering why he had been left out.

Al Smith spent the years after Roosevelt's smashing reelection very much a presence in the life of New York. He turned up at the Irish dinners around Saint Patrick's Day, at charitable events for Catholic causes, and earnest civic events like the state's constitutional convention in 1937, where he led a caucus of Democrats unhappy with the New Deal while his old roommate, Robert Wagner, led the pro–New Deal Democrats. He left the United States for the first time in 1937, traveling to Rome, where he was granted an audience with the pope and with Benito Mussolini; London, where he met with Winston Churchill; and then to Ireland, the place he considered his ancestral home even though Italy, through his father's family, had an equal claim on his affection. He seemed to enjoy his travels, but on his last night abroad he attended Mass in Ireland, and while on his knees he thanked God that he was born in the United States—"His country," as he called it.[38]

He still craved attention, still loved the stage, and the newspapers and newsreel cameras were happy to accommodate him, recording him singing old Bowery songs at a public appearance, capturing the image of Al and Katie leaving St. Patrick's Cathedral after Easter Mass, grinning broadly as he crossed Fifth Avenue to visit the Central Park Zoo, which Robert Moses had rebuilt and made splendid as a gift to the animal-loving man who rescued him from the high-minded ineffectiveness of good government. Moses presented his mentor with a badge designating him as the zoo's night watchman, and few things gave the aging, graying former governor more pleasure than to watch and feed and tease the animals of Central Park. He visited often at night, alone with God's creatures who never asked him about his religion or about drink or about Franklin Roosevelt.

The Al Smith of cheerful public performances was the Al Smith his children, especially his daughter, wanted everybody to remember and to cherish. But the bitter Al Smith mentioned in newspaper stories and passing into legend thanks to his harsh criticism of the New Deal was hard to ignore. A noted author named Emil Ludwig visited Smith in the Empire State Building as part of his research for a book about Franklin Roosevelt. Smith chewed on his cigar and said little. Ludwig came away with a picture of "an embittered misanthrope . . . at odds with himself and the world, not because he had lost the game, but because he felt he could no longer play it."[39]

In the White House, populated still with advisers who cherished the years they spent in service to Al Smith, Franklin Roosevelt appeared to move beyond the impulses that led him to try to punish Robert Moses and, by extension, Al Smith. He occasionally inquired about old Al with his labor secretary, Frances Perkins, who remained in touch with Smith with the full knowledge of the president. He surely must have talked about Smith with the man who helped him turn his ideas into law, Senator Robert Wagner. He once recalled with more than a little nostalgia how Al Smith used to resolve troublesome issues—everybody would be "sitting around a table," he said, until somebody came up with a solution. He reminded Perkins of another lesson he learned during his Albany years, not from Al Smith but from the Bowery boss Big Tim Sullivan, who served in the Senate with him. "Tim Sullivan used to say that the America of the future would be made out of the people who had come over in steerage and who knew in their own hearts and lives the difference between being despised and being accepted and liked," he told Perkins. Tim Sullivan, he said, "was right about the human heart."[40]

Franklin Roosevelt spent his life in first-class cabins, but he had absorbed the lessons he learned about those belowdecks, how they resented those who looked down at them. Those people went to the polls in 1932 and 1936 and voted for the Hudson Valley patrician with the common touch because they believed he accepted them and perhaps even liked them.

It was a measure of Al Smith's continued place in American public life that on October 1, 1939, he delivered a speech broadcast nationwide on radio urging Americans to "stand solidly" behind the man he spent so much time and energy deploring just three years earlier. But times had changed, and the evil Smith had warned against in early 1933, the evil of Hitler and the Nazis, had brought war to Europe for the second time in a quarter century. Smith came to Roosevelt's defense as the president sought to amend the country's neutrality laws to, in effect, allow the United States to sell arms to Great Britain and France a month after they declared war on Germany. Roosevelt, said Al Smith, "is so obviously right, so obviously on the side of common sense . . . that only those who lack an understanding of the issue will oppose him." His remarks had been advertised ahead of time and a group of protesters gathered outside a radio studio in Manhattan—the wrong one, as it turned out—carrying signs that read, "Al, are you going with the other crowd now?"[41]

Smith was barely off the air when a telegram arrived. "Very many thanks," wrote Franklin Roosevelt. "You were grand." Smith responded in a handwritten note, still a little chilly with its "Dear President" salutation. "I am sure you are going to win," he wrote, referring to the battle in Congress over the neutrality laws.[42]

The thaw was not enough to persuade Smith to support FDR's bid for a third term in 1940. He campaigned energetically for the Republican challenger, Wendell Wilkie, and made the most of Roosevelt's unprecedented break in the nation's hallowed two-term tradition. But there were no bitter recriminations after yet another Roosevelt victory, for there were issues at hand that were vastly more important than their relationship. Smith delivered another nationwide radio speech in January 1941 in support of Roosevelt's lend-lease plan to aid Britain, and he was rewarded with a telegram of thanks from his old acquaintance Winston Churchill.

Five months later, Smith again spoke on the radio to rally support for Roosevelt: "The president has made it perfectly clear the fact that with modern implements of war . . . we are sure to be next in line for invasion if the British fail," he said. Another telegram from the White House followed just after Smith finished, another crack in the ice.[43]

It was likely around this time that Frances Perkins told FDR that she would be traveling to New York and planned to stop by to see Al Smith. She always told him when she visited Smith, lest Roosevelt think she was plotting behind his back or colluding somehow with one of his most bitter critics.

"You're very good, aren't you," Roosevelt said. "You keep up that friendship."

Perkins wasn't used to the president engaging her with more than a few platitudes about Al Smith.

"I'm fond of him," she said. "I don't like him to feel he's got no friends in the old crowd."

The old crowd—Smith and Wagner and Perkins and Eleanor and Franklin and others, the Albany crowd that climbed the State Street hill when the century was young, worked the dimly lit hallways and elegant chambers of the gabled capitol building, argued for a new social contract, and resisted those who thought old ways were better. Franklin Roosevelt now thought of himself as part of that old crowd, even if his time in Albany was short and even if he was only a marginal figure at best while the others walked factory floors and tested fire escapes and wrote laws that sought to limit the exploitation of workers. Now, in the White House, he told stories of those days and made himself to be more important than he really was, on the side of issues that Al Smith championed, Smith and Wagner and Perkins and others like Big Tim Sullivan. The old crowd. The words seemed to soften the president, for he then said something to Perkins that she had never heard, not since they both left Albany for Washington.

"Tell Al that I think a lot of him and am grateful to him," Roosevelt said. "I wish he would come down and see me. I honestly mean that."[44]

The message was delivered, but Smith wasn't sure what to make of it. When he traveled to Washington a few days later, he called FDR's secretary, Grace Tully, mentioned that he was in town, and, while he didn't want to bother the president, well, he just wanted to pass along his good wishes.

"I know the president will want very much to see you," Tully said.[45]

The president did want to see him and he told Tully to make the arrangements. But the president was a busy man and his calendar was always full. How long, Tully asked, should the appointment last? "Oh, as long as he wants," the president said. "Several hours."

And why not? They hadn't spoken to each other in years. A lot of water under the bridge.

eighteen

PEACE

THE TWO MEN WHO MET each other for the first time in a lovely townhouse in Albany in 1911 were reunited on June 9, 1941, in the White House, and, like their first meeting, Al Smith and Franklin Roosevelt had little to say about it. The president had returned that morning, a Monday, after a weekend cruise aboard the USS *Potomac*, and greeted Smith at 12:30. Smith didn't stay for hours. He stayed for minutes, fifteen of them, and when he left reporters asked him what he and Roosevelt talked about. Smith didn't let on. He had come by, he said, simply to shake the president's hand and wish him well.

"Are all the hatchets buried now, governor?" one reporter asked.

"There never was any hatchet," Smith said.[1]

They met again slightly more than a month later, on July 23, and once again neither man revealed much about what was said. That they were together again so soon after their reunion of early June suggested, if nothing else, that the gulf between them had narrowed somewhat.

Within months Roosevelt led the nation into war, and Smith put aside his grievances and hurts for good. During his annual birthday chat with reporters on December 30, 1941, three weeks after Pearl Harbor, Smith seemed more buoyant and optimistic than he had been in years, puffing on a cigar and looking splendid at age sixty-eight in a dark blue suit with a red carnation in his lapel. The country, he said, was united, and, just as important, isolationism was dead and buried. Many of his Liberty League friends had opposed Roosevelt's support for the British as they defied Hitler's blitz and prepared for the invasion that never came. Smith was on Roosevelt's side before Pearl Harbor and it likely was no coincidence that because of his support when it was needed, he had met with the president twice in the space of a few weeks in the middle of 1941.

The day was coming, Smith said during his birthday interview, when the United States would realize the mistake it made in not joining the League of Nations. He said that after the war was won America would join "some form of organization to weld the democracies together, and if some dictator sticks his head over the fence we'll all sock him." There was no longer a Liberty League for Smith to quit, but his support for Roosevelt during the president's struggle to help the Allies and now his vision of America joining a postwar international organization marked a break with the league's funders and most prominent founders.[2]

Even with a world war raging, the White House offered Franklin Roosevelt no refuge from New York politics, and very suddenly and quite unexpectedly Al Smith was part of the conversation. In early 1942, New York governor Herbert Lehman, the man Smith and Roosevelt agreed upon when they were being disagreeable to each other in 1932, decided he had served long enough in Albany and would not seek reelection that year. Smith, Roosevelt, and Lehman represented twenty years of unbroken Democratic rule on the second floor of the capitol in Albany, and the party and the president believed it was imperative to keep the record intact—a loss in Franklin Roosevelt's home state would be embarrassing and, worse yet from their perspective, a morale booster for Republicans. The GOP was prepared to nominate a young, ambitious prosecutor named Thomas Dewey, who gave Lehman a run for his money in 1938 when he was just thirty-six years old. Roosevelt's top political aide, Ed Flynn, was in charge of the Democratic National Committee now, and he met with the president in the summer of 1942 to discuss the situation in New York. Flynn emerged from a meeting on July 8 to say that Roosevelt had two nonnegotiable traits for any Democrat seeking his support to be Lehman's successor and the latest steward of the Smith-Roosevelt legacy: the candidate, Flynn said, had to be a liberal and had to have been a supporter of the president's defense policies before Pearl Harbor. Roosevelt had a list of four people who met the test, Flynn said. One of them was Al Smith.[3]

Flynn must have savored the chance to drop Smith's name into the conversation, even if it was likely no more than a token gesture, for like so many in the old Albany crowd he had never lost his affection for the former governor. He and the other Smith people in the Roosevelt White House had watched with horror and confusion as the man they so admired campaigned against their boss in 1936 and 1940. But the war had changed what Smith said about Franklin Roosevelt, and even if he couldn't reconcile himself to the New Deal, he stood by Roosevelt when others did not. And now people were saying that Franklin Roosevelt might be trying to nudge Al Smith into running for governor again.

The following day, Smith was back at the White House—his third visit in less than a year—for a private conversation with the president that led the press to conclude that they were talking about the upcoming race for governor in New York and Smith's own prospects for a return to Albany. The meeting was held at Smith's request, and it was a measure of its importance that it was squeezed between a morning meeting with Admiral Ernest King, Roosevelt's chief of naval operations, and a late-morning conversation with Secretary of War Henry Stimson. Reporters descended on Smith as he left the White House to ask what he and Roosevelt had discussed. Did the president ask him to run for governor?[4]

"I don't remember," Smith said.

Did he have an announcement to make?

"No," he said.

Would he be open to running for governor again?

"No, too old."

A reporter noticed that Smith was wearing a white Panama hat, not his brown derby. Why was that?

"The derby is too hot in summer," Smith said, and he was on his way, giving up nothing. Perhaps there was nothing to give. Still, he seemed to be very much back in the game.[5]

There was no comeback, of course. Al Smith was indeed too old to think about returning to Albany fifteen years after he handed off the mansion on Eagle Street and the second-floor office in the capitol to Franklin Roosevelt. The reconciliation with Roosevelt, his continued place as a revered son of New York City, and his growing brood of grandchildren seemed to bring him a measure of peace. He and Katie spent their nights playing cards, often with guests and just as often with their own rules. He continued to maintain his office in the Empire State Building while serving on charitable boards, selling war bonds, and promoting Catholic causes.

He asked for another meeting with Roosevelt, this one on March 16, 1943. If the president ever needed a reminder that the home fires always needed tending, never mind great events that were unfolding thousands of miles away, March 16, 1943, would have done the trick. General George Patton's tanks were moving against Erwin Rommel's Afrika Korps in Tunisia, reports of devastating shipping losses in the North Atlantic were pouring into the War Department, and the Nazis were finishing up their extermination of the Jewish ghetto in Warsaw. But on March 16, the day before Saint Patrick's Day, a parade of New Yorkers made their way into Roosevelt's office to talk about local politics. New York City mayor Fiorello La Guardia came by first, in late morning (among the mayor's concerns was a shortage of poultry meat in New York City). Smith arrived at 12:30 after sharing a cab with British foreign secretary Anthony Eden and British ambassador Lord Halifax, who dropped him off on their way to the State Department. As usual, Smith was coy about his conversation with Roosevelt. "I just came in for a little talk," he said. And after Smith left, the head of the shriveled, mortally wounded Tammany Hall machine, Michael Kennedy, met with the president for more than an hour, a circumstance Smith surely found amusing, for he was among the dwindling, graying few who remembered the effete Roosevelt of 1911 and his nose-in-the-air contempt for Tammany Hall and machine politicians. But now, as president of the United States, Roosevelt spent an hour in conversation with the machine's boss—in the White House, talking about jobs! And just two hours earlier, he had entertained Tammany's greatest and most effective enemy, Mayor La Guardia. Who else but Frank Roosevelt could pull off such a stunt? You had to tip your derby to the man. He had learned a lot since the old days.[6]

Al Smith turned seventy on December 30, 1943, a Thursday, and he did so in a style to which New Yorkers had become accustomed: he brought in the city's newspaper reporters and spent a portion of the day, cigar stuck in the corner of his mouth, remembering the past, expounding on the present, and envisioning the future. He was asked whether he thought Franklin Roosevelt might run for a fourth term in 1944. Now was not the time for such talk, he said: "Let's polish off Adolf and Hirohito and then go back to politics."[7]

A note from the man himself, dated December 27, was on his desk. It referred to a reception planned for Smith later in the day. The president wished he could have been there. "Dear Al," Roosevelt's letter read,

> Our friends tell me that you are about to attain the dignity of three score years and ten.
>
> That has been known from time immemorial as the Scriptural age. It is a noble age by every manner of reckoning. On that account a man's friends like to make it the occasion of a testimonial on his behalf. I wish it were possible for me to join those who are honoring you next Thursday evening. But I shall be thinking of you on that happy occasion, and I send you hearty congratulations and warmest personal greetings.[8]

Other letters poured in from Republicans and Democrats alike, each one outdoing the other in praise for the child of the sidewalks of New

York who had nearly made it to the pinnacle of American politics. Most chose to avoid even the slightest reference to the unpleasantness of Smith's later years, not just his split with Roosevelt but the wounds incurred in 1928. But New York's Roman Catholic archbishop, Francis Spellman, simply couldn't resist. Al Smith, Spellman said, had shown his fellow Americans "how to rise above those who, in their prejudiced minds, betrayed the principles upon which our country was founded."[9]

A few weeks after his birthday, Smith decided to put aside one reminder of that difficult campaign of 1928: He auctioned off the brown derby—one of them, anyway—that he made famous during his whistle-stop speeches and campaign rallies that year. Proceeds went to the war effort. The brown derby fetched $150,000, paid for by New York's hotel and restaurant workers' union, men and women who washed dishes and bussed tables and who saw in Al Smith a piece of themselves.

The union donated the derby back to Smith, and he promptly said he'd never wear it again. Instead, he said, he'd put it someplace where he could point to it and tell visitors, "Here's the most expensive hat in the world"—Al Smith's brown derby.[10]

Katie Smith got sick in April 1944 and was taken to Saint Vincent's Hospital, a favorite charitable cause of both Smith and his friend Raskob. Smith was told she had pneumonia; in fact, she had cancer, and she died at six o'clock in the morning on May 5, two days before their forty-fourth wedding anniversary. The Al Smith who seemed so energetic and healthy during his birthday interview just four months earlier seemed like a very old man as he slumped in the front pew of St. Patrick's Cathedral for Katie's funeral mass. She had never aspired to be a partner in Smith's career as Eleanor had been for Franklin, but Smith's friends knew Al and Katie had a marriage, not an arrangement or an understanding. In Al's eyes, she was ever the sixteen-year-old he met in a parlor in the Bronx one day in the nineteenth century, and of the many sorrows and hurts heaped upon him in 1928, the worst were the cackling attacks on Katie, mostly about her matronly appearance.

A telegram from the White House arrived within hours of Katie's death. "I want you to know that I am thinking of you in your great loss and wish it were in my power to do something to lighten a grief so overwhelming," it read. "From a full heart I offer you and the children this assurance of deepest sympathy." The message was signed by Franklin Roosevelt, but the words were not the president's but those of an aide, William Hessett, who thought it right and important to reach out to Smith immediately rather than wait for the president to dictate his own thoughts—Roosevelt was in South Carolina in early May, and the clock was ticking for the coming invasion of Normandy. Regardless of its origins, the telegram under Roosevelt's name offered Smith solace when there was little to be had.[11]

He was tired. Friends like Robert Moses noticed and whispered their concerns to each other. But he soldiered on, summoning the press to the Empire State Building on May 25, just three weeks after Katie's death, to publicize a letter signed by governors, members of Congress, labor leaders, writers, and Smith himself, calling on the United States and its allies to accept refugees fleeing extermination in Europe. No person who participates in crimes against Jews, the letter read, should be allowed to escape punishment. Smith called for Allied governments to broadcast warnings to Nazi collaborators in occupied countries that they would face the wrath of humanity when Hitler was defeated.

He threw what energy he had left into the war that Franklin Roosevelt was commanding, and when he appeared on stage at a bond rally in mid-June, a band struck up "The Sidewalks of New York," no longer a campaign song but a tribute to the man who had grown up on those sidewalks. "I've heard that song before," Smith deadpanned.[12]

He performed well, but Robert Moses was right: he was tired. He checked into St. Vincent's Hospital in late June, and almost immediately a telegram arrived from a very busy Roosevelt, wishing him a speedy return to health. Smith assured him that he was fine and he was soon released.

Officially he was suffering from heart and lung congestion, but a later biographer learned from family members that the old governor had cirrhosis. He was back in the hospital in August, and the White House kept a careful watch over the patient from afar. On September 13, Roosevelt aide Steve Early sent a memo to the president, who was in Quebec with Winston Churchill to talk about the war and the peace that would follow, advising him of Smith's condition. "Al Smith is seriously ill—not expected to live." A telegram from Quebec was dispatched to Smith's bedside the same day. "I am thinking of you and know if you follow the doctor's orders you will be feeling yourself again," Roosevelt wrote. "Winston is with me and joins heartily in good wishes." Smith was in no shape to acknowledge the president and prime minister, so his daughter, Emily, sent Roosevelt a thank-you note.[13]

The press reported that Smith was rallying but the opposite was true, and his doctor announced on October 2 that the governor was "gravely ill." Franklin and Eleanor Roosevelt dispatched a dozen red roses to their ailing old friend. They arrived at around the same time Al Smith died, on October 4, 1944, at the age of seventy.[14]

His people wept and mourned as they would have for a family member or a close friend, which he indeed seemed to be. More than 160,000 people lined up outside St. Patrick's Cathedral on a dreary wet fall day to wait for their chance to walk by his coffin, placed in the center aisle near the altar. His family had planned to keep the coffin closed but the public demanded one last look at that familiar face, imagining that gold-toothed smile, conjuring memories of that unapologetically New York voice. The coffin stayed open, and so did the cathedral, long into the night of October 6, until the last mourner passed the bier at one in the morning. Later on that Saturday morning, as a bright autumn sun shone on all the black suits and dresses, the old crowd reassembled in the cathedral for Al Smith's funeral: two of his Albany roommates, Robert Wagner and Jimmy Walker; Eleanor Roosevelt, without her husband, who was in Hyde Park but was ill; Jim Farley, who got his first taste of power working for Smith in the early 1920s; Samuel Seabury, Jimmy Walker's tormentor and the man who once described Al Smith as the best of a bad lot; Ed Flynn, like Smith a protégé of the old Tammany boss Charles Francis Murphy, now the most important dispenser of political advice to the president of the United States. Frances Perkins issued a moving statement about the man who always told her the truth. So did the president: "To the populace, he was a hero," Roosevelt wrote. "Frank, friendly, and warmhearted, honest as the noonday sun, he had the courage of his convictions, even when his espousal of unpopular causes invited the enmity of powerful adversaries."[15]

The *New York Times* summed up the man's appeal and his legacy in two sentences: "From a newsboy and fishmonger to four times Governor of the Empire State and the candidacy of his party for President, the rise of Alfred E. Smith has no exact parallel in American history. There have been country boys in plenty, such as Lincoln and Garfield, who rose to the heights, but no other city urchin, earning a precarious living in the streets in his early days, ever rose so superior to his lack of youthful advantages and had so distinguished a public career."[16]

Thirty-five thousand people gathered on the sidewalks of New York near St. Patrick's to watch as Smith's coffin was carried down the cathedral steps and placed inside a hearse. From the cathedral in midtown they brought him to a cemetery in Queens, crossing the East River, his swimming hole and playground so many years ago, a river that had long since ceased to be a barrier between separate and rival cities. The Brooklyn Bridge of Al Smith's youth was as majestic as ever, but now it was simply the loveliest of a handful of great spans connecting the island of his birth with Brooklyn and Queens. They buried him next to Katie in old Calvary Cemetery in Long Island City, with its breathtaking view of the East Side of Manhattan.

Less than a month later, a gaunt and exhausted Franklin Roosevelt delivered one of the final speeches of his 1944 reelection campaign in Boston's Fenway Park on the Friday night before the nation went to the polls. He devoted the first several minutes of his speech not to the pressing issues of 1944 and his own achievements during a dozen memorable years in office but to Al Smith and the ways he had challenged and changed

America. The president reminded his audience that he had visited Boston in 1928 to urge voters to support Smith's doomed presidential candidacy. "And you did vote for that eternally 'Happy Warrior.'. . . And while I am speaking of that campaign of 1928, let me remind you that, having nominated Al Smith for the second time for the presidency, I was then running at his request for the governorship of New York. . . . And when I talked here in Boston in 1928 I talked about racial and religious intolerance which was then—as unfortunately it still is to some extent—a menace to the liberties of America. And all the bigots in those days were gunning for Al Smith."

But now, he said, "the Murphys and the Kellys, the Smiths and the Joneses, the Coens, the Carusos, the Kowalskis, the Schultzes, the Olsens and the Swobodas and . . . the Cabots and the Lowells" were fighting side by side in a common cause. "And it's our duty to them to make sure that, big as this country is, there is no room in it for racial or religious intolerance. And there is no room for snobbery."[17]

The following Tuesday, Franklin Roosevelt won reelection to a fourth term over another ambitious New York governor, Thomas Dewey. The achievement was historic but the mood was subdued, for the victor was a sick man whose blank stares and slacking jaw led the nation's urban political bosses to replace his third-term vice president, Henry Wallace, with a more reliable senator from Missouri, Harry Truman, for they knew Franklin Roosevelt would expire before his fourth term did. He met with Frances Perkins after a long cabinet meeting on the day before his fourth inauguration. "He had the pallor, the deep gray color, of a man who had been long ill," Perkins would later write. "He supported his head with his hand as though it were too much to hold it up. His lips were blue. His hand shook." Roosevelt begged her not to resign, as she wished to do. They both had tears in their eyes as they spoke. She did not resign.[18]

He took the oath the following day in front of a small crowd on the south portico of the White House. His inaugural address was the shortest since George Washington's second, amounting to no more than five hundred words. He was soon off to the Crimea—bringing along his trusted political adviser, Ed Flynn—to meet with Josef Stalin and Winston Churchill at Yalta to plan for the coming postwar world, and when he returned and addressed a joint session of Congress about the talks, he did so while seated in front of a desk rather than standing. Sitting, he told his audience almost apologetically, relieved him from the chore of encasing his legs in ten pounds of steel. It was the first time in his dozen years as president that he acknowledged his disability. Members of Congress, regardless of party, gave him an ovation.

He died six weeks later, on April 12, 1945, while in Warm Springs, as the armies he commanded moved closer to victory, as the nation he led was on the verge of becoming something for which a word had to be invented—a superpower. His body was brought to Washington and lay in state in the East Room as the mighty and the famous bowed their heads and tried to recall a day when Franklin Roosevelt was not president of the United States. He was then brought home to Springwood aboard a seventeen-car train that arrived in the Hudson Valley not long after dawn on April 15, hugging the eastern bank of the river he loved, passing under a new suspension bridge connecting Dutchess and Ulster Counties, a bridge he and Al Smith dedicated together on a fine late-summer day in 1930. The train hissed to a stop near the manor house, and the remains of Franklin Roosevelt were transported up the estate's steep embankment, shaded by the oak and hemlock trees he loved so well.

He was laid to rest in a rose garden on the bluff overlooking Crum Elbow, as the brine of the harbor met the runoff from the mountains, as city and country came together beneath the placid surface of a once unbridgeable chasm.

ACKNOWLEDGMENTS

MORE THAN A DECADE AGO, my old boss at the *New York Ob-server*, Peter Kaplan, took me out to lunch, ordered his usual tuna on toast and black coffee, looked me in the eye, and said, "I have an idea for a book for you." He paused and said, simply, "Frank and Al." That was all he had to say—the arc of the story, and its importance, didn't have to be stated. It was obvious, at least to the two of us. We both had been born about a decade after Frank and Al died, but we had in common an abid-ing appreciation for these two great New Yorkers. Sadly, I wasn't able to begin this story until many years later, and Peter died in 2013 at the age of fifty-nine. But his insights and encouragement were with me through-out my research and writing.

Peter and Arthur Carter, the founder and former publisher of the *Ob-server*, were responsible for training and supporting dozens of journalists who are now in positions of influence and leadership at a time when free-dom of the press is under attack. These journalists and their colleagues are not enemies of the people—they are relentless, determined, and in-defatigable seekers of the truth. I am proud to have worked with so many of them, and am eternally grateful for the wisdom and courage of both Peter Kaplan and Arthur Carter.

In telling the story of Frank and Al, I have been similarly blessed. My editor, Elisabeth Dyssegaard, needed no introduction to the characters who populate these pages. Her guidance and knowledge turned an unruly manuscript into a story with lessons for our own time.

Her assistant, Laura Apperson, and the sales and publicity staff at St. Martin's Press were extraordinarily helpful and enthusiastic. Donna Cherry, senior production editor, made everything run smoothly. Copy editor Ryan Masteller asked all the right questions and often provided the answers, and for that I'm thankful.

The bulk of my research took place in one of my favorite places on earth, the Franklin D. Roosevelt Museum and Library in Hyde Park, New York. My thanks to the library's former deputy director, Bob Clark; archivists Kirsten Carter, Sarah Navins, and Virginia Lewick; archives technician Patrick Fahy; and public program specialist Cliff Laube. I was lucky enough to conduct research at another favorite place, the Museum of the City of New York. Thanks to deputy director Sarah Henry, director of public programs Frances Rosenfeld, and Lauren Robinson.

I'm grateful to the archivists, educators, and support staff at all of the institutions I visited in the course of researching this book. They include the New York Public Library, the New York State Library, the New York State Archives, the Library of Congress, and the Columbia University Rare Book and Manuscript Library.

Countless friends, acquaintances, and colleagues have offered advice, encouragement, and the occasional libation when the first two were not enough. They include Pete Kelly, Peter Quinn, Sridhar Pappu, Jim Quinn, Josh Benson, Kathleen O'Brien, Dan Goldberg, Jack McEneny, Jay Dillon, Dan Barry, Ellen O'Brien Kelly, Joe Trinity, and Mary Trinity.

Janet and Al Faicco and Joanne and Don Sanbeg allowed me to take them on a tour of FDR's home and to rehearse some of the stories that later became part of this book. Their enthusiasm was a source of strength when words were hard to come by.

The story of Frank and Al was previewed in my doctoral dissertation, which was researched and written under the guidance of John Whiteclay Chambers II, Warren Kimball, and David Greenberg of Rutgers University and Mark Lender of Kean University.

I'm grateful to my extraordinary colleagues at Politico, especially Joe Schatz, John Appezzato, and David Giambusso, for giving me the time and space I needed. Thanks, too, to Politico's Albany bureau—Jimmy Vielkind, Bill Mahoney, Keshia Clukey, Marie French, and Nick Niedzwiadek—for their patience when I regaled them with stories about New York politics in the early twentieth century. There was a point to those stories—really, there was.

Thanks, too, to the faculty and staff at New York University's Glucksman Ireland House for their support and encouragement.

My agent and friend John Wright believed in this book from the very beginning, and that sometimes took a good deal of faith and determination.

My wife, Eileen Duggan, and children, Katie and Conor, have joined me on visits to places where the spirits of Frank and Al live on. It is a most unusual hobby. I thank them for indulging me.

NOTES

A NOTE ON SOURCES

The great *New York Times* writer Dan Barry described his book on the longest baseball game ever played, *Bottom of the 33rd,* as a work of "informed imagination." I can think of no better way to describe some of *Frank and Al.* For example, I don't know for certain how Al Smith's Tammany friends reacted when Franklin Roosevelt sent him a letter of endorsement in 1918, or whether Charles Francis Murphy had a good laugh over FDR's suggestion that his ally William Church Osborn ought to run for governor that year. But I have spent nearly two decades reading about and thinking about the characters in this book. I can only imagine how Murphy reacted to Roosevelt's impudence, circa 1918, or what Smith's friends made of FDR's endorsement that year. I can only imagine, and I did.

The sources below speak for themselves.

Except where indicated, all correspondence between Frank and Al is contained in the collection labeled Family, Business, and Personal Papers in the Franklin D. Roosevelt Library in Hyde Park, New York.

PROLOGUE

1. This account of Al Smith in Albany is based on several biographies and articles. Specific details are taken from Robert Slayton, *Empire Statesman: The Rise and Redemption of Al Smith* (New York: The Free Press, 2001), 74–78; William Kennedy, *O Albany!: Improbable City of Political Wizards, Fearless Ethnics, Spectacular*

   Aristocrats, Splendid Nobodies, and Underrated Scoundrels (New York: Penguin, 1985), 182–84; *Albany Evening Journal,* January 21, 1911.

2. *New York Times,* July 29, 1911.

3. *New York Times,* January 23, 1911.

4. R. W. Barkley to Franklin D. Roosevelt, January 26, 1911, Franklin D. Roosevelt Papers as State Senator, Franklin D. Roosevelt Library (hereafter, FDR Papers, FDRL).

5. *The Reminiscences of Frances Perkins,* Columbia Center for Oral History; Christopher M. Finan, *Alfred E. Smith: The Happy Warrior* (New York: Hill & Wang, 2002), 81.

6. FDR diary, FDR Papers as State Senator, FDRL.

7. Geoffrey C. Ward, *A First-Class Temperament: The Emergence of Franklin Roosevelt, 1905–1928* (New York: Vintage Books, 1989), 126.

8. Robert Caro, *The Power Broker: Robert Moses and the Fall of New York* (New York: Vintage Books, 1975), 285.

9. Slayton, *Empire Statesman,* 398.

CHAPTER ONE: RIVER FAMILIES

1. Tom Lewis, *The Hudson: A History* (New Haven: Yale University Press, 2007), 258–61.

2. *New York Times,* May 15, 1878.

3. Al Smith, *Up to Now: An Autobiography* (New York: Viking Press, 1929), 22.

4. Matthew and Hannah Josephson, *Al Smith: Hero of the Cities* (Boston: Houghton Mifflin, 1969), 21.

5. *New York Times,* October 7, 1894; Mike Wallace and Edwin C. Burrows, *Gotham: A History of New York to 1898* (New York: Oxford University Press, 1998), 1025; Thomas Kessner, *Capital City: New York City and the Men behind America's Rise to Economic Dominance, 1860–1900* (New York: Simon & Schuster, 2004), 193.

6. Al Smith, "New York Is My America," Private Papers of Alfred E. Smith, Box 41, New York State Library, Albany, NY.

7. Richard O'Connor, *The First Hurrah: A Biography of Alfred E. Smith* (New York: G. P. Putnam's Sons, 1970), 17.

CHAPTER TWO: FATHERS, MOTHERS, AND SONS

1. Sara Roosevelt's diary is contained in the Rita Halle Keelman Papers, Box 2, FDRL.

2. Jean Edward Smith, *FDR* (New York: Random House, 2008), 19.

3. Robert Slayton, *Empire Statesman: The Rise and Redemption of Al Smith* (New York: The Free Press, 2001), 10.

4. Al Smith, *Up to Now: An Autobiography* (New York: Viking Press, 1929), 25.

5. *New York Times,* January 19, 1925.

6. Matthew and Hannah Josephson, *Al Smith: Hero of the Cities* (Boston: Houghton Mifflin, 1969), 35.

7. Josephson and Josephson, *Al Smith*, 42–43.

8. Emily Smith Warner, *The Happy Warrior: The Story of My Father, Alfred E. Smith* (New York: Doubleday & Co., 1956), 27.

9. Sara Roosevelt diary, Keelman Papers, FDRL.

CHAPTER THREE: YOUNG MEN IN A HURRY

1. Emily Smith Warner, *The Happy Warrior: The Story of My Father, Alfred E. Smith* (New York: Doubleday & Co., 1956), 30–31.

2. Matthew and Hannah Josephson, *Al Smith: Hero of the Cities* (Boston: Houghton Mifflin, 1969), 48–49, 53.

3. Alfred E. Smith Papers, Museum of the City of New York.

4. Elliot Roosevelt, ed., *The Roosevelt Letters, Being the Personal Correspondence of Franklin Delano Roosevelt*, vol. 1 (London: George G. Harrap & Co., 1949), 391.

5. Roosevelt, *Roosevelt Letters*, 394.

6. Geoffrey C. Ward, *Before the Trumpet: Young Franklin Roosevelt, 1882–1905* (New York: Vintage Books, 1985), 290.

7. Kenneth Davis, *FDR: The Beckoning of Destiny, 1882–1928* (New York: G. P. Putnam's Sons, 1971), 150.

8. *New York Times*, January 17, 1925.

9. Richard O'Connor, *The First Hurrah: A Biography of Alfred E. Smith* (New York: G. P. Putnam's Sons, 1970), 48–49.

10. Jean Edward Smith, *FDR* (New York: Random House, 2008), 59.

CHAPTER FOUR: ALBANY

1. Al Smith, *Up to Now: An Autobiography* (New York: Viking Press, 1929), 69–70.

2. Smith, *Up to Now*, 76.

3. Smith, *Up to Now*, 76; Christopher M. Finan, *Alfred E. Smith: The Happy Warrior* (New York: Hill & Wang, 2002), 57.

4. Smith, *Up to Now*, 74–75.

5. Smith, in *Up to Now*, says he was not assigned to these committees until 1905, but committee assignments listed in *Documents of the Assembly of the State of New York, 1904*, vol. 1, 41–48, lists all committee assignments and had Smith on Banks as well as Public Lands and Forestry.

6. Ray Tucker, "The Story of Al Smith," *American Review of Books*, February 1928.

7. Smith, *Up to Now*, 75.

8. Kenneth Davis, *FDR: The Beckoning of Destiny, 1882–1928* (New York: G. P. Putnam's Sons, 1971), 213.

9. Elliot Roosevelt, *FDR: His Personal Letters, 1905–1928* (New York: Duell, Sloan and Pearce 1948), 157.

10. Ernest K. Lindley, *Franklin D. Roosevelt: A Career in Progressive Democracy* (Indianapolis: Bobbs-Merrill, 1931), 78.

11. Letter to FDR, November 9, 1910, unknown signature, FDR Papers as State Senator, FDRL.

CHAPTER FIVE: LEADERSHIP

1. Al Smith, *Up to Now: An Autobiography* (New York: Viking Press, 1929), 90; Robert Caro, *The Power Broker: Robert Moses and the Fall of New York* (New York: Vintage Books, 1975), 121.

2. *New York Times*, January 30, 1907; February 24, 1909.

3. George Martin, *Madame Secretary: Frances Perkins* (Boston: Houghton Mifflin Harcourt, 1983), 81–84.

4. Robert Slayton, *Empire Statesman: The Rise and Redemption of Al Smith* (New York: The Free Press, 2001), 84.

5. Caro, *Power Broker*, 122.

6. *New York Times*, December 17, 1910.

7. FDR diary, FDR Papers as State Senator, FDRL.

8. FDR diary, FDR Papers as State Senator, FDRL.

9. J. Joseph Huthmacher, *Senator Robert F. Wagner and the Rise of Urban Liberalism* (New York: Atheneum, 1971), 13; Leon Keyserling Oral History, Harry S. Truman Presidential Library, www.trumanlibrary.org/oralhist/keyserl.htm.

10. Geoffrey C. Ward, *A First-Class Temperament: The Emergence of Franklin Roosevelt, 1905–1928* (New York: Vintage Books, 1989), 159.

11. Samuel Beskin to FDR, January 3, 1911; W. J. Kiernan to FDR, February 25, 1911, FDR Papers as State Senator, FDRL.

12. Harvey Hinman to FDR, March 20, 1911; FDR to Rev. J. J. Cowles and Rev. W. L. Hughes, June 20, 1911; C. F. Shaffer to FDR, February 12, 1911; FDR to Augustus Walker, April 14, 1911, FDR Papers as State Senator, FDRL.

13. *New York Times*, January 22, 1911.

14. *New York Times*, June 8, 1911; Ward, *First-Class Temperament*, 154.

15. *The Reminiscences of Frances Perkins*, Columbia Center for Oral History.

16. *The Reminiscences of Frances Perkins*, Columbia Center for Oral History.

17. *New York Times*, April 1, 1911.

18. FDR to Paul Fuller, April 14, 1911, FDR Papers as State Senator, FDRL.

CHAPTER SIX: FIRE

1. Al Smith, *Up to Now: An Autobiography* (New York: Viking Press, 1929), 99.

2. Frances Perkins talked about how moved Smith was in the aftermath of the fire. See George Martin, *Madam Secretary: Frances Perkins* (Boston: Houghton Mifflin Harcourt, 1983), 88–90.

3. The account of Smith's remarks is taken from Martin, *Madam Secretary*, 88–89, and from a lecture by Frances Perkins on September 30, 1964, a copy of which is in Cornell University's Kheel Center for Labor-Management Documentation and Archives, https://trianglefire.ilr.cornell.edu/primary/lectures/FrancesPerkinsLecture.html?CFID = 2062762&CFTOKEN = 85602757 (accessed August 8, 2016).

4. Matthew and Hannah Josephson, *Al Smith: Hero of the Cities* (Boston: Houghton Mifflin, 1969), 133–34.

5. *New York Times*, March 13, 1913.

6. Robert Slayton, *Empire Statesman: The Rise and Redemption of Al Smith* (New York: The Free Press, 2001), 96.

7. Josephson and Josephson, *Al Smith*, 130–31.

8. *New York Times*, March 2, 1912.

9. *The Reminiscences of Frances Perkins*, Columbia Center for Oral History.

10. Langdon Marvin to FDR, January 31, 1912, FDR Papers as State Senator, FDRL.

11. Marvin to FDR, February 15, 1912, FDR Papers as State Senator, FDRL.

12. FDR to Marvin, March 1, 1912; Marvin to FDR, March 4, 1912, FDR Papers as State Senator, FDRL.

13. Jean Edward Smith, *FDR* (New York: Random House, 2008), 98.

14. Theodore Roosevelt to FDR, March 18, 1913, FDR Papers as Assistant Secretary of the Navy, FDRL.

15. Frank Freidel, *Franklin D. Roosevelt: A Rendezvous with Destiny* (New York: Back Bay Books, 1990), 20.

16. FDR to Abram Elkus, February 13, 1913, FDR Papers as State Senator, FDRL.

CHAPTER SEVEN: CHANGING TIMES

1. Richard O'Connor, *The First Hurrah: A Biography of Alfred E. Smith* (New York: G. P. Putnam's Sons, 1970), 70.

2. Robert Slayton, *Empire Statesman: The Rise and Redemption of Al Smith* (New York: The Free Press, 2001), 98.

3. O'Connor, *First Hurrah*, 77.

4. O'Connor, *First Hurrah*, 80–81.

5. Al Smith, *Up to Now: An Autobiography* (New York: Viking Press, 1929), 142; *New York State Constitutional Convention, Revised Record* (Albany: J. B. Lyon, 1916), 2975.

6. Christopher M. Finan, *Alfred E. Smith: The Happy Warrior* (New York: Hill & Wang, 2002), 103.

7. Smith, *Up to Now*, 140.

8. O'Connor, *First Hurrah*, 86.

9. Slayton, *Empire Statesman*, 113.

10. One such example, Stanley Weintraub, *Young Mr. Roosevelt: FDR's Introduction to War, Politics, and Life* (New York: Da Capo Press, 2013), views Roosevelt's years in the Wilson administration as a critical part of his political maturation.

11. William Gibbs McAdoo to FDR, April 29, 1913; FDR to McAdoo, May 9, 1916; McAdoo to FDR, February 16, 1917, FDR Papers as Assistant Secretary of the Navy, FDRL.

12. For examples of FDR's plotting, see George Davidson to FDR, November 21, 1913; Mark Richards to FDR, February 16, 1914; and Chester Platt to FDR, May 23, 1914, FDR Papers as Assistant Secretary of the Navy, FDRL.

13. McAdoo to FDR, August 15, 1914, FDR Papers as Assistant Secretary of the Navy, FDRL.

14. The campaign letter is included with McAdoo to FDR, August 15, 1914, FDR Papers as Assistant Secretary of the Navy, FDRL.

15. Jean Edward Smith, *FDR* (New York: Random House, 2008), 124.

16. *New York Sun*; *New York Times*, July 5, 1917.

17. Finan, *Alfred E. Smith*, 107.

18. J. Joseph Huthmacher, *Senator Robert F. Wagner and the Rise of Urban Liberalism* (New York: Atheneum, 1971), 41.

19. Geoffrey C. Ward, *A First-Class Temperament: The Emergence of Franklin Roosevelt, 1905–1928* (New York: Vintage Books, 1989), 182.

20. Frank Freidel, *Franklin D. Roosevelt: The Apprenticeship* (Boston: Little Brown & Co., 1952), 343.

21. *New York Times*, July 25, 1918.

22. *New York Times*, July 25, 1918.

23. *New York Times*, October 21, 1918.

24. FDR to Al Smith, October 14, 1918; Smith to FDR, October 19, 1918.

CHAPTER EIGHT: BRIDGE BUILDING

1. The Malbone Street disaster and the subsequent trials of BRT officials and Luciano were covered extensively in the New York press. For some examples, see the *New York Times* and *New York Sun*, November 2, 3, 4, 5, 1918, and *New York Times*, March 19, April 5 and 6, 1919.

2. *New York Times*, November 2, 1918.

3. *New York Times*, January 3, 1933.

4. Geoffrey C. Ward, *A First-Class Temperament: The Emergence of Franklin Roosevelt, 1905–1928* (New York: Vintage Books, 1989), 417.

5. *New York Times*, November 6, 1918; Al Smith, *Up to Now: An Autobiography* (New York: Viking Press, 1929), 164.

6. Smith, *Up to Now*, 165.

7. *New York Times*, November 7, 1918.

8. Tom Foley to James Farley, December 2, 1918, James A. Farley Papers, Library of Congress.

9. FDR to Al Smith, December 27, 1918.
10. Smith to FDR, January 6, 1919.
11. *New York Times*, January 18, 1919.
12. Joseph Proskauer, *A Segment of My Times* (New York: Farrar, Straus, 1950), 42.
13. See, as examples of the growing relationship between FDR and Smith, FDR to Smith, March 17, 1919, April 2, 1919, April 23, 1919; and Smith to FDR, March 13, 1919.
14. *New York Times*, January 2, 1919.
15. George Martin, *Madam Secretary: Frances Perkins* (Boston: Houghton Mifflin Harcourt, 1983), 143–144.
16. *New York Times*, November 3, 1919.
17. *New York Times*, January 14, 1920.
18. Richard O'Connor, *The First Hurrah: A Biography of Alfred E. Smith* (New York: G. P. Putnam's Sons, 1970), 117; *New York Times*, February 12, 1920.
19. Henry Moskowitz, ed., *Progressive Democracy: Addresses and State Papers of Alfred E. Smith* (New York: Harcourt, Brace and Company, 1928), 278.
20. *New York Times*, February 12, 1920.
21. Jean Edward Smith, *FDR* (New York: Random House, 2008), 173.
22. In his biography of Smith, Robert Slayton suggests that the photographs were of victims of starvation in Armenia. See *Empire Statesman: The Rise and Redemption of Al Smith* (New York: The Free Press, 2001), 140–44.
23. O'Connor, *First Hurrah*, 110.
24. Slayton, *Empire Statesman*, 145.
25. *New York Times*, October 30, 1919.
26. O'Connor, *First Hurrah*, 190.

CHAPTER NINE: DEFEAT

1. Robert Slayton, *Empire Statesman: The Rise and Redemption of Al Smith* (New York: The Free Press, 2001), 196.
2. Edward J. Flynn, *You're the Boss: The Practice of American Politics* (New York: Collier, 1962), 80.
3. *Baltimore Evening Sun*, July 1, 1920.
4. Emily Smith Warner, *The Happy Warrior: The Story of My Father, Alfred E. Smith* (New York: Doubleday & Co., 1956), 122.
5. Marion Elizabeth Rogers, ed., *The Impossible H. L. Mencken: A Selection of His Best Newspaper Stories* (New York: Anchor Books, 1991), 248.
6. *Official Report of the Proceedings of the Democratic National Convention* (Indianapolis: Bookwalter-Ball Printing Co., 1920), 136–40.
7. Frances Perkins, *The Roosevelt I Knew* (New York: Viking Press, 1946), 27; Geoffrey C. Ward, *A First-Class Temperament: The Emergence of Franklin Roosevelt, 1905–1928* (New York: Vintage Books, 1989), 509.

8. *Official Report of the Proceedings*, 141.
9. *New York Times*, July 2, 1920.
10. *New York Times*, July 1, 1920.
11. *Official Report of the Proceedings*, 444–45.
12. *New York Times*, August 10, 1920.
13. Ward, *First-Class Temperament*, 532.
14. *New York Times*, October 31, 1920.
15. Smith to FDR, November 8, 1920; FDR to Smith, November 9, 1920.

CHAPTER TEN: RESURRECTION

1. FDR to William Gibbs McAdoo, April 23, 1922, FDR Family, Business and Personal Papers, FDRL.
2. McAdoo to FDR, May 29, 1922, FDR Family, Business and Personal Papers, FDRL.
3. FDR to Langdon Marvin, September 3, 1921, FDR Family, Business and Personal Papers, FDRL.
4. FDR to Neal Brewster, June 20, 1922, FDR Papers, 1920–28, FDRL.
5. FDR to Al Smith, July 28, 1922.
6. *New York Times*, May 2, 1922.
7. *New York Times*, February 12, 1922.
8. Robert Slayton, *Empire Statesman: The Rise and Redemption of Al Smith* (New York: The Free Press, 2001), 137.
9. Slayton, *Empire Statesman*, 152; *New York Times*, August 7, 1922.
10. *New York Times*, August 7, 1922.
11. FDR to Smith, August 14, 1922.
12. Smith to FDR, August 15, 1922.
13. *New York Times*, August 16 and 17, 1922.
14. McAdoo to FDR, August 23, 1922, FDR Family, Business and Personal Papers, FDRL.
15. James A. Farley, *Behind the Ballots: The Personal Story of a Politician* (New York: Harcourt, Brace, 1938), 33.
16. Matthew and Hannah Josephson, *Al Smith: Hero of the Cities* (Boston: Houghton Mifflin, 1969), 271.
17. Josephson and Josephson, *Al Smith*, 271; Farley, *Behind the Ballots*, 37.
18. *New York Evening Post*, September 30, 1922.
19. Geoffrey C. Ward, *A First-Class Temperament: The Emergence of Franklin Roosevelt, 1905–1928* (New York: Vintage Books, 1989), 644.
20. Smith to FDR, October 8, 1922.
21. FDR to Smith, October 15, 1922.
22. Slayton, *Empire Statesman*, 155,
23. FDR to Joseph Davies, November 18, 1922, FDR Papers, 1920–1928, FDRL.

CHAPTER ELEVEN: THE DARNED OLD LIQUOR QUESTION

1. Matthew and Hannah Josephson, *Al Smith: Hero of the Cities* (Boston: Houghton Mifflin, 1969), 283.
2. *New York Times*, January 2, 1923.
3. FDR to Al Smith, May 23, 1923.
4. Robert Slayton, *Empire Statesman: The Rise and Redemption of Al Smith* (New York: The Free Press, 2001), 201.
5. FDR to Smith, May 21, 1923.
6. Edward J. Flynn, *You're the Boss: The Practice of American Politics* (New York: Collier Books, 1962), 55.
7. *New York Times*, June 1, 1923.
8. *New York Times*, June 10, 1923.
9. *New York Times*, June 11, 1923.
10. FDR to William Jennings Bryan, June 20, 1923, FDR Family, Business and Personal Papers, FDRL.
11. Jean Edward Smith, *FDR* (New York: Random House, 2008), 204.
12. See coverage of FDR's activities in *New York Times*, May 3 and 15, December 3, 1922; Smith's visit is covered in the *New York Times*, August 26, 1923.
13. Geoffrey C. Ward, *A First-Class Temperament: The Emergence of Franklin Roosevelt, 1905–1928* (New York: Vintage Books, 1989), 683.
14. *New York Evening Post*, January 23, 1924.
15. FDR to H. J. Adamson, January 28, 1924, FDR Papers, 1920–1928, FDRL.
16. Daniel Roper to FDR, August 22, 1923; January 21, 1924, FDR Papers, 1920–1928, FDRL.
17. *New York Times*, February 12, 1924.
18. *New York Times*, April 15, 1924.
19. *New York Times*, April 16, 1924.
20. Robert K. Murray, *The 103rd Ballot: Democrats and the Disaster in Madison Square Garden* (New York: Harper & Row, 1976), 19; *New York Times*, September 10, 1924.
21. For coverage of the Klan, see *New York Times*, March 22, April 6 and 27, May 31, 1924.
22. *New York Times*, April 26, 1924.
23. *New York Times*, April 26, 1924.

CHAPTER TWELVE: THE HAPPY WARRIOR

1. *New York Herald-Tribune*, May 1, 1924.
2. *New York Times*, May 6, 1924.
3. Babe Ruth to FDR, May 9, 1924, FDR Papers Pertaining to the 1924 Campaign, FDRL.
4. Anonymous letter to FDR, May 26, 1924, FDR Papers Pertaining to the 1924 Campaign, FDRL.

5. G. Deah to Al Smith, June 26, 1924, FDR Papers Pertaining to the 1924 Campaign, FDRL.

6. *New York Times*, October 26, 1923.

7. Philip M. Chase, *William Gibbs McAdoo: The Last Progressive*, unpublished PhD diss., University of Southern California, 237, http://digitallibrary.usc.edu/cdm/ref /collection/p15799coll127/id/140194 (accessed December 2, 2017).

8. *The Reminiscences of Joseph Proskauer*, Columbia Center for Oral History.

9. The exchange over the "Happy Warrior" speech is taken from Proskauer's oral history.

10. Geoffrey C. Ward, *A First-Class Temperament: The Emergence of Franklin Roosevelt, 1905–1928* (New York: Vintage Books, 1989), 695.

11. Kenneth Davis, *FDR: The Beckoning of Destiny, 1882–1928* (New York: G. P. Putnam's Sons, 1971), 754; *New York Times*, June 24, 1924; Robert K. Murray, *The 103rd Ballot: Democrats and the Disaster in Madison Square Garden* (New York: Harper & Row, 1976), 104.

12. Murray, *103rd Ballot*, 117.

13. *New York Times*, June 26, 1924.

14. Murray, *103rd Ballot*, 126.

15. James Roosevelt and Sidney Shalett, *Affectionately, F.D.R.: A Son's Story of a Lonely Man* (New York: Harcourt, Brace & Co., 1959), 205.

16. The dramatic story of FDR's journey from his seat to the podium is told in many biographies, based in part on James Roosevelt's memoir, cited above. However, in a long account in the *New York Times* on June 27, 1924, journalist Elmer Davis wrote that "Roosevelt was brought to the platform in a wheelchair" and then, using crutches, he "walked" to the podium with the help of James A. Lynch of Poughkeepsie. James Roosevelt's firsthand account is likely more reliable.

17. *New York Times*, June 27, 1924.

18. George Martin, *Madam Secretary: Frances Perkins* (Boston: Houghton Mifflin Harcourt, 1983), 184–85.

19. Murray, *103rd Ballot*, 177.

20. Ward, *First-Class Temperament*, 697.

CHAPTER THIRTEEN: UNCIVIL WAR

1. *New York World*, July 7, 1924; Frank Freidel, *Franklin D. Roosevelt: The Ordeal* (Boston: Little, Brown, 1954), 177.

2. Robert K. Murray, *The 103rd Ballot: Democrats and the Disaster in Madison Square Garden* (New York: Harper & Row, 1976), 147.

3. Quotes from the day's speeches are taken from transcripts in *New York Times*, June 29, 1924.

4. Murray, *103rd Ballot*, 163.

5. *New York Times*, June 30, 1924.

6. The letter was addressed to the Rev. J. H. Dooley of Corpus Christi Church in

Manhattan. Dooley forwarded it to Smith's campaign headquarters on June 30, 1924. It is found in FDR Papers Pertaining to the 1924 Campaign, FDRL.

7. Letters found in FDR Papers Pertaining to the 1924 Campaign, FDRL.

8. Robert Slayton, *Empire Statesman: The Rise and Redemption of Al Smith* (New York: The Free Press, 2001), 214. Bryan's use of the phrase "You do not represent the future of this country" is cited in several accounts of his speech but does not appear in the transcript published in the *New York Times*, July 3, 1914.

9. Murray, *103rd Ballot*, 173.

10. Murray, *103rd Ballot*, 175.

11. *New York Herald-Tribune*, July 2, 1924.

12. Martha Duitz to Al Smith, July 2, 1924, FDR Papers Pertaining to the 1924 Campaign, FDRL.

13. *New York Times*, July 5, 1924.

14. James A. Farley, *Behind the Ballots: The Personal Story of a Politician* (New York: Harcourt, Brace, 1938), 43.

15. *New York Times*, July 9, 1924.

16. *Baltimore Evening Sun*, July 14, 1924.

17. Freidel, *Franklin D. Roosevelt: The Ordeal*, 180.

18. Al Smith, *Up to Now: An Autobiography* (New York: Viking Press, 1929), 292.

19. Eleanor Roosevelt, *This I Remember* (New York: Harper & Brothers, 1949), 31; *New York Times*, November 2, 1924.

20. *New York Times*, October 31, 1924.

21. Eleanor Roosevelt to Al Smith, April 7, 1925, FDR Family, Business and Personal Papers, FDRL.

CHAPTER FOURTEEN: THE CHALLENGE OF NEW AMERICA

1. Richard O'Connor, *The First Hurrah: A Biography of Alfred E. Smith* (New York: G. P. Putnam's Sons, 1970), 160; *New York Times*, November 3, 1925.

2. Al Smith to FDR, June 25, 1925.

3. Robert Caro, *The Power Broker: Robert Moses and the Fall of New York* (New York: Vintage Books, 1975), 287, 291.

4. FDR to Smith, September 17, 1926.

5. *New York Times*, July 5, September 27, 1926.

6. *New York Times*, September 28, 1924.

7. *New York Times*, January 2, 1927.

8. Smith to FDR, May 7, 1926.

9. FDR to Smith, May 7, 1925; FDR to Smith, May 20, 1927; Smith to FDR, May 27, 1927.

10. FDR to Smith, June 20, 1927; Smith to FDR, June 28, 1927; O'Connor, *First Hurrah*, 182–83.

11. FDR to A. J. Berres, November 22, 1927, FDR Papers, 1920–1928, FDRL; O'Connor, *First Hurrah*, 171.
12. FDR to Smith, March 10, 1927.
13. O'Connor, *First Hurrah*, 178.
14. Smith to FDR, March 22, 1927.
15. FDR to Ellery Sedgwick, March 19, 1927, FDR Papers, 1920–1928, FDRL.
16. O'Connor, *First Hurrah*, 178; Robert Moses, *A Tribute to Governor Smith* (New York: Simon and Schuster, 1962), 21.
17. Alfred E. Smith, "Catholic and Patriot: Governor Smith Replies," *Atlantic Monthly*, May 1927.
18. FDR to Smith, no date, likely early May 1927.
19. Smith to FDR, May 10, 1927.
20. FDR to A. J. Berres, November 22, 1927, FDR Papers, 1920–1928, FDRL.
21. *The Nation*, July 4, 1928.
22. Christopher M. Finan, *Alfred E. Smith: The Happy Warrior* (New York: Hill & Wang, 2002), 191–92; O'Connor, *First Hurrah*, 184.
23. Wilbur Bryant to FDR, October 3, 1927; FDR to Bryant, October 15, 1927, FDR Papers, 1920–1928, FDRL.
24. FDR to Smith, January 28, 1928; Smith to FDR, February 3, 1928.
25. Robert Slayton, *Empire Statesman: The Rise and Redemption of Al Smith* (New York: The Free Press, 2001), 254.
26. *New York Times*, June 27, 1928.
27. *New York Times*, June 23, 1928.
28. Geoffrey C. Ward, *A First-Class Temperament: The Emergence of Franklin Roosevelt, 1905–1928* (New York: Vintage Books, 1989), 784.
29. Slayton, *Empire Statesman*, 247.
30. *New York Times*, June 28, 1928.
31. *New York World*, June 28, 1928.
32. Ward, *First-Class Temperament*, 785.
33. *New York Times*, June 29, 1928.
34. Slayton, *Empire Statesman*, 258.
35. Slayton, *Empire Statesman*, 256–59; *New York Times*, June 30, 1928.
36. FDR to Sara Roosevelt, July 14, 1928, Elliot Roosevelt, ed., *FDR: His Personal Letters* (New York: Duell Sloan and Pearce, 1918), 639–41.
37. Ward, *First-Class Temperament*, 788.

Chapter Fifteen: Confronting Old America

1. *New York Times*, August 22 and 23, 1928.
2. Bernard L. Shientag, *Campaign Addresses, Governor Alfred E. Smith, 1928* (Albany: J. B. Lyon, 1929), 1–27.

3. Christopher M. Finan, *Alfred E. Smith: The Happy Warrior* (New York: Hill & Wang, 2002), 206.

4. Shientag, *Campaign Addresses*; also see *New York Times*, August 23, 1928.

5. For examples of Klan activity, see *New York Times*, August 28, September 11, 19, and 25, 1928. For the Pope's interest in the post office, see Robert Slayton, *Empire Statesman: The Rise and Redemption of Al Smith* (New York: The Free Press, 2001), 310.

6. Clip from the *Fellowship Forum*, no date, Private Papers of Alfred E. Smith, New York State Library, Albany, NY.

7. Slayton, *Empire Statesman*, 290.

8. *New York Times*, August 26, September 10, 1928.

9. *New York Times*, September 11, 1928.

10. Matthew and Hannah Josephson, *Al Smith: Hero of the Cities* (Boston: Houghton Mifflin, 1969), 386.

11. Joseph Proskauer, *A Segment of My Times* (New York: Farrar, Straus, 1950), 62; *New York Times*, September 21, 1928.

12. Josephson and Josephson, *Al Smith*, 389.

13. Geoffrey C. Ward, *A First-Class Temperament: The Emergence of Franklin Roosevelt, 1905–1928* (New York: Vintage Books, 1989), 787fn; *New York Times*, September 9, 1928.

14. *New York Times*, September 27, 1928.

15. Ward, *First-Class Temperament*, 790.

16. *New York Times*, October 2, 1928.

17. Ward, *First-Class Temperament*, 792.

18. *New York Times*, October 3, 1928.

19. Ward, *First-Class Temperament*, 795; Kenneth Davis, *FDR: The New York Years, 1928–1933* (New York: Random House, 1994), 1.

20. *New York Times*, October 3, 1928.

21. *New York Evening Post*, October 5, 1928.

22. *New York Times*, October 7, 1928.

23. Eleanor Roosevelt, *This I Remember* (New York: Harper & Brothers, 1949), 47.

24. George Martin, *Madam Secretary: Frances Perkins* (Boston: Houghton Mifflin Harcourt, 1983), 197.

25. *New York Times*, October 16, 17 and 21, 1928.

26. *New York Times*, October 29, 1928.

27. *The Nation*, October 3, 1928; Slayton, *Empire Statesman*, 316.

28. *New York Times*, October 7 and 3, 1928.

29. Martin, *Madam Secretary*, 190.

30. Martin, *Madam Secretary*, 202.

31. Slayton, *Empire Statesman*, 318.

32. *New York Times*, November 4, 1928.

33. *New York Times*, November 6, 1928.

34. *New York Times*, November 7, 1928.

35. Smith's daughter, Emily Smith Warner, said in her book, *The Happy Warrior: The Story of My Father, Alfred E. Smith* (New York: Doubleday & Co., 1956), that Smith appeared at the 69th Regiment Armory, home of the legendary Fighting 69th. But contemporary newspaper accounts place him at the 71st Regiment Armory. See *New York Times*, November 7, 1928.

36. Ward, *First-Class Temperament*, 797.

37. *The Reminiscences of Frances Perkins*, Columbia Center for Oral History.

38. Blanche Wiesen Cook, *Eleanor Roosevelt: The Early Years* (New York: Penguin, 1993), 379.

39. *New York Evening Post*, November 5, 1928.

40. Irish-American novelist and essayist Peter Quinn tells the story of flags coming down in his Bronx neighborhood in *The Irish in America: Long Journey Home*, episode 3, "Up From City Streets," directed by Thomas Lennon, aired January 28, 1998, on PBS.

41. Joseph Tumulty to Thomas McCarthy, November 8, 1928; Tumulty to Al Smith, November 7, 1928, Tumulty Papers, Library of Congress.

42. *New York Evening Post*, November 7, 1928.

43. Tribute book found in the Papers of Alfred E. Smith, Museum of the City of New York.

44. For an analysis of Smith's impact on voting patterns, see Samuel Lubell, *The Future of American Politics* (Garden City, NY: Doubleday, 1951).

45. *New York Times*, November 9, 1928.

46. *The Reminiscences of Frances Perkins*, Columbia Center for Oral History.

47. FDR to Smith, December 3, 1928; Smith to FDR, December 7, 1928; Martin, *Madam Secretary*, 208; *The Reminiscences of Frances Perkins*, Columbia Center for Oral History.

48. Robert Caro, *The Power Broker: Robert Moses and the Fall of New York* (New York: Vintage Books, 1975), 296.

49. *New York Times*, January 2, 1929.

50. *New York Times*, January 2, 1929; archival footage of the opening of FDR's speech in *The Irish in America: Long Journey Home*, episode 3.

51. FDR to Smith, February 8, 1929, September 17, 1929.

52. Slayton, *Empire Statesman*, 360.

53. Slayton, *Empire Statesman*, 360; *The Reminiscences of Frances Perkins*, Columbia Center for Oral History.

Chapter Sixteen: Frank or Al

1. *New York Times*, May 2, 1931.

2. Archival footage in *New York: A Documentary Film*, directed by Ric Burns, episode 9.

3. *New York Times*, May 2, 1931.

4. FDR to Smith, February 4, 1930; Smith to FDR, no date, FDR Papers as Governor, FDRL.

5. *New York Times*, October 1, 1930.

6. Jean Edward Smith, *FDR* (New York: Random House, 2008), 249.

7. See *New York: A Documentary Film*, episode 9.

8. Kenneth Davis, *FDR: The New York Years, 1928–1933* (New York: Random House, 1994), 157.

9. *New York Times*, July 1, 1930.

10. *New York Times*, July 1, 1930; Edward J. Flynn, *You're the Boss: The Practice of American Politics* (New York: Collier Books, 1962), 96.

11. FDR to Al Smith, February 28, 1931, FDR Papers as Governor, FDRL.

12. George Martin, *Madam Secretary: Frances Perkins* (Boston: Houghton Mifflin Harcourt, 1983), 218.

13. *New York Times*, March 7, 1931.

14. Martin, *Madam Secretary*, 218.

15. *New York Times*, November 2, 1931.

16. *New York Times*, November 2 and 3, 1931.

17. FDR to Smith, November 10, 1931, FDR Papers as Governor, FDRL.

18. *New York Times*, November 19, 1931.

19. Davis, *FDR: The New York Years*, 249.

20. Flynn, *You're the Boss*, 100.

21. *New York Times*, January 15, 1932.

22. *New York Times*, January 27, 1932.

23. *New York Times*, January 25, 1932.

24. *New York Times*, February 8, 1932.

25. A sampling of the nation's editorials was published in the *New York Times*, February 9, 1932.

26. *New York Times*, February 9, 1932.

27. James Hoey to James A. Farley, May 4, 1932, Farley Papers, Library of Congress.

28. *New York Times*, February 27, 1932.

29. *New York Times*, March 31, 1932.

30. *New York Times*, April 9, 1932.

31. Robert Caro, *The Power Broker: Robert Moses and the Fall of New York* (New York: Vintage Books, 1975), 187.

32. *New York Times*, February 10, 1932.

33. *New York Times*, April 14, 1932.

34. The roundup of editorial comments was published in the *New York Times*, April 15, 1932.

35. *New York Times*, April 15, 1932.

36. Edward House to FDR, April 14, 1932, FDR Papers as Governor, FDRL.

37. Robert Slayton, *Empire Statesman: The Rise and Redemption of Al Smith* (New York: The Free Press, 2001), 366.

38. William Gibbs McAdoo to Joseph Tumulty, February 24, 1932, Tumulty Papers, Library of Congress.

39. Claude Bowers to Edward J. Flynn, October 16, 1947, Flynn Papers, FDRL.
40. *New York Times*, June 22, 1932.
41. Flynn, *You're the Boss*, 108.
42. James A. Farley, *Behind the Ballots: The Personal Story of a Politician* (New York: Harcourt, Brace, 1938), 139.
43. *New York Times*, July 2, 1932.
44. Emily Smith Warner, *The Happy Warrior: The Story of My Father, Alfred E. Smith* (New York: Doubleday & Co., 1956), 261.
45. *New York Times*, July 2, 1932.
46. Slayton, *Empire Statesman*, 373.

CHAPTER SEVENTEEN: FRANK VS. AL

1. James A. Farley, *Behind the Ballots: The Personal Story of a Politician* (New York: Harcourt, Brace, 1938), 169–70.
2. Oliver E. Allen, *The Tiger: The Rise and Fall of Tammany Hall* (Reading, MA: Addison-Wesley, 1993), 253.
3. Kenneth Davis, *FDR: The New York Years, 1928–1933* (New York: Random House, 1994), 355.
4. *New York Times*, September 22, 1932.
5. *New York Times*, September 5, 1932.
6. Farley, *Behind the Ballots*, 176–77; *New York Times*, October 5, 1932.
7. Christopher M. Finan, *Alfred E. Smith: The Happy Warrior* (New York: Hill & Wang, 2002), 289; *New York Times*, October 25, 1932.
8. *New York Times*, October 29, 1932.
9. *New York Times*, November 5, 1932.
10. Al Smith to FDR, December 28, 1932, Grace Tully Papers, FDRL.
11. *New York Times*, January 3, 1933.
12. *New York Times*, January 3, 1933.
13. Davis, *FDR: The New York Years*, 430–32.
14. *New York Times*, March 5, 1933.
15. *New York Times*, April 8, 1933.
16. *New York Times*, March 28, 1933.
17. Robert Slayton, *Empire Statesman: The Rise and Redemption of Al Smith* (New York: The Free Press, 2001), 378–80; *New York Times*, July 24, 1979.
18. *New York Times*, October 5, 1933.
19. *New York Times*, October 24, 1933.
20. Slayton, *Empire Statesman*, 378.
21. *New York Times*, November 25 and 27, 1933.
22. *New York Times*, December 3, 1933.
23. Smith to FDR, December 26, 1933; Smith to FDR, March 21, 1934; FDR to Smith, March 27, 1934, President's Personal File, FDRL.

24. Emily Smith Warner, *The Happy Warrior: The Story of My Father, Alfred E. Smith* (New York: Doubleday & Co., 1956), 265.

25. Eleanor Roosevelt to Smith, December 18, 1935; Smith to Eleanor Roosevelt, December 18, 1935, January 5, 1936, Eleanor Roosevelt Papers, FDRL.

26. *New York Times*, January 26, 1936.

27. Christopher M. Finan, *Alfred E. Smith: The Happy Warrior* (New York: Hill & Wang, 2002), 319.

28. Matthew and Hannah Josephson, *Al Smith: Hero of the Cities* (Boston: Houghton Mifflin, 1969), 457.

29. *New York Times*, January 27, 1936.

30. Robert Moses, *A Tribute to Governor Smith* (New York: Simon and Schuster, 1962), 39–40; Joseph Proskauer, *A Segment of My Times* (New York: Farrar, Straus, 1950), 72–73; *The Reminiscences of Frances Perkins*, Columbia Center for Oral History.

31. Smith to Herbert Lehman, April 5, 1933, Lehman Papers, Columbia University, http://lehman.cul.columbia.edu/lehman/document_id = ldpd_leh_0849_0020 ?&q = chicago + AND + file_unittitle_t%3A%22Smith%2C + Alfred + E .%22 + AND + unitdate_iso%3A%5B1933-04-05T23%3A59%3A59Z + TO + % 2A%5D;&items = 3&itemNo = 0 (accessed July 17, 2016).

32. Edward J. Flynn, *You're the Boss: The Practice of American Politics* (New York: Collier, 1962), 162–63.

33. Warner, *Happy Warrior*, 274.

34. *New York Times*, February 28, 1935.

35. Smith to FDR, telegram, September 24, 1936, President's Personal File, FDRL.

36. *New York Times*, October 2, 1936.

37. *New York Times*, November 4, 1936.

38. Copies of the articles are in the Private Papers of Al Smith, New York State Library, Albany, NY.

39. Josephson and Josephson, *Al Smith*, 464.

40. Reference to Smith is in President's Personal File, 200, FDRL; Frances Perkins, *The Roosevelt I Knew* (New York: Viking Press, 1946), 13.

41. *New York Times*, October 2, 1939.

42. FDR to Smith, October 1, 1939; Smith to FDR, October 2, 1939, President's Personal File, FDRL.

43. *New York Times*, May 29, 1941; FDR to Smith, May 29, 1941, President's Personal File, FDRL.

44. George Martin, *Madam Secretary: Frances Perkins* (Boston: Houghton Mifflin Harcourt, 1983), 397.

45. Slayton, *Empire Statesman*, 398.

CHAPTER EIGHTEEN: PEACE

1. *New York Times*, June 10, 1941.
2. *New York Times*, December 31, 1941.
3. *New York Times*, July 9, 1942.
4. See memo from Marvin (Mac) McIntrye, June 17, 1942, President's Personal File; Reference to Al Smith's meeting is recorded in the White House log, available online: http://www.fdrlibrary.marist.edu/daybyday/daylog/july-9th-1942/.
5. *New York Times*, July 10, 1942.
6. *New York Times*, March 17, 1943; Roosevelt log for March 16, 1943, http://www.fdrlibrary.marist.edu/daybyday/daylog/march-16th-1943/.
7. *New York Times*, December 31, 1943.
8. FDR to Al Smith, December 27, 1943, President's Personal File, FDRL.
9. *New York Times*, December 31, 1943.
10. *New York Times*, February 18, 1944.
11. FDR to Smith, May 4, 1944; Memo from William Hessett, May 4, 1944, President's Personal File, FDRL.
12. Christopher M. Finan, *Alfred E. Smith: The Happy Warrior* (New York: Hill & Wang, 2002), 344.
13. See Finan, *Alfred E. Smith*, 354, about cirrhosis; Memo for the President from Steve Early, September 13, 1944; FDR to Smith, September 13, 1944, President's Personal File, FDRL.
14. *New York Times*, October 3, 1944.
15. *New York Times*, October 7 and 8, 1944.
16. *New York Times*, October 4, 1944.
17. *New York Times*, November 5, 1944.
18. Frances Perkins, *The Roosevelt I Knew* (New York: Viking Press, 1946), 393.

BIBLIOGRAPHY

LETTERS AND MANUSCRIPT COLLECTIONS

Columbia University Rare Book and Manuscript Library, New York
    Papers of Herbert Lehman and Frances Perkins
Cornell University, Kheel Center for Labor-Management Documentation and Archives
Franklin D. Roosevelt Library (FDRL), Hyde Park, New York
    Papers of Edward J. Flynn, Grace Tully, Louis Howe, Rita Halle Keelman, Herbert Claiborne Pell and Eleanor Roosevelt
    Papers of Franklin D. Roosevelt, including:
        Family, Business and Personal Papers
        Papers as Assistant Secretary of the Navy
        Papers as State Senator
        Papers, 1920–1928
        Papers Pertaining to the Campaigns of 1924 and 1928
        Papers as Governor of New York
        President's Official File
        President's Personal File
        President's Secretary's File
        Vertical File
Library of Congress, Washington, DC
    Papers of Joseph Tumulty and James A. Farley
New York Public Library, New York City
    Papers of William Bourke Cockran and Robert Moses
Museum of the City of New York
    Alfred E. Smith Papers
New York State Archives, Albany, New York
    Public Papers of Alfred E. Smith
New York State Library, Manuscripts and Special Collections, Albany, New York
    Private Papers of Alfred E. Smith

ORAL HISTORY INTERVIEWS

Columbia Center for Oral History, Columbia University, New York

Reminiscences of Edward J. Flynn, Jeremiah T. Mahoney, Frances Perkins, and Joseph Proskauer

GOVERNMENT PUBLICATIONS

Documents of the Assembly of the State of New York, vol. 1. Albany: Oliver Quayle, 1904.

New York State Constitutional Convention, Revised Record. Albany: J.B. Lyon, 1916.

Official Report of the Proceedings of the Democratic National Convention, 1920. Indianapolis: Bookwalter-Ball Printing Co., 1920.

Official Report of the Proceedings of the Democratic National Convention, 1924. Indianapolis: Bookwalter-Ball Printing Co., 1924.

Preliminary Report of the Factory Investigating Commission, vols. 1 and 2. Albany: J. B. Lyon Co., 1912.

Report of the Reconstruction Commission to Governor Alfred E. Smith on Retrenchment and Reorganization in the State Government. Albany: J. B. Lyon Co., 1919.

PUBLISHED COLLECTIONS OF CORRESPONDENCE AND DOCUMENTS

Moskowitz, Henry, ed. *Progressive Democracy: Addresses and State Papers of Alfred E. Smith.* New York: Harcourt, Brace and Company, 1928.

Roosevelt, Elliot, ed. *The Roosevelt Letters, Being the Personal Correspondence of Franklin Delano Roosevelt*, vol. 1. London: George G. Harrap & Co., 1949.

———. *FDR: His Personal Letters, 1905–1928.* New York: Duell, Sloan and Pearce, 1948.

Rosenman, Samuel, ed. *The Public Papers and Addresses of Franklin D. Roosevelt.* New York: Macmillan, 1939.

Shientag, Bernard L. *Campaign Addresses, Governor Alfred E. Smith, 1928.* Albany: J. B. Lyon, 1929.

BOOKS: MEMOIRS, BIOGRAPHIES, GENERAL HISTORIES

Allen, Oliver E. *The Tiger: The Rise and Fall of Tammany Hall.* Reading, MA: Addison-Wesley, 1993.

Allswang, John M. *Bosses, Machines, and Urban Voters.* Baltimore: Johns Hopkins University Press, 1986.

Bowers, Claude: *My Life.* New York: Simon and Schuster, 1962.

Buenker, John. *Urban Liberalism and Progressive Reform.* New York: W. W. Norton, 1973.

Caro, Robert. *The Power Broker: Robert Moses and the Fall of New York.* New York: Vintage Books, 1975.

Cook, Blanche Wiesen. *Eleanor Roosevelt: The Early Years.* New York: Penguin, 1993.

Cross, Robert D. *The Emergence of Liberal Catholicism in America.* Cambridge: Harvard University Press, 1958.

Dallek, Robert. *Franklin D. Roosevelt: A Political Life.* New York: Viking, 2017.

Davis, Kenneth S. *FDR: The Beckoning of Destiny, 1882–1928.* New York: G. P. Putnam's Sons, 1972.

———. *FDR: The New York Years, 1928–1933.* New York: Random House, 1994.

De Kay, James Tertius. *Roosevelt's Navy: The Education of a Warrior President, 1882–1920.* New York: Pegasus Books, 2012.

Farley, James A. *Behind the Ballots: The Personal Story of a Politician.* New York: Harcourt, Brace, 1938.

Fenster, Julie M. *FDR's Shadow: Louis Howe, The Force That Shaped Franklin and Eleanor Roosevelt.* New York: Palgrave Macmillan, 2009.

Finan, Christopher M. *Alfred E. Smith: The Happy Warrior.* New York: Hill & Wang, 2002.

Flynn, Edward J. *You're the Boss: The Practice of American Politics.* New York: Collier Books, 1962.

Fowler, Gene. *Beau James: The Life and Times of Jimmy Walker.* New York: Viking Press, 1949.

Freidel. Frank. *Franklin D. Roosevelt: The Apprenticeship.* Boston: Little, Brown & Co., 1952.

———. *Franklin D. Roosevelt: The Ordeal.* Boston: Little, Brown, 1954.

———. *Franklin D. Roosevelt: A Rendezvous with Destiny.* New York: Bach Bay, Books, 1990.

Golway, Terry. *Machine Made: Tammany Hall and the Creation of Modern American Politics.* New York: Liveright, 2014.

Greenwald, Richard A. *The Triangle Fire, the Protocols of Peace, and Industrial Democracy in Progressive Era New York.* Philadelphia: Temple University Press, 2005.

Handlin, Oscar. *Al Smith and His America.* Boston: Little, Brown, 1958.

Henderson, Thomas M. *Tammany Hall and the New Immigrants: The Progressive Years.* New York: Arno Press, 1976.

Higham, John. *Strangers in the Land: Patterns of American Nativism, 1960–1925.* New Brunswick, NJ: Rutgers University Press, 2004.

Huthmacher, J. Joseph. *Senator Robert F. Wagner and the Rise of Urban Liberalism.* New York: Atheneum, 1971.

Josephson, Matthew and Hannah. *Al Smith: Hero of the Cities.* Boston: Houghton Mifflin, 1969.

Kazin, Michael. *A Godly Hero: The Life of William Jennings Bryan.* New York: Anchor Books, 2006.

Kennedy, William. *O Albany!: Improbable City of Political Wizards, Fearless Ethnics, Spectacular Aristocrats, Splendid Nobodies, and Underrated Scoundrels.* New York: Penguin, 1985.

Kessner, Thomas. *Capital City: New York City and the Men Behind America's Rise to Economic Dominance, 1860–1900.* New York: Simon & Schuster, 2004.

LaCerra, Charles. *Franklin Delano Roosevelt and Tammany Hall of New York.* New York: University Press of America, 1997.

Lewis, Tom. *The Hudson: A History.* New Haven: Yale University Press, 2007.

Lichtman, Allan J. *Prejudice and the Old Politics: The Presidential Election of 1928.* Lanham, MD: Lexington Books, 2000.

Lindley, Ernest K. *Franklin D. Roosevelt: A Career in Progressive Democracy.* Indianapolis: Bobbs-Merrill, 1931.

Lubell, Samuel. *The Future of American Politics.* Garden City, NY: Doubleday, 1951.

Martin, George. *Madam Secretary: Frances Perkins.* Boston: Houghton Mifflin Harcourt, 1983.

Mitgang, Herbert. *The Man Who Rode the Tiger: The Life and Times of Judge Samuel Seabury.* New York: J. B. Lippincott, 1963.

Morris, Charles. *American Catholic.* New York: Times Books, 1997.

Moses, Robert. *A Tribute to Governor Smith.* New York: Simon and Schuster, 1962.

Murray, Robert K. *The 103rd Ballot: Democrats and the Disaster in Madison Square Garden.* New York: Harper & Row, 1976.

Nevins, Allen. *Herbert Lehman and His Era.* New York: Scribner, 1963.

O'Connor, Richard. *The First Hurrah: A Biography of Alfred E. Smith.* New York: G. P. Putnam's Sons, 1970.

Perkins, Frances. *The Roosevelt I Knew.* New York: Viking Press, 1946.

Perry, Elisabeth Israels. *Belle Moskowitz: Feminine Politics and the Exercise of Power in the Age of Alfred E. Smith.* New York: Oxford University Press, 1987.

Proskauer, Joseph. *A Segment of My Times.* New York: Farrar, Straus, 1950.

Rogers, Marion Elizabeth, ed. *The Impossible H. L. Mencken: A Selection of His Best Newspaper Stories.* New York: Anchor Books, 1991.

Rollins, Alfred Brooks. *Roosevelt and Howe.* New York: Knopf, 1962.

Roosevelt, Eleanor. *This I Remember.* New York: Harper & Brothers, 1949.

Roosevelt, Franklin D. *The Happy Warrior: Alfred E. Smith.* Boston: Houghton Mifflin, 1928.

Roosevelt, James, and Sidney Shalett. *Affectionately, F.D.R.: A Son's Story of a Lonely Man.* New York: Harcourt, Brace & Co., 1959.

Scoop, Daniel. *Mr. Democrat: Jim Farley, the New Deal, and the Making of Modern American Politics.* Ann Arbor: University of Michigan Press, 2006.

Slayton, Robert. *Empire Statesman: The Rise and Redemption of Al Smith.* New York: The Free Press, 2001.

Smith, Alfred E. *Up to Now: An Autobiography.* New York: Viking Press, 1929.

Smith, Jean Edward. *FDR*. New York: Random House, 2008.

Von Drehle, David. *Triangle: The Fire that Changed America*. New York: Grove Press, 2005.

Wallace, Mike and Edwin C. Burrows. *Gotham: A History of New York to 1898*. New York: Oxford University Press, 1998.

Ward, Geoffrey C. *Before the Trumpet: Young Franklin Roosevelt, 1882–1905*. New York: Vintage Books, 1985.

———. *A First-Class Temperament: The Emergence of Franklin Roosevelt*. New York: Vintage Books, 1989.

Warner, Emily Smith. *The Happy Warrior: The Story of My Father, Alfred E. Smith*. New York: Doubleday & Co., 1956.

Weintraub, Stanley. *Young Mr. Roosevelt: FDR's Introduction to War, Politics, and Life*. New York: Da Capo Press, 2013.

Weiss, Nancy Joan. *Charles Francis Murphy, 1858–1924: Respectability and Responsibility in Tammany Politics*. Northampton, MA: Smith College Press, 1968.

Wesser, Robert F. *A Response to Progressivism: The Democratic Party and New York Politics, 1902–1918*. New York: New York University Press, 1986.

Zacks, Richard. *Island of Vice: Theodore Roosevelt's Doomed Quest to Clean Up Sin-Loving New York*. New York: Doubleday, 2002.

SOURCES ACCESSED ONLINE

Herbert H. Lehman Collections, Columbia University, http://lehman.cul.columbia.edu

Oral History of Leon Keyserling, Harry S. Truman Presidential Library, http://www.trumanlibrary.org/oralhist/keyserl.html

NEWSPAPERS AND PERIODICALS

Albany, New York
Albany Evening Journal

Baltimore, Maryland
Baltimore Evening Sun

Boston
Atlantic Monthly

New York City
New York American
New York Evening Post

New York Herald-Tribune
New York Sun
New York Times
New York World
The Nation

DOCUMENTARY FILMS

Lennon, Thomas, dir. *The Irish in America: Long Journey Home.* Episode 3, "Up From City Streets." Aired January 28, 1998, on PBS.

Burns, Ric, dir. *New York: A Documentary History.* Part 9. PBS, 1999.

UNPUBLISHED DISSERTATIONS

Chase, Philip M. *William Gibbs McAdoo: The Last Progressive.* Unpublished PhD diss., University of Southern California. http://digitallibrary.usc.edu/cdm/ref/collection /p15799coll127/id/140194 (accessed December 2, 2017).

Evers, John T. *Investigating New York: Governor Alfred E. Smith, the Moreland Act, and Reshaping New York Government.* Unpublished PhD diss., University at Albany, 2013.

INDEX